Non-Governmental Organizations in the Global System

Non-Governmental Organizations in the Global System

George Kaloudis

LEXINGTON BOOKS
Lanham • Boulder • New York • London

Published by Lexington Books
An imprint of The Rowman & Littlefield Publishing Group, Inc.
4501 Forbes Boulevard, Suite 200, Lanham, Maryland 20706
www.rowman.com

6 Tinworth Street, London SE11 5AL, United Kingdom

British Library Cataloguing in Publication Information Available

Library of Congress Cataloging-in-Publication Data
Names: Kaloudis, George Stergiou, 1952- author.
Title: Non-governmental organizations in the global system /
   George Kaloudis.
Description: Lanham, Maryland : Lexington Books, 2021. |
   Includes bibliographical references. | Summary: "In Nongovernmental
   Organizations in the Global System George Kaloudis examines the
   important and paradoxical role NGOs play in the global system"—
   Provided by publisher.
Identifiers: LCCN 2020055117 (print) | LCCN 2020055118 (ebook) |
   ISBN 9781793627360 (cloth) | ISBN 9781793627377 (epub)
   ISBN 9781793627384 (pbk)
Subjects: LCSH: Non-governmental organizations. | International relations.
Classification: LCC JZ4841 .K35 2021 (print) | LCC JZ4841 (ebook) |
   DDC 341.2—dc23
LC record available at https://lccn.loc.gov/2020055117
LC ebook record available at https://lccn.loc.gov/2020055118

For our family in the United States and Greece.

Contents

Acknowledgments

This work would not have been completed without the constant encouragement of my wife Penelope, the intellectual stimulation of my colleagues at Rivier University, the support of the staff at Regina Library, Rivier University, and the interest in the project of Mr. Joseph Parry and his colleagues at Lexington Books. I also want to thank our children Stergos and Naomi for always showing interest in my work. I must also thank our daughter-in-law, Meghan, my brothers Antonis and Lefteris, and my sisters Christina and Popi for their keen interest in all my endeavors. George and Stevie, you are always in my mind.

Abbreviations

APC: Association for Progressive Communication
ARF: Asia-Pacific-wide ASEAN Regional Forum
ASEAN: Association of Southeast Asian Nations
ASEE: Alashan Society Entrepreneur Ecology Association
BRAC: Bangladesh Rural Advancement Committee
CARE: Cooperative for Assistance Everywhere
CBOs: Community-Based Organizations
CEF: Connecting Europe Facility
CHAI: Clinton Health Access Initiative
CIFF: Children's Investment Fund Foundation
CRS: Congressional Research Service
CTBT: Comprehensive Test Ban Treaty
CTBTO: Preparatory Commission for the Comprehensive Nuclear-Test-Ban
   Treaty Organization
DFID: The UK Department for International Development
DONGOs: Donor-organized non-governmental organizations
ECOSOC: Economic and Social Council
ENGOs: Environmental nongovernmental organizations
ERIO: European Roma Information Office
ERRC: European Roma Rights Center
ERSA: Economic Reform and Structural Adjustment programs
ESF: European Social Fund
EU: European Union
FAO: Food and Agriculture Organization
FATA: Federally Administered Tribal Areas of Pakistan
FCTC: Framework Convention on Tobacco Control
FEE: Foundation for Environmental Education

FFP: Food for Peace
GINAN: Ghanaian Infant Nutrition Action Network
GONGOs: Government-organized nongovernmental organizations
GOs: Governmental organizations
GROs: Grassroots organizations
IAEA: International Atomic Energy Agency
ICAO: International Civil Aviation Organization
ICC: International Criminal Court
ICDA: International Coalition for Development Action
ICG: International Crisis Group
ICRC: International Committee of the Red Cross
IFAD: International Fund for Agricultural Organization
IICD: International Institute for Communication Development
IISD: International Institute for Sustainable Development
ILO: International Labor Organization
IMF: International Monetary Fund
IMO: International Maritime Organization
INGOs: International nongovernmental organizations
IOM: International Organization for Migration
IRC: International Rescue Committee
ITU: International Telecommunication Union
IUCN: International Union for Conservation of Nature and Natural Resources
LNGOs: Local nongovernmental organizations
MDD: Music, dance, and drama
MTP: Mini TASO Project
NED: National Endowment for Democracy
NGOs: Nongovernmental organizations
NNGOs: Northern nongovernmental organizations
NPT: Nuclear Non-Proliferation Treaty
ODA: Official Development Assistance
OFDA: Office of Foreign Disaster Assistance
OHCHR: Office of the High Commissioner for Human Rights
OLS: Operation Lifeline Sudan
OPCW: Organization for the Prohibition of Chemical Weapons
PLHIV: People living with HIV and AIDS
PTBT: Partial Test Ban Treaty
REC: Regional Environmental Center for Central and Eastern Europe
RHOs: Rights-holder organizations
SEE: South-Eastern Europe
SNGOs: Southern nongovernmental organizations
TANs: Transnational advocacy networks
TASO: The AIDS Support Organization

UN: United Nations
UNAIDS: The Joint United Nations Program on HIV/AIDS
UNCED: United Nations Conference on Environment and Development
UNDP: UN Development Program
UNEP: UN Environmental Program
UNESCO: UN Educational, Scientific and Cultural Organization
UNFCCC: UN Framework Convention on Climate Change
UNFPA: UN Population Fund
UNHRC: UN High Commissioner for Refugees
UNICEF: UN Children's Fund
UNIDIR: UN Institute for Disarmament Research
UNIDO: UN Industrial Development Organization
UNITAR: UN Institute for Training and Research
UNOPS: UN Office for Project Services
UNRWA: UN Relief and Works Agency for Palestine Refugees
UNSSC: UN System Staff College
UNTAC: UN Transitional Authority in Cambodia
UNWTO: UN Tourism Organization
UPU: Universal Postal Union
USAID: US Agency for International Development
USIP: US Institute of Peace
WABA: World Alliance on Breastfeeding Action
WANGOs: World Association of Non-Governmental Organizations
WCTU: Women's Christian Temperance Union
WFP: World Food Program
WHO: World Health Organization
WIPO: World Intellectual Property Organization
WMO: World Meteorological Organization
WTO: World Trade Organization
WWF: World Wildlife Fund
YMCA: Young Men's Christian Association

Introduction

The Treaty of Westphalia ended the Thirty Years' War in 1648, a war between Protestants and Catholics at the heart of Europe. The Westphalian settlement signified the beginning of modern international relations and the "plenipotentiaries creatively fused diverse ideas to put international order on a new footing."[1] This new international system is often referred to as the Westphalian order and dominated world politics for the next 350 years. The Westphalian order was based on two main principles: the principle of statehood and the principle of sovereignty. The Westphalian order was a state-centric system and the rulers of Europe agreed that each had the right to govern their territories without outside interference.[2] The Westphalian order was a system of governance that set in place the "rules of the game," that is, how states were to relate to and behave toward each other. But "[the] steady concentration of power in the hands of the states that began in 1648 with the Peace of Westphalia is over, at least for a while."[3] During the past few decades, the global system has been transformed in numerous ways including the multiplicity of non-state actors that at times cooperate with the state and at other times challenge the state. And even though "current global politics are largely dependent on the actions and strategies of nation-states, nation-states are not the only actors at work."[4] The most powerful factor contributing to the decline of states and the emergence of non-state actors is the technological revolution with its serious political and social consequences. "By drastically reducing the importance of proximity, the new technologies change people's perceptions of community." These technologies connect people with much greater ease "while separating them from natural and historical associations within nations."[5]

The technological revolution can also have the opposite effect, enhancing "political and social fragmentation by enabling more and more identities and interests scattered around the globe to coalesce and thrive." The new technologies often divide people, separating the masses from elites who possess wealth and who have power by commanding technology's power. Those elites not only they are wealthy and powerful, they tend to have more in common with their counterparts in other countries than with the common people in their own countries. Even more important, the new technologies "disrupt hierarchies, spreading power among more people and groups." They link people much faster than ever before and they favor decentralized networks. Non-state actors of various kinds have adopted the network model. "Governments, on the other hand, are quintessential hierarchies, wedded to an organizational form incompatible with all that new technologies make possible." Non-state actors are not new, but they have never before reached their present strength.[6] Among the plethora of non-state actors are thousands, if not millions, of nongovernmental organizations (NGOs) which play a significant role in the global system and whose role is likely to increase in the future. The proliferation of NGOs is of such scale, scholars refer to it as the "global associational revolution."[7] By considering NGOs throughout much of the world, this work focuses on the reasons for the growth of NGOs particularly since the end of the Cold War, the functions of NGOs, assessment of NGOs, and their place in the global system. This work also shows the ambivalent and often paradoxical role of NGOs, which is reflected in the works of scholars and the actual behavior of NGOs themselves.

The approach adopted by this work is broader than the approach of works by other authors in order to expose the reader to as many issues as possible related to NGOs. The objective is to present material in a balanced, unbiased, and critical manner. Also, the specific references to various scholars throughout the text is for the purpose of attaching specific names to arguments and to attract the attention of the reader. In addition, some sections in this work are lengthier than others (i.e., those on civil society, democratization, etc.) because they deal with matters of most importance to people around the world. Furthermore, much emphasis is given to NGOs in nondemocratic states such as China, Russia, and others because there is an inclination by many to minimize the role of NGOs in such states.

Before anything else is articulated, it is necessary to define an acceptable NGO (as opposed to unacceptable, i.e. Al-Qaeda, ISIS, etc.) because NGOs are often defined to fit the research agendas of scholars. The term NGOs was coined by the United Nations (UN) after World War II. After 1945, scholars began to use the term about societal actors that were international bodies and engaged in the UN system. But especially since the 1980s, the term NGO began to be used in relationship to all kinds of societal actors engaged in the UN system, nationally and internationally. Before the word NGO was utilized widely, other terms were used. Terms such as "private organizations," "international pressure groups," and "voluntary agencies."[8]

In spite, the widespread usage of the term NGO and the greater interest on the subject, there are, albeit with many similarities, numerous definitions of NGOs. Craig Warkentin defines NGOs as "private, voluntary, nonprofit associations whose membership and organizational activities cross national borders."[9] Shamina Ahmed and David M. Potter define an NGO as "any international organization which is not established by inter-governmental agreement ..." According to them, an NGO cannot be for profit, it cannot advocate violence, and it cannot be a political party, a school, or a university.[10] Cornelia Beyer defines NGOs as "non-state, non-profit, non-violent organizations with the main objective of pursuing political and/or social change without striving for governmental power."[11] Dianne Otto says that NGOs "are organizations that aim to represent values and aspirations associated with peoples rather than states, including the promotion of human rights, gender and race equality, environmental protection, sustainable development, indigenous rights, nonviolent conflict resolution, participatory democracy, social diversity, and social and economic justice."[12] Kerstin Martens provides a comprehensive definition of NGOs by stating that NGOs possess the following characteristics:

...NGOs are formal (professionalized) independent societal organizations whose primary aim is to promote common goals at the national or the international level.

NGOs are societal actors because they originate from the private sphere. Their members are individuals, or local, regional, national branches of an association...-and usually do not (or only to a limited extent) include official members, such as governments, governmental representatives, or governmental institutions. NGOs promote common goals because they work for the promotion of public goods, from which their members profit and/or the public gains. NGOs can be professionalized because they may have paid staff with specifically trained skills, but they are not profit-oriented. NGOs are independent because they are primarily sponsored by membership fees and private donations. They may receive financial funding from official institutions, but only to a limited extent, so that they are not under the control of governmental institutions. NGOs are formal organizations because NGOs have at least aminimal organizational structure which allows them to provide for continuous work. This includes a headquarters, permanent staff, and constitution (and also a distinct recognized legal status in at least one state).[13]

The United Nations definition of an NGO encompasses six principles: an NGO should support the mission of the United Nations; an NGO should be a representative body; an NGO cannot be a profit-making organization; an NGO cannot advocate violence; an NGO must not interfere in the domestic affairs of states; and an NGO must not be established by an intergovernmental agreement.[14]

It is imperative to also state the definition of NGOs included in the World Association of Non-Governmental Organizations' (WANGOs') *Code of Ethics & Conduct for NGOs*. According to WANGO:

> [An] NGO is considered in its broadest context: a not-for-profit, non-governmental organization. The term non-profit is used in the sense of "not-for-profit-distributing" in that any profits are invested back into the public mission of the organization, and are not distributed for the benefit of the board, staff or shareholders—thus distinguishing the NGO sector from the business sector. The term non-governmental is used in the sense that the organization is independent of government—it is not controlled by a governmental entity nor is it established by an intergovernmental agreement. Included in the definition are large, international organizations and small, one-person operations, those that are secular as well as those that are faith-based, and both membership and non-membership groups.[15]

These definitions have much in common: NGOs cannot be for-profit organizations, must be independent of government, must not interfere in the domestic affairs of states, must not advocate violence, etc. But at the same time these definitions are problematic because if one were to closely follow the traits that characterize an NGO, many of the entities regarded as NGOs will be excluded from consideration. In a significant number of countries, both democratic and nondemocratic, because of the functions they perform and the services they offer, they are involved in the internal affairs of states. What is for NGOs to do in failed states? What is for NGOs to do when governments are unable or unwilling to perform necessary functions or offer essential services? Must they attempt to interfere in a state's affairs? There is no doubt that for NGOs to be as effective as possible, they ought to be as neutral as possible whenever possible. It should also be kept in mind that there are some NGOs that advocate a degree of political violence (i.e. protests and demonstrations) to fulfill their mission and achieve their objectives.

Because of the prevailing circumstances, our definition of NGOs is more broad to include not only the category of NGOs that matches the general definition of NGOs, but also NGOs that operate in countries where many restrictions are imposed upon them and even government-organized NGOs (GONGOs) as long as they do some of what is expected of independent NGOs. Despite the problematic nature of many of these NGOs, they often offer citizens a variety of opportunities and they often perform useful functions regularly identified by the stereotypical NGOs. So, an entity could be an

NGO even if it does interfere in the domestic affairs of states, it participates in for-profit activities, or it operates under strict governmental controls as long as it functions as an agent to protect the environment, to offer relief, to contribute to social and economic environment, to promote human rights, etc.

To further elaborate the point about NGOs in general and GONGOs, the idea of government-organized NGOs is perplexing to many people. "How can an organization be simultaneously government-organized and non-governmental in the same breath? The paradoxical nature of this organizational form has meant that scholars and practitioners alike often disagree on what a GONGO is and how they fit within the realm of civil society. ... But far too frequently discussions center on organizational authenticity; neither GONGOs specifically, nor NGOs in authoritarian contexts [often in democratic ones as well], are believed to be 'real' NGOs. [Reza Hasmath et al. argue that] this 'is it or isn't' debate is unhelpful."[16]

But as Hasmath et al. assert, scholars have difficulty providing a precise definition even for traditional NGOs. In addition, it is often noted that NGOs are nongovernmental in nature and not dependent on government for financial support. However, this is not the case — "even grassroots NGOs are increasingly reliant upon government support." Furthermore, "GONGOs are growing in number and influence primarily because of the context in which NGOs, more broadly, are needed. This is notably the case where the government lacks specialization and capacity to do the work themselves, where it is hesitant to allow for the flourishing of a truly independent NGO sector, but also where these organizations themselves have limited options other than the government for financial support and general patron. Therefore, [the] inclination is to suggest that in many political institutional environments strong evolutionary pressures urge organizations to become closer to the government."[17]

As is already evident, NGOs differ from each other in the functions they perform, the levels at which they operate, and in their structures, goals, and membership. NGOs are involved in but not limited to matters related to charitable, religious, research, human rights, and environmental endeavors. Some have very few unpaid staff while others have multimillion-dollar budgets. Some are primarily voluntary organizations with no government association while others are created and supported by governments. Some are single-issue organizations operating in a specific area, and others are far more expansive with a presence across the globe. For these reasons, it should be acknowledged that there are many kinds of acceptable NGOs, and among them are the following: Northern NGOS (NNGOs), founded in developed countries; Southern NGOs (SNGOs), founded in developing countries; government-organized NGOs (GONGOs) established by governments; donor-organized NGOs (DONGOs); and international NGOs (INGOS) as opposed to local NGOs (LNGOs).

  NGOs operate in a complex environment. Since the immense growth of NGOs since the 1980s, many scholars have glorified NGOs because to them, they are nongovernmental, not-for-profit, and trying to liberate people from oppressive governments and the grip of the market. Through NGOs, these scholars "envision an alternative form of social organization, one that is more altruistic, more cooperative, and less hierarchical than governments and for-profit organizations." But NGOs are "shaped as much by how they are imagined as by what they actually do. These organizations confront a profound contradiction between the global visions of transformation that animate them and the complex, obdurate material and social realities they encounter on the ground. By their presence, development NGOs assert an imagined shared citizenship in an emerging global polity. As organizations, however, these NGOs must attempt to bridge the gap between their lofty goals and the variegated lives and often parochial aspirations of those individuals and communities they seek to transform."[18]

  It should be pointed out that even though different people using different measurements come up with a different list, at least according to Mia Lazzarini, the following are the top 10 influential NGOs in reverse order:

10. Clinton Health Access Initiative (CHAI) — Headquarters: Portland, Oregon
CHAI's main goal is to save the lives of people with HIV/AIDS in developing countries. CHAI makes efforts to decrease the costs of medical treatment, to increase access to lifesaving technologies, and to help governments build high quality care. CHAI has more than 1,500 employees and operates in more than 30 countries.

9. Cure Violence — Headquarters: Chicago, Illinois
This NGO is committed to stopping violence by "detecting and disrupting conflicts, identifying and treating high risk individuals, and changing social norms. The organization has seen community violence decreased by up to 70 percent by employing such strategies." Cure Violence operates mostly in the U.S., Latin America, the Middle East, and North Africa.

8. PATH — Headquarters: Seattle, Washington
PATH focuses on the health of especially women and children. It works with countries in Africa and Asia to deal with their greatest health needs and to "disrupt the cycle of poor health."

7. Mercy Corps — Headquarters: Portland, Oregon
This NGO has worked in more than 40 countries to help people who face hardship and other kinds of disasters. It provides assistance related to disaster preparedness and emergency responses, education, and equality for women and children. Mercy Corps was founded in 1979 as Save the Refugees Fund, which was established by Dan O'Neill to help Cambodian refugees fleeing famine, genocide, and war.

6. CERES Coalition — Headquarters: Boston, Massachusetts

It promotes sustainable business practices and solutions by mobilizing investor and business leaders with the purpose of building a healthier global economy. This coalition has 10 important principles, "among them is the protection of the biosphere, sustainable use of natural resources, energy conservation, risk reduction, and environmental education."

5. International Rescue Committee (IRC) — Headquarters: New York City
The IRC was founded in 1933 at the request of Albert Einstein to help people devastated by conflict and disaster. The IRC works with people facing the worst humanitarian crises.

4. Heifer International — Headquarters: Little Rock, Arkansas
This NGO tries to eliminate hunger and poverty by focusing on increasing the assets and incomes of communities, by improving food security and nutrition, and by paying attention to environmental sustainability. "Heifer envisions that change will be manifested through women's empowerment and social capital."

3. Partners in Health — Headquarters: Boston, Massachusetts
Partners in Health works with governments and the world's leading academic and medical institutions to strengthen health systems. By establishing these kinds of networks, this NGO has two main goals: "to bring the benefits of modern medical science to those most in need of them, and to serve as an antidote to despair."

2. Bill and Melinda Gates Foundation — Headquarters, Seattle, Washington
The Foundation is committed to improving the lives of people all over the world. It focuses "on the areas of greatest need and on the ways they can do the most good. The Foundation seeks to solve complex problems and demands the coordination of leaders, governments, communities, and individuals around the world in order to drive change on a global scale."

Foundation for Environmental Education (FEE) — Headquarters: Copenhagen, Denmark
The FEE's mission is to educate people "in order to protect the environment as well as the people who live in it, the communities that depend on it, businesses who profit from it, and the ecosystems that rely on it."[19]

NOTES

1. Charles W. Kegley and Gregory A. Raymond, *Exorcising the Ghost of Westphalia: Building World Order in the New Millennium* (Upper Saddle River, New Jersey: Prentice Hall, 2002), 128.

2. Anthony McGrew, "Globalization and global politics," in *Globalization of World Politics: An Introduction to International Relations*, eds. John Baylis, et al., 4th ed. (Boulder, Colorado: Lynne Rienner Publishers, 2008), 23–24.

3. Jessica T. Mathews, "Power Shift," in *The Globalization Reader*, eds. Frank J. Lechner and John Boli (Malden, MA: Blackwell Publishing, 2004), 270.

4. Marc Abeles, "Rethinking NGOs: The Economy of Survival and Global Governance," *Indiana Journal of Global Legal Studies* 15, no. 1 (January 2008): 241.

5. Mathews, 271.

6. Ibid., 271.

7. Euiyoung Kim, "The Limits of NGO-Government Relations in South Korea," *Asian Survey* 49, no. 5 (September/October 2009): 873.

8. Kerstin Martens, "Mission Impossible? Defining Nongovernmental Organizations," *Voluntas: International Journal of Voluntary and Nonprofit Organizations* 13, no. 3 (September 2002): 271–272.

9. Craig Warkentin, *Reshaping World Politics: NGOs, the Internet, and Global Civil Society* (New York: Rowman & Littlefield Publishers, 2001), 3.

10. Shamina Ahmed and David M. Potter, *NGOs in International Politics* (Boulder, Colorado: Kumarian Press, 2013), 8.

11. Cornelia Beyer, "Non-Governmental Organizations as Motors of Change," *Government and Opposition* 42, no. 4 (2007): 514.

12. Dianne Otto, "Non-Governmental Organizations in the United Nations System: The Emerging Role of International Civil Society," *Human Rights Quarterly* 18 (1996): 112.

13. Martens, 282.

14. Peter Willetts, "Transnational Actors and International Organizations in Global Politics," in *The Globalization of World Politics*, eds. John Baylis, Steve Smith, and Patricia Owens, 4th ed. (Boulder, Colorado: Lynne Rienner Publishers., 2008), 340.

15. Code of Ethics and Conduct for NGOs, WANGO, accessed November 11, 2019, www.wango.org/codeofethics.a.spx.

16. Reza Hasmath, et al., "Conceptualizing Government-Organized Non-Governmental Organizations," *Journal of Civil Society* 15, no. 3 (2019): 267.

17. Ibid., 268, 280–281.

18. Susan Cotts Watkins, Ann Swidler, and Thomas Hannan, "Outsourcing Social Transformation: Development NGOs as Organizations," *Annual Review of Sociology* 38 (2012): 286.

19. Mia Lazzarini, "The Top 10 Influential NGOs," PeopleBrowsr, accessed January 6, 2020, www.peoplebrowsr.com/blog/the-top-ten-influential-ngos.

Chapter 1

Reasons for the Growth of Non-Governmental Organizations

After having set the stage for the layout of this work, it is vital to first consider the forces that led to the emergence and growth of NGOs. Even though the end of the Cold War is regarded as a watershed moment related to the growth of NGOs, what followed the Treaty of Westphalia could be an important reason for the rise of organizations and institutions resembling today's NGOs. Before the Treaty of Westphalia there was no separation of church and state, and the Church, other than family members assisting each other, was an important vehicle in helping people in need. But the rise of the modern state, the secularization of politics, and especially the rise of private wealth contributed to the proliferation of these organizations. The escalation of warfare, the greater destructiveness of war, social problems resulting from industrialization, etc. led to an acute need for organizations to supplement the role of the state in offering services. The International Committee of the Red Cross (ICRC) is an example of such an organization. Henri Dunant, a Swiss banker, and four other Geneva residents founded it during the second half of the 19th century. At the battle of Solferino, Italy, in 1859 Durant saw thousands of soldiers dying on the battlefield because of inadequate medical services. These experiences propelled Durant to seek the help of locals to care for the soldiers. In 1862 he published what he observed at Solferino and by 1863 he had so much support that the Geneva Society for Public Welfare assisted him in founding the International Committee for the Relief of the Wounded. In 1875 this organization became the International Committee of the Red Cross.[1]

There are, of course, many other reasons, both internal and external, for the growth of NGOs during the last thirty to forty years. According to Manuel Castells, globalization is one of the reasons for the emergence of NGOs as important actors in global politics. He states that today's global world is characterized by the following: 1. the existence of a global economy; 2. a global

1

media system; 3. irreversible environmental damage caused by unsustainable development; 4. globalization of human rights; and 5. global security as a shared problem. "Overall, the critical issues conditioning everyday life for people and their governments in every country are largely produced and shaped by globally interdependent processes that go beyond the realm of countries as defined by the territories under the sovereignty of a given state. Under such conditions, a number of processes constitute the new landscape of global politics. There is a growing gap between the space where the issues are defined (global) and the space where the issues are managed (the nation-state). This is at the source of four distinct, while related, political crises that affect the institutions of national governance."[2]

The crises confronting democratic states are: 1. Crisis of efficiency: problems cannot be sufficiently managed by individual governments (i.e., global warming and regulation of financial markets). 2. Crisis of legitimacy: "political representation is increasingly distant." There is greater separation between political representatives and those being represented; this is a situation worsened by the media with its emphasis on scandals and access to power by the privileged. 3. Crisis of identity: as people see their nation and culture becoming disjointed by the forces of globalization, "their claim to autonomy takes the form of resistance identity and cultural identity politics as opposed to their identity as citizens." 4. Crisis of equity: globalization often increases inequality between countries and among social groups within countries. The absence of global regulatory regimes to manage global inequality places great strain upon welfare states. And countries without welfare states have even greater difficulty compensating for the increasing inequality. Because of these crises and the inability of governments to do much about them, non-state actors, among them NGOs, become the voices for the voiceless.[3] Of course, such crises are not the property of democratic countries alone. The same crises and more face many nondemocratic states — among the reasons for the growth of NGOs there as well.

Kim Reimann provides more reasons for the growth of NGOs in the late 1980s and early 1990s with the end of the Cold War. NGOs have proliferated in numbers because of "expanding opportunities for resource mobilization and political access." As international organizations and institutions have expanded to deal with global issues, they have sought the cooperation of NGOs as service providers and advocates. In addition, greater international funding opportunities have created an environment conducive to NGO growth.[4]

NGOs need funding to survive and fulfill their mission and governments have been among the most important donors in the form of grants and other forms of assistance. Among national governments, the United States government has been the world leader in providing aid and assistance. The current aid system was established by the 1961 Foreign Assistance Act. According to this law, aid is defined as "the unilateral transfers of US resources by the US government to or for the benefit of foreign entities." The resources dispensed included not only goods and funding but also technical assistance, educational programs, health care, and other kinds of services. Recipients of this aid are governments, local businesses, charitable groups, international organizations, and of course NGOs.[5]

Even though estimates vary depending on the source, according to the nonpartisan Congressional Research Service (CRS), the total spending, which included military and security assistance, was approximately $49 billion in 2016. This accounts for about 1.2 percent of the federal budget. Funding levels were the highest following World War II when the United States was heavily involved in reconstructing European economies. In the 1990s, aid levels were cut because of the collapse of the Soviet Union; in 1997 aid spending was less than $20 billion, or 0.8 percent of the budget. Aid was significantly increased after the 9/11 attacks, surpassing 1.4 percent of the budget by 2007.[6]

The goals of foreign aid are multiple with national security being the most important with the aim of providing stability, supporting allies, promoting democracy, and assisting in counterterrorism efforts abroad. There are, of course, other reasons for providing aid beyond national security. These include providing humanitarian relief during natural disasters, assisting in efforts to reduce poverty, and promoting health care and other development programs. The United States attempts to achieve these goals through an array of programs. According to CRC calculations, foreign aid in 2016 was distributed as follows:

Long-term development aid (42 percent) went toward funding projects that promoted economic growth in developing countries. More than half of this assistance funded health programs related to HIV/AIDS and family health.

Military and security aid (33 percent) went toward helping allies purchase American military equipment, training military personnel from other countries, and assisting in peacekeeping missions.

Humanitarian aid (14 percent) was spent to provide relief during humanitarian crises. This included relief efforts by the State Department and Defense Department as well as purchases of American agricultural goods and supporting organizations such as the International Red Cross and the United Nations High Commissioner for Refugees.

Political aid (11 percent) was designed to promote political stability, economic reforms, and democratic institutions.[7]

American foreign assistance is managed by a complex system of more than twenty federal agencies. "The 1961 Foreign Assistance Act created the US government's primary aid organization, the US Agency for International

Development (USAID). The agency administers the bulk of US development and humanitarian aid, managing nearly $20 billion in funds and employing more than nine thousand staff around the world. [President] Trump's proposed budgets, in 2017 and 2018, sought to slash USAID funds by nearly a third, but were rejected by Congress. USAID is a semi-independent agency, operating under the policy guidance of the president, the State Department, and the National Security Council. It receives its funding through the State Department budget.... The Department of Defense plays a major role as the agency primarily responsible for implementing traditional military aid, though the State Department also funds and influences many security assistance programs. The Department of Health and Human Services implements many health-related programs ... The Treasury Department helps manage funding of global financial institutions, as well as programs for debt relief and economic reforms in poor countries. There is also a plethora of other agencies and autonomous organizations, including the Millennium Challenge Corporation, the Peace Corps, and the African Development Foundation, involved in aid work."[8]

United States funds for NGOs are channeled primarily through USAID as well as the National Endowment for Democracy (NED) and the United States Institute of Peace (USIP). Most USAID funds go through universities, NGOs, and contractors. The CRS in 2015 reported that only 4 percent of USAID assistance went directly to governments. According to the report, 49 percent of the aid was directed toward American nonprofit organizations, for-profit companies, and American educational institutions. About 29 percent went to international organizations such as the Global Fund and numerous United Nations agencies. Even though not all aid flows through USAID, more than 60 percent of it does.[9] The NED provides more than 1,200 grants to support NGOs that are "dedicated to the cultural values, institutions, and organizations of democratic pluralism." The NED is primarily funded by the US Congress and it is subject to oversight by Congress, the State Department, and independent financial audit. The USIP is an "independent, nonpartisan institution established and funded by Congress ... [and its] goal is to create a world without violent conflict."[10]

The United Nations system is made up of the United Nations itself and many programs, funds, and specialized agencies, all with their leadership and budget. The programs and funds are financed through voluntary contributions while the specialized agencies are independent organizations funded by voluntary and assessed contributions. NGOs helped establish the United Nations and they have worked with the United Nations ever since. The United Nations Charter has arrangements for United Nations and NGOs consultations, which are described in the Economic and Social Council (ECOSOC) in Article 71. Actual NGO participation in the United Nations system has expanded dramatically because of "(1) the public parliamentary character of social relationships at the various UN headquarters, (2) widening UN system agendas, (3) the technological revolution in communications and (4) growing demand of people throughout the world to play a role in shaping political decisions that affect their lives."[11]

NGOs have become engaged in almost all issues and agendas in the United Nations system. They perform various roles in public meetings of decision-making bodies, and they also play a role in preparing public meetings. At the same time,

> their relations with secretariats involve an even broader range of activities, including regular meetings, representation on committees, involvement in symposia, receiving papers posted on UN websites, joint research, joint implementation and monitoring of UN programs and even standing in for UN agencies.
>
> NGO involvement in UN conferences away from headquarters has broadened NGO participation, and served to relax restraints on NGO participation and encourage NGOs to develop their own parallel assemblies. These developments have led to the involvement of an increasing number of NGOs at the UN headquarters and demands for fewer restraints on UN participation there. It has also fostered the development of a People's Millennium Forum at UN Headquarters and visions of a permanent People's Assembly alongside the present General Assembly of states.[12]

NGOs have the greatest influence regarding the environment, women's rights, development, and human rights. In these areas, NGOs use the media and lobbying of individual governments to set the agenda at the UN. The degree of influence varies depending on the issue under consideration. Governments and NGOs often negotiate comfortably enough about the environment, development, and maybe women's issues. However, in some other areas such as disarmament, NGOs are kept on the sidelines. As for human rights issues, NGOs have had to fight every step of the way and one of the major reasons for this has been the matter of sovereignty.[13]

Since its inception and through many of its agencies the United Nations has also been a major funder of NGOs and United Nations agencies have included NGOs as partners and contractors while offering services all over the globe.

Below is a list of Funds and Programs, Specialized Agencies, and other entities and bodies working with and funding NGOs:

FUNDS AND PROGRAMS

- The United Nations Development Program (UNDP)

- The United Nations Environment Program (UNEP)
- The United Nations Population Fund (UNFPA)
- The United Nations Human Settlements Program (UN-Habitat)
- The United Nations Children's Fund (UNICEF)
- The World Food Program (WFP)

UN SPECIALIZED AGENCIES

These agencies are independent organizations working with the United Nations through negotiated agreements. Some were created before World War I; some were associated with the League of Nations, some were created at the same time the United Nations was created, and some were created by the United Nations to meet emerging needs.

- The Food and Agriculture Organization (FAO)
- The International Civil Aviation Organization (ICAO)
- The International Fund for Agricultural Development (IFAD)
- The International Labor Organization (ILO)
- The International Monetary Fund (IMF)
- The International Maritime Organization (IMO)
- The International Telecommunication Union (ITU)
- The United Nations Educational, Scientific and Cultural Organization (UNESCO)
- The United Nations Industrial Development Organization (UNIDO)
- The World Tourism Organization (UNWTO)
- The Universal Postal Union (UPU)
- The World Health Organization (WHO)
- The World Intellectual Property Organization (WIPO)
- The World Meteorological Organization (WMO)
- The World Bank

OTHER ENTITIES AND BODIES

- The Joint United Nations Program on HIV/AIDS (UNAIDS)
- The United Nations High Commissioner for Refugees (UNHCR)
- The United Nations Institute for Disarmament Research (UNIDIR)
- The United Nations Institute for Training and Research (UNITAR)
- The United Nations Office for Project Services (UNOPS)

- The United Nations Relief and Works Agency for Palestine Refugees (UNRWA)
- The United Nations System Staff College (UNSSC)
- UN Women

RELATED ORGANIZATIONS

- The Preparatory Commission for the Comprehensive Nuclear-Test-Ban Treaty Organization (CTBTO)
- The International Atomic Energy Agency (IAEA)
- The International Organization for Migration (IOM)
- The Organization for the Prohibition of Chemical Weapons (OPCW)
- The United Nations Framework Convention on Climate Change (UNFCCC)
- The World Trade Organization (WTO)

A significant number of scholars focus on the undemocratic elements of the UN system which make it difficult for individuals and non-state actors to have a greater impact in international legal processes. "This structure institutionalizes the longstanding antipathy of states towards the idea of NGOs and individuals assuming an autonomous role in international affairs." Despite these difficulties, as already mentioned, NGOs have had a major effect on global affairs. "Concern with the environment, for women's equality, and for disarmament would not have achieved international expression without the backdrop of social and political understandings promoted by NGOs. This civil activity has supported a 'quiet revolution' in the UN system.... [It] has enabled non-governmental input to enrich the soft law processes of the General Assembly, to contribute informally to areas within the responsibility of the Security Council, and to influence international legislative processes, particularly in the area of human rights."[15]

Another intergovernmental organization that has increased its support of NGOs is the European Union. In addition to the desire of individual European Union members to support NGOs, what has become the European Union has had its own foreign assistance program since the 1960s and began funding NGOs in the mid-1970s. Other Western democratic states are also important sponsors of NGOs. Industrial democratic states have especially funded NGOs involved in international development and humanitarian crises.[16] The number of countries afflicted by calamities and in need of such assistance is overwhelming. The most recent examples of such countries include Syria, Libya, Greece, and many others, which means a role for the European Union and its individual members.

Nearly 80 percent of the European Union funding to NGOs is managed by the members themselves, while the rest is managed by the European Commission and other European Union bodies. Below is a list of projects funded by the European Union.

SOCIAL INCLUSION, GENDER, AND EQUAL OPPORTUNITIES

NGOs doing work in these areas may receive support from the European Social Fund (ESF).

CULTURE AND MEDIA

The Creative Europe program funds projects related to European the audio-visual, cultural, and creative sectors. This program is composed of two subprograms: Culture and MEDIA. The former subprogram supports coop-eration projects, literary translation, networks and platforms, while the latter provides funding to help the European Union film industry.

FOSTER CITIZENSHIP AND CIVIC PARTICIPATION

The Europe for Citizens program has two important goals: to help people understand what the European Union is all about and to promote European citizenship as well as to improve conditions for democratic and civic partici-pation at the European Union level.

RESEARCH AND INNOVATION

"Societal Challenges, a component of the *Horizon 2020* research and innova-tion program, provides funding for projects covering areas such as health, demographic change, food security, sustainable agriculture and forestry and marine, maritime and inland water research."

DEVELOPMENT AND HUMANITARIAN AID

"NGOs can get funding under most of the thematic or regional programs man-aged by the Commission's department dealing with international cooperation and development (DEVCO). NGOs are also eligible for funding for humanitarian aid and civil protection activities through the Commission's department dealing with humanitarian aid and civil protection (ECHO)."

TRANSPORT, ENERGY, AND ICT

Funding is available to NGOs for projects related to the Connecting Europe Facility (CEF).[17]

A further reason for the proliferation of NGOs is private foundations. In 2013, the strength of these foundations was felt even more than previously as many of them have become the largest donors to nonprofit organizations and have created opportunities for NGOs in countries around the globe. Many private foundations fund NGOs involved in international development, service, and advocacy making them significant sources for new partnerships and opportunities for NGOs. Here is a list of the top ten United States charitable foundations, which have contributed billions to NGOs.

THE BILL AND MELINDA GATES FOUNDATION

The foundation supports projects around the world that are trying to solve some of the most pressing healthcare problems including HIV/AIDS, polio, and Malaria. The foundation also plans to help about 150 million of the poorest families in Sub-Saharan Africa and Asia to lift themselves out of poverty.

OPEN SOCIETY FOUNDATIONS

These Foundations fund programs ranging from public health to education and business development. They are committed "to the global struggle for open society and responding quickly to the challenges and opportunities of the future." Their mission is to "build vibrant and tolerant democracies where governments are accountable to citizens."

THE FORD FOUNDATION

The founding charter of the foundation states that resources should be used in such a way to promote "scientific, educational and charitable purposes." Today, the foundation sustains programs in dozens of countries. It delivers three major programs: "World Peace and the establishment of law and justice," "Freedom and democracy," and "Advancing the economic well-being for people everywhere."

THE WILLIAM AND FLORA HEWLETT FOUNDATION

The foundation provides funding to solve social and environmental problems across the globe. Currently, the foundation focuses on issues related to limiting the risk of climate change, improving education for young people, and improving reproductive health and rights.

THE CHILDREN'S INVESTMENT FUND FOUNDATION (CIFF)

This foundation aims at improving the lives of children in developing countries by transforming the environments in which children live. In addition, CIFF tries to lobby governments so that they put in place policies that will benefit children. The foundation emphasizes four major projects: climate, education, hunger alleviation, and child survival.

THE UNITED NATIONS FOUNDATION

This foundation brings together governments and different sectors to deal with significant international challenges. It provides funds and it also behaves as a platform for connecting people to help the United Nations solve worldwide problems. The foundation endeavors to create partnerships, to grow constituencies, to mobilize resources, and to advocate changes to support the United Nations mission. The foundation works with NGOs around the world on four primary areas: energy and climate, global health, the United Nations and women, and population.

THE JOHN D. AND CATHERINE T. MACARTHUR FOUNDATION

The foundation supports people and organizations interested in "building a more just, verdant, and peaceful world." The foundation also tries to promote human rights, "advance global conservation and security, make cities better places, and understand how technology is affecting children and society." By providing funding to individuals and organizations, the foundation promotes "the development of knowledge, nurtures individual creativity, strengthens institutions, helps improve public policy, and provides information to the public, primarily through support for public interest media."

THE CONRAD N. HILTON FOUNDATION

The foundation provides funding to nonprofit organizations that work on relieving suffering, helping the distressed and the destitute. Its mission is to cooperate with locally based organizations to help in the following areas: helping children affected by HIV/AIDS, supporting older youth in foster care, preventing substance abuse, and providing safe access to clean water in developing countries.

THE ROCKEFELLER FOUNDATION

The foundation helps to promote work that "expands opportunity and strengthens resilience to social, economic, health and environmental challenges." The foundation works with NGOs as well as governments aimed at meeting four important goals: revalue ccosystems, advance health, secure livelihoods, and transform cities.

THE GORDON AND BETTY MOORE FOUNDATION

The foundation makes the effort "to advance environmental conservation, scientific research, and patient care around the world." It devotes some of its funding "to experimentation, focused innovation, and agile response to time-sensitive, high-impact opportunities in its areas of focus."[18]

The availability of more funding is, of course, beneficial to NGOs. But at the same time, there are problems associated with it. NGOs in especially nondemocratic societies are under extreme pressure from their governments regarding many of their roles as well as their financial dependence upon foreign donors. Governmental pressure put aside, LNGOs are often frustrated with Western governmental agencies such as USAID and the European Commission. "These agencies often come ... with agendas rooted in specific foreign policy objectives seeking 'partners' to unquestioningly carry out programs that seldom resonate with the political situation on the ground."[19]

Such developments are changing the nature of NGOs and their sources of funding. NGOs that receive funding from foreign donors have three options available to them: to become GNGOs, to alter their mandate to accommodate foreign donors, or to try to remain true to their mission while facing downsizing or closure because of the absence of funding. As part of the first option, NGOs can become part of government disinformation campaigns. As part of the second, NGOs serve "the funders' 'project objectives'" in the region. The third, "which some of the older and better-established NGOs have chosen, is to set their own agendas and to raise their money accordingly. They have decided that foreign funds are welcome if a donor wishes to support a program they have designed. If not, they do not wish to take the money."[20]

One of the most interesting and presently one of the most significant reasons for the growth of NGOs is the number of failed, or near failed, states in Africa, the Balkans, the Middle East, the former Soviet Union, and elsewhere in the world. Failed states have increased the level of chaos and uncertainty to which NGOs and other organizations and institutions have tried to respond. The humanitarian emergencies resulting from failed states are defined by the following characteristics: the collapse of central government authority; ethnic or religious conflict and human rights abuses; food insecurity and starvation; high rates of inflation and unemployment; and massive numbers of internally displaced people and refugees. Such emergencies have caused a shift of resources from sustainable development to life-saving humanitarian interventions. As such, the amount of funding provided by USAID to UN organizations, the International Organization for Migrations, the International Committee of the Red Cross, and other NGOs rose dramatically beginning in the 1980s and 1990s.[21]

In 1989 the Office of Foreign Disaster Assistance (OFDA) and Food for Peace, both USAID offices, offered $297 million for humanitarian relief. This amount was raised to $1.2 billion by 1993. A very complex system emerged to respond to these emergencies and to spend this money. The system is composed of NGOs, UN agencies, and the ICRC, with NGOs being the most complex, especially when it comes to humanitarian emergencies.[22]

Natural disasters, the rise in the number of citizen demonstrations, and the role of the media are additional reasons for the growing number of NGOs. Multiple examples could be cited to illuminate the point. Two among many are what happened in China in 2008 and thereafter and what happened in Greece primarily since 1999. On May 12, 2008, an earthquake measuring 7.9 on the Richter scale struck the western part of Sichuan Province, causing severe damage and the death of approximately 70,000 people. The social response to this calamity was unexpected. There was a dramatic increase in volunteers, civic organizations, and enterprises, and media donated their time, money, and materials to the relief and reconstruction efforts. While some of the organizations were INGOs or GNGOs, many were grassroots associations. The response was so great, some media reports spoke of 2008 as the "Year of the Volunteer" or the "Year of Civil Society."[23]

The unprecedented response from volunteers and organizations demonstrates that civil society in China has made progress. In the past, during disasters the government monopolized relief efforts with minimum participation by ordinary citizens. But have these developments led to significant change in state-society relations? Studies of civil society responses to calamities show that, in the short run, the shortcomings of the state are exposed and present civic associations with an opportunity to play an important role. In some cases, disasters have led to changes in law related to civic organizations. In other cases, calamities have had limited impact on state-society relations, "as the upsurge in NGO activity and volunteering was not sustained."[24]

[Nonetheless,] the Sichuan earthquake was a watershed event for China's associational sphere. It triggered an unprecedented display of public-spiritedness, charitable giving, volunteering and networking in Chinese society. The extensive horizontal networking among a diverse community of NGOs produced the strongest expression to date of a nascent Chinese civil society not captured by the corporatist state. Civil society associations do not necessarily have to assume an oppositional role vis-a-vis the state. Indeed, ... cooperation and partnerships with the state were an important part of the NGO response. The rapid emergence of NGO networks is also an indication of the social capital that has accumulated over the past decade or so in China's associational community. This reserve of social capital is impressive, given the long-standing problems in the NGO community such as weak organizational capacity, fragmentation and lack of legitimacy, in addition to the constraints imposed by an authoritarian state which remains suspicious of NGOs. While this social capital may not lead to democratization, it shows that NGOs are able to come together to address broader issues that transcend their own parochial interests.[25]

A subsequent study confirms the optimism expressed by Shawn Shieh and Guosheng Deng, and it also confirms some of their reservations about NGOs and Chinese civil society. Kang Yi, in his examination of developments in the Sichuan Province after the earthquake, notes that at first there was cooperation between local governments and NGOs, but after 2010 local government support of LNGOs diminished significantly. One the one hand, various governmental policies recognized the role of social organizations and encouraged them to pursue funding from the government and domestic foundations. But the 2017 Foreign NGO Management Law restricted the activities of foreign NGOs in China and made it very difficult for LNGOs to access foreign funding.[26]

After the earthquake, some locals in the Sichuan Provide established their own NGOs without support from the government. The absence of connections with government officials and their lack of financial resources made their survival difficult. To overcome these problems, they decided to expand their networks, and in the process not only made friends in different parts of the globe, but also became exposed to foreign civil society practices and knowledge. At first, local government authorities paid little attention to these new social organizations, and generally regarded them positively. But as these grassroots organizations began to grow and to gain greater community support, local governments intervened in their development and compelled them demonstrate loyalty.[27]

Foreign NGOs also played an important role during the post-earthquake period by providing relief to the victims, and by helping in the rehabilitation and reconstruction of the area. Their presence was appreciated by the residents and local authorities. But this did not last for very long. Even though government authorities tolerated a degree of NGO independence as long they "could harness the resources of these organizations for their own benefit," tensions began to emerge with the passing of time. "Local authorities not only continuously asked these NGOs to contribute resources and ideas to fulfil governmental agendas, but also increasingly intervened in their operations to ensure that they followed the directives of local authorities."[28]

The passing of the Chinese Charity Law, which relaxed registration and fundraising requirements for LNGOs, gave rise to philanthropic foundations. These foundations supported the development of grassroots organizations and provided funding to them. But even these foundations "scarcely deviated from the agenda of the state, as they relied on the permission and support of the authorities."[29]

Yi concludes his work by making the following sobering comments:

[Although] after the earthquake the Chinese government ... embraced a more open associational environment, it remains unclear whether Chinese NGOs can flourish and contribute to the rise of a civil society in the western sense of the term. In fact, most of these NGOs have limited aspirations that do not extend to promoting civil society as a political space: they simply wish to avoid trouble and complement the state in serving populations in need. Moreover, the narrowing of funding sources has caused anxiety and driven NGOs to compete for the favor and patronage of donors. Recently established NGOs are likely to become government or business-like organizations before they can demonstrate their unique value.... Still, not everything is lost. The new funding game that sees the coexistence of government and business rationales, as well as recent developments like the facilitated channels for philanthropic public fundraising and NGOs' versatile strategies for self-sufficient growth, may still open new windows of opportunity for Chinese NGOs.[30]

Christos Frangonikopoulos, in his article about NGOs in Greece notes that participation in NGOs increased since the 1980s. By the mid-1990s, 1,200 NGOs operated in Greece. By 1999 there were about 2,400 NGOs. The deadly 1999 earthquake in Athens led many NGOs to offer food, clothes, and health services to the victims. NGOs, both Greek and non-Greek, also offered welfare services to immigrants and others in need. Among the most active non-Greek NGOs were Doctors without Borders (Medecins sans Frontiers — MSF) and Doctors of the World. As for Greek NGOs, those which played the most visible role were Klimaka (Scale), Praksis (Action), Orthodox Church-related NGOs such as Apostoli (Mission), Helpida (Hope), Hamogelo tou Paidiou (Children's Smile), Diktyo Dikaiomaton tou Paidiou (Network for Children's Rights), Hellenic League of Human Rights, Minority Groups Research Center, Merangopoulos Foundation, Antigone, Institute for Rights, Equality and Diversity, and Greek Forum of Migrants.[31]

In the summer of 2007, NGOs played an important role in response to the forest fire in Parnitha near Athens. Using social media, NGOs mobilized citizens to protest the lack of strong environmental legislation. Today there are about 300 environmental NGOs. Some of these NGOs are small NGOs affiliated with large international NGOs such as the World Wildlife Fund (WWF) and Greenpeace. Many of these NGOs are in Athens and Thessaloniki, but there a few others that are active in small islands as well as mountainous areas. The serious financial crisis that began in 2009 stimulated many Greeks to mobilize even more and offer their services. Social networks and self-help groups have sprung up across Greece and especially the major cities to provide food, shelter, medical services, etc. "Characteristic examples are the exchange and distribution networks of goods and services for vouchers or online credit, which in 2013 numbered 22. Significant is also the operation of 11 social medical centers and 7 social pharmacies, established by volunteering doctors, nurses, pharmacists and social workers. Indicative is also the increasing ... network of volunteers which serve as intermediaries between supermarkets, restaurants and bakeries in order to supply food to soup kitchens, shelters, orphanages, homes for the elderly and other charitable organizations."[32]

However, at least in the case of Greece, "this increase in civic engagement in NGOs should not be understood as a reflection of Greece's social and political norms. In 2011, and despite the acute social consequences of the economic crisis, only 14 percent of Greeks participated in voluntary activities, in contrast to 26 percent of Italians, 15 percent of Spaniards and 12 percent of Portuguese (European Union [EU]-27 average: 24 per cent)."[33] There are many reasons for this outcome.

One of the reasons for such mindset is the importance of family and relatives regarding mutual aid and support. As a result, the level of social trust and membership in associations and other social networks is very low. Only during the summer Olympics of 2004 there was an increase in voluntarism. And at the time it was the beginning of a new period for voluntarism in

Greece. But research conducted after 2004 has revealed that Greeks "care for their fellow citizen only occasionally, or under extenuating circumstances, and during natural disasters."[34]

Another reason why Greeks think as they do about voluntarism is the "existence of a clientilistic and antagonistic political party system [that] does not allow for the growth of an autonomous civil society and NGO sector ... [The] polarization of the political debate, as well as the dominant role of the state in the economy have not only turned politics into a struggle for office, but have also significantly reduced the space for the development of NGOs as the party in power uses the state to develop clientilistic networks that under-mined meritocracy and interpersonal trust."[35]

NGOs, in Greece and much of the rest of the world, seek media attention in order to advance their goals and to frame the public debate. The mass media on the other hand operate with one important goal in mind, to increase their ratings, viewership, and readership. In the case of Greece, media organiza-tions prioritize information coming mostly from the government, large busi-nesses, entertainment, and sports. Journalists are given assignments related to important ministries and very few of them are assigned to specific NGOs. Consequently, the organization of news works against NGOs. NGOs need the media to gain greater visibility while the media does not need NGOs to survive.[36]

Under the prevailing circumstances "and in a society where the steady and long-term occupation with voluntary work is not the priority of citizens, the recognizability of NGO[s] inevitably is directed by the mass media. The mass media afford limited space to the projection of NGOs, and when they do so they do not deepen their analysis on the need of NGOs to promote voluntarism and solutions to long-standing social and economic problems. NGOs benefit from favorable projection of their activities during emotion-ally charged periods (Christmas, Easter, physical disasters and humanitarian tragedies). At the same time and when considering that most Greek NGOs are dependent upon financing and grants, they are also projected as mongers of public money."[37]

The Greek media has devoted much time to exposing questionable transac-tions between NGOs and the state. While many transactions between NGOs and the state were under investigation, "the entire sector has become a scape-goat for all cases of political corruption that have ravaged the country since the mid-1990s. The entire NGO sector has been discredited as a result. To illustrate, a recent public opinion poll reported that 78.2 percent of Greek citi-zens do not trust NGOs when it comes to national progress and prosperity."[38]

The situation between NGOs and the media in Greece and several other countries should not prevent us from realizing the significant role played by the technological revolution as related to the growth of NGOs. "The change in the speed of communication has been dramatic. Just as important, but rarely acknowledged, is that email, the Web and applications such as Facebook and Twitter are extremely inexpensive to operate. Global Communications can for the first time be used by the poor as well as the rich. ..."[39]

In the opinion of Peter Willetts,

[the] origins [of the internet] lie not in a military-developed command-and-control communications system, but in the vision and technical innovation of a small number of NGO activists in the 1980s who realized the potential of electronic communications to enhance the work of all NGOs. It is true, that in the 1960s, the Pentagon's Advanced Research Projects Agency funded university computer science departments to create a computer network. However, people-to-people, email networks—mainly for university staff and students — evolved in the 1970s, as an unplanned outcome and initially were not open to the public. The first global NGO electronic network, Interdoc, was built in 1984 by the International Coalition for Development Action (ICDA), at the request of their African and Latin American NGO members. This too was for private use by ICDA members only. In 1986, PeaceNet/EcoNet in San Francisco and GreenNet in London became Internet providers and took the first step in opening global email and electronic conferencing to the public. By 1990, before Tim Berners-Lee had produced the first Web page, these NGO pioneers had linked to advanced networks in five other countries and by telephone connections to many more. They went on to form the Association for Progressive Communication (APC), which provided a public network for NGO activists. Their technical lead meant both the World Bank and the UN first went onto the Internet by using the APC servers.[40]

The changing nature and context of conflicts since the end of the Cold War has been a contributing factor regarding the greater role of NGOs. The end of the Cold War, in the opinion of some scholars, has led to issues such as "governance, democratic legitimacy, social inclusion and economic equity ranking just as high as, if not higher than, traditional military and security priorities...." As a consequence, "conflict management can no longer be restricted simply to military-based strategies." This statement is illuminated by the difficulties encountered by the US-led coalition to rebuild Afghanistan and Iraq.[41]

What do these developments, for example, mean in the case of Southeast Asia? Even though the UN has played an important and successful role in Cambodia and East Timor, the region's reluctance toward interventionism should tamper people's expectations for greater civilian participation in peace operations. Two commonly cited objections in this regard are: "First, regional elites prefer state centrism, non-interference and 'soft' regionalism. ... The other concern derives from the fact that regional institutions such as the

Association of Southeast Asian Nations (ASEAN) and the Asia-Pacific wide ASEAN Regional Forum (ARF) continue to lack the institutional capacity as well as requisite collective will to contribute to peace operations, much less to tolerate civilian involvement in such missions."[42]

In spite these difficulties, at least two interrelated developments have taken place in Southeast Asia — institutional and attitudinal — to offer hope for greater civilian participation in peace operations in that part of the world.

> On the one hand, it is maintained that specific institutional changes, including those undertaken in response to certain post-Cold War challenges confronting the region, have engendered social conditions more or less favorable to NGO involvement in humanitarian intervention. Four areas of institutional change have been noted: (1) a limited recalibration of long-standing state-centric norms in response to various contemporary, nontraditional regional challenges; (2) the proliferation and rising influence of NGOs as a result of ongoing political liberalization within the region; (3) the potential enlistment of civil society (to be defined later) actors by governments in the regional war against terrorism; and (4) the growing pattern of formalization in the region, partly exemplified by ASEAN's strategic efforts, still incipient at this stage, to utilize hitherto untested mechanisms in strengthening regional resilience against region-wide threats that have the potential to cripple the region's economies and societies. On the other hand, it is also maintained that a parallel attitudinal adjustment in military opinions toward NGO activism in humanitarian intervention and particularly peace operations appears to be taking place. Civilian attitudes towards military counterparts are also changing, but at a slower pace.[43]

It is important at this juncture to include some of the reasons for the growing role of NGOs in conflict management. Among them are the accelerating coalitions of civil society groups and their insistence upon having a say related to issues from antipersonnel landmines to multinational corporations. The end of the Cold War led to the inclusion of more individuals and institutions in the process of conflict resolution. States and international organizations, after ignoring NGOs for a very long time, have realized that NGOs could play a significant role in societies facing strife. And on their part, NGOs have participated in conflict resolution efforts all over the world. This of course does not mean that there are no problems. The good thing though is that many NGOs recognize these difficulties. They recognize that they should "do no harm" and should do what will promote the interests of the people confronted with strife. NGOs have begun to recognize that working with international peacekeepers as partners and not as competitors is positive, and governments and peacekeepers can no longer ignore the importance of NGOs in conflict management.[44]

There is no doubt that the Internet has been of great benefit to NGOs and has contributed to their growth. NGOs can communicate with each other and their members more efficiently and with greater speed. This enhances their ability to mobilize the public across the globe. Despite all this, the "effect of the Internet should not be exaggerated. There would have been no Arab Spring without the existence of a young generation of disaffected, educated, unemployed individuals, who were willing to risk their lives by responding to the calls made on the Internet for them to demonstrate."[45]

Dramatic shift in the form of government has also been a contributing factor as related to the growth of NGOs. An example of such development, among many, is Cambodia. From 1975 to 1979, the Khmer Rouge regime caused great destruction and the death of two million people. The Khmer Rouge regime also closed and expelled members of international organizations present in Cambodia. Soon after the regime collapsed in 1979, several organizations such as UNICEF, World Food Program, the Food and Agriculture Organization, the International Committee of the Red Cross, and Oxfam returned to Cambodia to provide emergency relief assistance. By the early 1980s approximately two dozen NGOs were involved in the country.[46]

Increased foreign aid in the early 1990s gave rise to the number of INGOs and LNGOs from less than 100 in 1991 to about 1,000 in the early 2000s. In 2012 about 1,400 NGOs operated in Cambodia. The current funding of NGOs in Cambodia is not as robust as in the past when the country was regarded as "a donor darling." And while funding is decreasing, the need for such funding is greater due to the large number of NGOs. The competition for limited financial resources has caused the demise of many LNGOs while some INGOs have decided to move out of Cambodia. A 2012 study revealed that of the 3,000 NGOs registered in Cambodia only 1,350 were still active.[47]

LNGOs were involved in projects related to health, water sanitation, education, agriculture, and advocacy. The rise in the number of LNGOs was sustained by the United Nations Transitional Authority in Cambodia (UNTAC) and INGOs involved in promoting democracy, human rights, poverty reduction, and social development. "However, the growth and consolidation of LNGOs in Cambodia has provoked comments pointing out that LNGO proliferation was more a response to available donor funding or foreign initiatives than a gradual opening up of democratic space, the natural scaling up of grassroots organizations, the emergence of a culture of voluntarism/social activism or the organized charity of an established middle class. As many LNGOs did not evolve from the bottom up, these organizations were not based on the real needs of communities. The more so as with the increasing dependence on [international aid or Official Development Assistance] ODA the process of development in Cambodia is dominated by foreign agencies acting on behalf but in fact beyond the control of local people."[48]

A somewhat different perspective is presented by S. Ui et al. in their work on the role of NGOs in strengthening community participation at health centers in rural Cambodia. The authors note that after the persistent conflict ended in 1998 and elections were held in 2002, a pilot program was introduced to involve community participation in health care management as a way of improving national health. For this purpose, two committees were established: The Health Center Management Committee (HCMC) and Village Health Support Group (VHSG) as the vehicles for community participation. "The HCMC was to make decisions about the health center's services and management, while the VHSG was to exchange information and provide feedback between community members and the health center.... However, the functionality and sustainability of the committees have come into question, because such committees have only nominal existence at many health centers. The Cambodian Ministry of Health's efforts to activate the committees were limited, due to financial constraints. Most of the efforts related to local health committees in Cambodia involved international aid agencies or NGOs with intensive financial and technical inputs, and issues of sustainability are common after such projects phase out."[49]

Under these conditions, local NGOs in Cambodia have the potential of overcoming "the difficulties in community participation and sustainability, given their long-term commitments to specific localities and communities." They can do so by promoting community organizing and capacity building and application of experiences in health; through regular communication, monitoring, and management support to health centers; and by linking local actors for health. "Certain characteristics of local NGOs in Cambodia's provinces can enhance their effectiveness ... The process of building the capacity and confidence of a community takes a long time, and a local NGO with a long-term commitment to a certain geographical area can prepare the ground and facilitate the process.... Local NGOs often describe their very limited financial and material inputs as 'weaknesses.' However, such limitations could be strengths in the long run, because they can help to minimize attitudes of dependency upon NGOs and external agencies, both in communities and in government agencies."[50]

As demonstrated thus far, NGOs in Cambodia have played an ambivalent role with both positive and negative results. A further example of this situation is the role of civil society organizations and NGOs as related to transitional justice in Cambodia. The year 2019 signifies forty years after the end of the Khmer Rouge regime and fifteen years after the establishment in 2004 of the Extraordinary Chambers in the Courts of Cambodia (ECCC), also known as the Khmer Rouge tribunal.[51]

The geopolitics of the Cold War, the involvement of many countries in the affairs of Cambodia, and the political interests of the regimes succeeding the Khmer Rouge delayed negotiations between the United Nations and the government of Cambodia regarding accountability for crimes committed between 1975 and 1979 under the Khmer Rouge until 1997. The ECCC was able to secure the conviction of numerous individuals. "Besides the ECCC, civil society actors have significantly shaped the transitional justice process in Cambodia. Their work has been complimentary to the ECCC, in particular when it came to victim participation, legal services, psychosocial support and outreach, as civil society organizations provided many key services for the ECCC due to the tribunal's limited funding or mandate in this field. NGOs were able to make use of the attention of the international donor community on transitional justice in Cambodia that arose with the establishment of the ECCC, although they have now for the past few years faced significant 'donor fatigue.'"[52]

Given the current circumstances in Cambodia, many questions are raised about the transitional justice process and its long-term transformative potential. "With the dissolution of Cambodia's main political opposition party in 2017 and its exclusion from the 2018 election, the country has moved away from its scheduled trajectory towards democracy. In an increasingly authoritarian context, civil society organizations [and NGOs] ... working on human rights advocacy face significant difficulties to conduct their work ... [The] political situation in contemporary Cambodia ... raises questions regarding the legacies of the ECCC and the transitional justice process."[53]

Decisions by governments to introduce liberalization measures have been yet another reason for the growth of NGOs. Such an example is China. Since the 1980s, China has experienced an explosion of the NGO sector. In nearly three decades, the number of officially registered NGOs has grown to 440,000 — alongside many more unregistered ones. The significant growth is especially attributed to the social challenges resulting from the economic liberalization policies of the past few decades. The Chinese state gradually has withdrawn from the delivery of social and welfare services, which in turn allowed for the growth of NGOs. The changing Chinese landscape has caused many NGOs to become important players by receiving recognition for their contributions to society. These contributions range from "supplementing the state's role in providing social services to educating the public about various social issues."[54]

Local state authorities in China have decided to engage with NGOs because of their auxiliary role in providing services. For example, in 2012 the central government expressed its desire for greater participation by social organizations in different activities in cooperation with the state. While the role of the state in influencing NGO activities is highly suspect and should be scrutinized, it is important to understand how the government has "adopted and adapted corporatist measures in their engagement with NGOs.

... [Corporatist] measures continue to be employed by local authorities as an effective means of ensuring the potency and relevance of the local state in a rapidly changing sector. Notwithstanding, there is noticeable adaptation of corporatist measures — namely, the local state is utilizing subtle or tacit forms of approval to manage the sector."[55]

Among other factors that have contributed to the rise of NGOs in China are the impact of globalization, the Internet, the media, and INGOs. Before 1995, every Chinese NGO was created by the government. These NGOs had leaders chosen by the government, relied on the government for financial resources, and were controlled by the government, which, of course, led many to question the existence of an independent NGO sector. Since the mid-1990s, the number of NGOs has expanded tremendously. By 2012, there were 6.13 million of them. "A substantial number of grassroots NGOs initiated by citizens have emerged in a variety of areas, including women's rights, environmental protection and AIDS advocacy. It is estimated that the number of grassroots NGOs in China now exceeds one million."[56]

One often ignored and interesting factor influencing the development of Chinese NGOs is philanthropy. An increasing number of very wealthy Chinese are establishing their own NGOs or are funding already established ones. During the years of the Mao era, the Chinese government emphasized equality and forbade the accumulation of private wealth. But beginning in the early 1980s and after Deng Xiaoping allowed a few individuals to become wealthy, a new social class began to emerge in China. This class of wealthy people grew in numbers over the years. Before 1978, the Chinese government's attitude toward charity was negative and it banned or seized their assets. The initiation of reforms in the 1980s signaled a new period and the government's attitude toward charity changed. The establishment of the China Charity Federation in 1994 and the amendment of the "Regulations on the Management of Foundations" in 2004 caused the philanthropic sector to enter a new stage of development. "Previously, nearly all Chinese foundations had been established by the government. Wealthy individuals who wish to donate could only contribute to government-run charitable organizations, but the government-run charities had low accountability and efficiency, which greatly affected the willingness of the wealthy to donate. The 2004 revisions for the first time allowed enterprises and individuals to establish foundations, thus providing a new vehicle for the wealthy to engage in philanthropy. The new ability of the wealthy both to establish private foundations and to manage and use donated funds as they wished stimulated the wealthy's enthusiasm for donating. In addition, the Chinese Communist Party officially recognized the role of charity in social development, and the government began to actively encourage social donations.[57]

The following are four examples of the potency of philanthropy in China:

The Philanthropy of Cao Dewang

In 2009 and 2010, five southwest Chinese provinces experienced serious drought, which especially affected the poor in these places. In 2010, Cao Dewang, the chairman of Fuyao Group, and his son Cao Hui made personal donations to the China Foundation for Poverty Alleviation to help combat poverty in southwest China. "Cao Dewang has influenced the NGO sector in two ways. He has leveraged his large and public donations to promote the transparency and accountability of NGOs, which in turn helps to improve the trust in and support for NGOs from the government and the public and enhances the sustainability of China's NGO development. In addition, he has also actively shaped public policies by using personal relationships and funding research projects, which promote the improvement of the legal environment for NGOs and increase the impact of the NGO sector."[58]

Zhou Qingzhi and the Narada Foundation

In 2007, Zhou Qingzhi, another wealthy Chinese entrepreneur, and his colleagues funded the establishment of the Narada Foundation. Zhou himself continues to make yearly monetary contributions to the foundation for the purpose of promoting grassroots NGOs and NGO leadership. In this context, the Narada Foundation created the Ginkgo Fellow Program to cultivate future grassroots NGO leaders and the Bright Way Program to single out potential grassroots NGOs worthy of funding.[59]

Pan Jiangxue and the Adream Charitable Foundation

In 2002, Pan Jiangxue, a wealthy senior executive in the financial sector, visited Ngawa Prefecture in Sichuan Province and there she came across children without books and isolated from the rest of the world. She was so affected by what she saw, she and her associates established two Dream Centers, which were provided with libraries, computers, and other multimedia instruments so that the children could have access to educational material and not be isolated. The number of Dream Centers has increased with presence in many provinces across China and in 2008 Pan and her partners registered the Adream Charitable Foundation with the government. The foundation quickly became a model of transparency and efficiency for the philanthropic sector in China.[60]

Alashan Society Entrepreneur Ecology Association

The Alashan Society Entrepreneur Ecology Association (ASEE) is an environmental protection NGO established by sixty-four entrepreneurs in 2004. The initial reason for creating this association was to lessen the impact of desertification in the Alashan region in Inner Mongolia. After some early problems with running the association, ASEE's management was standardized and began to pursue new projects. The first is the Creating a Green Home Plan, which funds grassroots environmental-protection NGOs. The second is the Green Leadership Project, which provides training to young people interested in environmental protection and to nurture future leaders of environmental NGOs. The third is Cultivating Key Talent, which strives to provide mentorship to individuals who run newly established NGOs.[61]

It should be kept in mind that even though Chinese charities began to grow in the 1980s and 1990s, charity in China has a long history. [The] Confucian model of *ren* ... (benevolence) very much focused on the responsibility of those in power to care for the vulnerable. Buddhism stressed the ideals of charity and kindness. And during the Ming (1368–1644) and Qing (1644–1911) periods, "a new tradition of religiously inspired charities called *shantang* ... (benevolent associations)" joined the previously founded charities.[62]

When Christian missions arrived in China during the nineteenth century, "they presented this native tradition with both challenges and opportunities. Mission-run poor houses, schools and hospitals dwarfed even the largest *shantang*, and moreover enjoyed both endowed funding and a dedicated administrative structure, two institutional innovations that Chinese charities were quick to adopt." More hybrid Chinese charities were founded during the Republican era (1912–1949) because of the establishment of civic organizations as well as because of many crises, which the government was unable to deal with. As noted previously, beginning in 1949 with the founding of the People's Republic and until Deng Xiaoping rose to power, these developments were ended. "While the Republican regime had expressed reservations about the operation of private charities, the Communist government confronted these organizations adamantly and directly. Missionary institutions were closed almost immediately. Some native charities ... were purged; those that were not were effectively rendered redundant by virtue of a state that endeavored to take direct charge of the material equality and material welfare of the people."[63]

Although charities and NGOs in twenty-first century China and many other countries with similar political and institutional structures operate in a very limited space, a key to their success is their ability to "shape their own agendas to conform to government programs and demands, or at least to avoid public confrontation with them." Simultaneously, though, the strength of wealthy individuals and public opinion has emerged as a force to be reckoned with. While wealthy individuals have been able to carve out a powerbase, similarly these developments have led to a different aspect of the "intertwining of charity and public opinion: the mutual bolstering of state legitimacy and personal celebrity around worthy causes, the problems and promise of raising public awareness of issues outside the officially sanctioned framework, the role of foreign organizations, and the importance of charity to China's soft power abroad. The momentum with which public opinion gathers online is a force without precedent in China's history, and underscores the fact that even with draconian legislation waiting on the horizon, the Chinese state has perhaps more long-term interest than anyone else in ensuring the peaceful rise of the NGO sector."[64]

A less optimistic view related to the growth of grassroots organizations in China is presented by Anthony J. Spires et al. After having studied 263 grassroots organizations in Guangdong, Yunnan, and Beijing, and focusing on four important issues — HIV/AIDS, labor rights, environmental protection, and education — they concluded the following:

> The inspiring visions driving emergent NGOs have found fertile ground in China over the past decade. Yet, despite the blossoming of a support system for these grassroots groups, the reality is that the typical NGO operates at a very small scale and with extremely few resources. The services which such groups can provide and their ability to advocate on behalf of disadvantaged groups thus remain quite limited. Even though the number of NGOs will most likely increase over the next decade, we expect that, without substantive change in the political environment and more generous and stable financial support, the influence of grassroots NGOs will continue to be dwarfed by the sheer magnitude of China's diverse social needs. If grassroots NGOs are ever truly to flourish and to grow into something beyond the small, struggling green shoots that we see today, a great deal of deep and careful nurturing by many societal actors is essential.[65]

An approximate argument related to the state of NGOs in China is made by Hugo Winckler et al. They note that the Chinese government is "fine-tuning" the country's first law on NGOs, the "law on the Administration of Overseas Non-Governmental Organizations." Since the Arab Spring and the Orange Revolution in Ukraine, the Chinese government is convinced that the West is determined to cause regime change with the Chinese Communist Party being the target.[66]

This perceived hostility of the West provides the basis for the NGO law. Under this law, the Ministry of Public Security (MPS) could prevent INGOs from operating in China if it is decided that these organizations threaten Chinese national security. INGOs must have a government sponsor, and every year, they must have authorization from the MPS by submitting a work plan and a budget. This law has caused some NGOs to leave China, while others have decided to remain and operate under such restrictions. But at the same time, "there are nuances in China's position on how to administer foreign NGOs. Some of these organizations are valued for their contribution, especially in environmental affairs, as China faces up to a disastrous ecological crisis. Foreign NGOs have been involved in capacity building in many areas of China's development since the beginning of the reform era [under Deng Xiaoping], and China seems to want to avoid hindering their operations."[67]

Ghanem Bibi et al., in examining the multiplication of NGOs in the Arab world, argue that there are three main reasons: 1. They "constitute a necessity." 2. The political life in the Arab world is highly frustrating and NGOs are a way for people to become involved in campaigns having to do with women's rights, human rights, health, etc. 3. "[There] is outside pressure to allow more room for NGOs. The pressure is coming from more than one source, but mainly from the North, where NGOs are seen as another form of privatization of society."[68] Their argument, of course, is closely related to the appeal of the "Washington Consensus" especially beginning in the 1980s and 1990s.

The "Washington Consensus" is seen as synonymous with neoliberalism, a term coined in the 1980s by the free-market economist John Williamson. For governments in Latin America or elsewhere in the South to borrow money from the IMF, the World Bank, or any other neoliberal institutions they had to adhere to some stringent requirements. Among them were the following:

1. A guarantee of fiscal discipline, and a curb to budget deficit
2. A reduction of public expenditure, particularly in the military and public administration
3. Tax reform, aiming at the creation of a system with a broad base and with effective enforcement
4. Financial liberalization, with interest rates determined by the market
5. Competitive exchange rates, to assist expert-led growth
6. Trade liberalization, coupled with the abolition of import licensing and a reduction of tariffs
7. Promotion of foreign direct investment
8. Privatization of state enterprises, leading to efficient and improved performance
9. Deregulation of the economy
10. Protection of property rights[69]

Although adherence to these requirements led to general growth in numerous countries both in the North and South, these policies have also led to great disparities in income, loss of jobs, and states either unable or unwilling to provide the services and programs necessary for basic living. This has led to a vacuum filled by different organizations and institutions including NGOs.

A related argument regarding the growth of NGOs is made by Ruth Phillips and Susan Goodwin in their work on NGOs as central actors in contemporary welfare states. The authors note that over the past few years,

> The Australian welfare state has been significantly marketized, both through the privatization of state-based human services and through the contracting out of welfare services previously provided by the state.... It is in this context that human service NGOs have dramatically increased their activities as state-funded welfare and community service providers.
>
> In 2010, the Australian government, in recognition of the significant role of [NGOs] in delivering services, established the Office for the Not-for-profit Sector, and the Productivity Commission released a report that demonstrated enormous growth in the contribution of [NGOs] in Australia. The Productivity Commission report detailed the major shift in how social needs are provided in Australia. It found that the total government funding to the NGO human service sector increased from $10.1 billion in 1999—2000 to $25.5 billion in 2006—07. It also reported that in 46 percent of state and Commonwealth public sector agencies, NGOs account for 75 percent or more of the value of government funded services delivered by external organizations and that for a further 19 percent of public sector services agencies, NGOs account for between 50 and 74 percent of the value of these services' income.[70]

The neoliberal agenda is a conservative one and NGOs have been active in keeping certain political issues alive and challenging the agendas of those in power. In examining The Jesuit Refugee Service, Sydney, The NSW Red Cross, Amnesty International Australia, Sydney, Aid/Watch, Sydney, and The Center for Refugee Research, UNSW and The Australian Refugee Rights Alliance, Elaine Thomson concludes the following:

> If politics is, in part about agenda control, the NGOs studies here have demonstrated that there are ways in which to challenge the agendas set by governments and others in positions of power. Governments and their agendas in Australia are not insensitive to criticism especially, but not exclusively, in international forums.
>
> The NGOs provide alternative information and analysis. With internet access to such information, the environment in which those in power operate becomes less comfortable. Finally, the NGOs work at individual and community level where there is no one else, and this role may ultimately be the single most important element of a socially conscious ethical community.... Even now when terrorism as a mantra threatens to engulf all values, especially those of the most underprivileged, these NGOs continue to fight for the retention of a focus

on individual rights and for the greater good by promoting our humanity and remaining committed to social justice and equality ...[71]

Asef Bayat, in considering activism and social development in the Middle East, examines the strategies employed by grassroots organizations in the region to defend their rights and to improve their lives in the neoliberal era. The author correctly notes that before the 1980s, most Middle Eastern countries were either nationalist-populist (Egypt, Syria, Iraq, Libya, etc.) or pro-Western "rentier states" (Iran, Arab Gulf states). Income from oil allowed these states to provide social services to many of their citizens. Provision of social services was essential to these states in order to gain popularity among the peasants, workers, and the middle class. "The state acted as the moving force of economic and social development on behalf of the populace."[72]

The leaders of most if not all of these states were able to suppress civil society. Christopher Heurlin, in examining civil society under dictatorship in East Asia (the same could be applied in the Middle East as well as else-where), asserts that dictatorships utilize two strategies to deal with NGOs. "First, some dictatorships follow a corporatist strategy, in which business associations, development and social welfare organizations are co-opted into the state and controlled through a variety of strategies. Second, other dictatorships pursue an exclusionary strategy in which NGOs are marginal-ized and replaced with state institutions." The strategy used depends on the degree of "elite competition and the type of development strategy." One-party states tend to control elites more effectively and thus often adopt a corporat-ist strategy. "In personalist regimes dictators tend to fear the organizational and mobilizational potential of NGOs and thus tend to pursue exclusionary strategies."[73]

No matter what strategy was followed, the authoritarian nature of these states prevented meaningful political participation and the emergence of an effective civil society. "The regimes' etatist ideology and patrimonial tenden-cies rendered the state the main, if not the sole, provider of livelihoods for many citizens, in exchange for their loyalty." But the promotion by the IMF of the Economic Reform and Structural Adjustment programs (ERSA) has cause significant socioeconomic changes. Neoliberal policies have led to an increase in consumer goods and have enriched the upper strata of society. But at the same time, these policies have led to great income disparities and have caused serious changes in labor markets. In the meantime, states are no longer as generous regarding their social responsibilities.[74]

The above-mentioned sociopolitical developments were followed "by the globalization of the ideas of human rights and political participation, which have placed economic rights and citizen participation on the political agenda and subsequently helped to open new spaces for social mobilization. The inability of populist states to incorporate or suppress the new social forces (lower-middle and middle classes) that they have helped to generate has led to the growth of civil society institutions. When states are unable to meet the needs of these classes, they resort to (and encourage the establishment of) civil associations to fulfill them.... Despite the authoritarian nature of many states, human rights activists, artists, writers, religious figures, and professional groups have brought pressure to bear on the governments for accountability and openness."[75] This was the beginning of things to come in the 2000s.

The outbreak of protests in 2000 in northern Africa and the Middle East led to the ousting of long-lasting authoritarian regimes including the Mubarak regime. Even though there was initial success, most of these movements ended in failure. Despite the ultimate outcome, the fact that there were such outbreaks in some of the most repressive parts of the world shows that a few changes in the political culture of the region had taken place. New forms of opposition politics emerged, which gave rise "to protest movements as an arena for coalition building and dynamic processes of networking, involving different political factions and ideological programs." A new generation of activists used different strategies and tactics, which produced "a richer and more pluralist political culture of opposition. In particular, a potentially sig-nificant conclusion ... is that it is not so much the networks per se in which these groups take part that have created a new dynamic and inclusive politi-cal culture, but more the actual processes of networking itself." In addition, the "linkages and networking, essential to coalition-building, need not be a formal, predictable process."[76]

Sheila Carapico presents an interesting list of factors that have contributed to the dramatic growth of NGOs primarily in the Arab world in the 1990s. Some of the factors overlap with the ones discussed earlier in this chapter. Before Carapico discusses the reasons for the growth in the number, scope, and functions of NGOs, she makes a notable reference to the polarized views scholars and laypeople hold about NGOs. To some, NGOs are "agents of political, economic and social change, influencing the allocation of scarce resources in their own societies and the images national regimes project abroad. But to others, NGOs are the promoters of failed economic policies and are nothing more than the "stooges of Western imperialism. ..." The for-mer view is the "developmentalist view of NGOs as agents of liberalization" and the latter is the "Orientalist stereotype of Arab society as either passive or violent but incapable of civic behavior ..." The following are among the mul-tiplicity of internal and external reasons for the exponential growth of NGOs:

Political policies. That is the decisions by governments to suppress opposition political parties, unions, cooperatives, and other channels of civic engagement; the greater space given to religious, charitable, and other associations; and government budget cuts in social services despite the need for such services.

Social trends. That is the "effects of urbanization and education, on the one hand, and anomie and detachment from 'roots,' on the other; the intellectual and political aspirations of millions of university graduates; the even higher ambitions of many hundreds of holders of European or American degrees; and the cosmopolitanization of human rights, environmental and feminist concerns, particularly among urban elites."

Economics. In the past, international organizations such as the World Bank, the United Nations, the International Monetary Fund, and other kinds of donors provided grants and loans in support of development programs only to national governments, but in recent years these organizations have done the same with NGOs.

Politics. Peace-process related funding from the United States, Europe, Canada, and other donors is now more available to support civic engagement and education activities in the Middle East. Funding in support of democratization efforts undertaken by NGOs has also come to the Middle East. (As will be discussed later in this book, there are scholars who disagree at least in part with the democratizing role of NGOs). And finally, the inclusion of NGOs in international conferences on human rights, environmental concerns, and concerns regarding women "has raised the consciousness of these issues among Arab, Iranian and Turkish elites and has stimulated NGO formation and animation."[77]

As demonstrated thus far, numerous reasons have led to the dramatic growth of NGOs. When attempting to study the matter, and when considering specific states and the place of NGOs in their space, one must be mindful that likely more than one factor has contributed to this development.

NOTES

1. International Committee of the Red Cross, *Britannica Online Encyclopedia*, 1, accessed January 6, 2020, https://britannica.com/print/article/290788.. The ICRC is now one element of a large network that includes national Red Cross and Red Crescent societies as well as the International Federation of the Red Cross and Red Crescent Societies. The governing body of the ICRC is the committee, which consists of more than twenty-five members all of whom are Swiss in part because of the origins of the Red Cross in Geneva and to establish neutrality so any country that might need help can receive it. The governing body meets ten times a year to make sure the organization fulfills its mission of promoting humanitarian law and to ensure that the Fundamental Principles of the ICRC are abided by.

2. Manuel Castells, "Global Governance and Global Politics," *Political Science and Politics* XXXVIII, no. 1 (2004): 10.

3. Ibid., 10.

4. Kim D. Reimann, "A View from the Top: International Politics, Norms and Worldwide Growth of NGOs," *International Studies Quarterly* 14, no. 1 (2006): 46.

5. "How Does the US Spend Its Foreign Aid?" *Council on Foreign Relations*, 2, https://www.cfr.org/backgrounder/how-does-us-spend-its-foreign-aid

6. Ibid., 2–3.

7. Ibid., 3–5.

8. Ibid., 5–6.

9. "Most US Foreign Aid Flows through US Organizations," *PolitiFact Global News Service*, 2-3, accessed January 2, 2020, https://www.politifact.com/global-news/statements/2017/mar/08/rejshah.yes-most-us-foreign-aid-flows-through-us-orginizat/.

10. "NGO Monitor: Making NGOs Accountable," 1-8, accessed January 2, 2020, https://www.ngomonitor.org/funder/united_states/.

11. Chadwick F. Alger, "Evolving Roles of NGOs in Member State Decision-Making in the UN System," *Journal of Human Rights* 2, no. 3 (September 2003): 422.

12. Ibid., 422.

13. Willetts, 3–4.

14. "Funds, Programs, Specialized Agencies and Others," *United Nations*, 1–4, accessed January 2, 2020, https://www.un.org/en/sections/about-un/funds-programmes-specialized-agencies-and-others/.

15. Otto, 127.

16. Reimann, 51–52.

17. "Funding Opportunities for NGOs," *European Union*, 1-2, accessed January 8, 2020, https://ec.europa.eu/info/funding-tenders/how-eu-funding-works/who-eligible-funding/funding-opportunities-ngos_en.

18. "The World's Top Ten Charitable Foundations", 1-6, accessed December 5, 2019,https://www.fundsforngos.org/foundation-funds-for-ngos/worlds-top-ten-wealthiest-charitable-foundations.

19. Julia Pitner, "Critiquing NGOs: Assessing the Last Decade," *Middle East Report,* no. 214 (Spring 2000): 35.

20. Ibid., 36–37.

21. Andrew S. Natsios, "NGOs and the UN System in Complex Humanitarian Emergencies: Conflict or Cooperation?" In *The Politics of Global Governance: International Organizations in an Interdependent World*, ed. Paul F. Diehl (Boulder, Colorado: Lynne Rienner Publishers, 2005), 381–382.

22. Ibid., 382–383.

23. Shawn Shieh and Guosheng Deng, "An Emerging Civil Society: The Impact of the 2008 Sichuan Earthquake on Grassroots Associations in China," *The China Journal,* no. 65 (January 2011): 181.

24. Ibid., 182.

25. Ibid., 194.

26. Kang Yi, "Sichuan, Year Zero?" In *Dog Days: Made in China Yearbook 2018*, eds. Ivan Franceschini et al. (Canberra, Australia: ANU Press, 2019), 196–197.

27. Ibid., 197.

28. Ibid., 198.

29. Ibid., 198–199.

30. Ibid., 199.

31. Christos A. Frangonikopoulos, "Politics, the Media and NGOs: The Greek Experience," *Perspectives on European Politics and Society* 15, no. 4 (2014): 607.

32. Ibid., 607–608.

33. Ibid., 608.

34. Ibid., 608–609.

35. Ibid., 609.

36. Ibid., 611–612.

37. Ibid., 611–613.

38. Christos A. Frangonikopoulos and Stamatis Poulakidakos, "Revisiting the Public Profile and Communication of Greek NGOs in Time of Crisis," *International Journal of Media and Cultural Politics* 11, no. 1 (2015): 121.

39. Peter Willetts, "The Role of NGOs in Global Governance," *World Politics Review* (September 27, 2011): 2, https://www.worldpoliticsreview.com/articles/10147/the-role-ngos-in-global-governance.

40. Ibid., 1–2.

41. See Seng Tan, "NGOs in Conflict Management in Southeast Asia," *International Peacekeeping* 12, no. 1 (Spring 2005): 49.

42. Ibid., 50.

43. Ibid., 63.

44. Ibid., 51–53.

45. Willetts, 2.

46. Sothy Khieng and Heidi Dahles, "Resource Dependence and Effects of Funding Diversification Strategies among NGOs in Cambodia," *Voluntas: International Journal of Voluntary and Nonprofit Organizations* 26 (2015): 1416.

47. Ibid., 1416–1417.

48. Ibid., 1416.

49. S. Ui et al., "Strengthening Community Participation at Health Centers in Rural Cambodia: Role of Local Non-Governmental Organizations (NGOs)," *Critical Public Health* 20, no. 1 (March 2010): 97–98.

50. Ibid., 110–112.

51. Julie Bernath and Ratana Ly, "Forward to the Working Paper Series on Cambodia," *Swisspeace* (2019): 7.

52. Ibid., 8–9.

53. Ibid., 10.

54. Jennifer Y. J. Hsu and Reza Hasmath, "The Local Corporatist State and NGO Relations in China," *Journal of Contemporary China* 23, no. 87 (2014): 516.

55. Ibid., 516–517.

56. Guosheng Deng, "The Influence of Elite Philanthropy on NGO Development in China," *Asian Studies Review* 39, no. 4 (2015): 554–555.

57. Ibid., 555–558.

58. Ibid., 559, 562.

59. Ibid., 562.

60. Ibid., 564–565.

61. Ibid., 565–566.

62. Thomas David DuBois, "Before the NGO: Chinese Charities in Historical Perspective," *Asian Studies Review* 39, no. 4 (2015): 542.

63. Ibid., 542.

64. Ibid., 551.

65. Anthony J. Spires, Lin Tao, and Kin-man Chan, "Societal Support for China's Grassroots NGOs: Evidence from Yunnan, Guangdong and Beijing," *The China Journal*, no. 71 (January 2014): 90.

66. Hugo Winckler et al., "China: Waging 'Lawfare' on NGOs," *European Council on Foreign Relations* (2015): 1.

67. Ibid., 1–2.

68. Ghamen Bibi, Julie Peteet, and Joe Stork, "The NGO Phenomenon in the Arab World," *Middle East Report*, no. 193 (March–April 1995): 26.

69. Manfred B. Steger and Ravi K. Roy, *Neoliberalism: A Very Short Introduction* (New York: Oxford University Press, 2010): 19–20.

70. Ruth Phillips and Susan Goodwin, "Third Sector Social Policy Research in Australia: New Actors, New Politics," *Voluntas: International Journal of Voluntary and Nonprofit Organizations* 25 (2014): 573.

71. Elaine Thompson, "The Role of NGOs in Challenging the Conservative Agenda: Some Empirical Studies," *Social Alternatives* 23, issue 1 (2004): 43, 48.

72. Asef Bayat, "Activism and Social Development in the Middle East," *International Journal of Middle East Studies* 34, no. 1 (February 2002): 1.

73. Christopher Heurlin, "Governing Civil Society: The Political Logic of NGO-State Relations Under Dictatorship," *Voluntas: International Journal of Voluntary and Nonprofit Organizations* 21, issue 2 (June 2010): 220.

74. Bayat, 2.

75. Ibid., 2.

76. Maha Abderlraman, "The Transnational and the Local: Egyptian Activists and Transnational Protest Networks," *British Journal of Middle Eastern Studies* 38, no. 3 (December 2011): 407–408, 424.

77. Sheila Carapico, "NGOs, INGOs, GO-NGOs and DO-NGOs: Making Sense of Non-Governmental Organizations," *Middle East Report*, no. 214 (Spring 2000): 12–13.

Chapter 2

Functions of Non-governmental Organizations

It is to be expected that after examining the multiplicity of factors that contributed to the rise and growth of NGOs one must study the primary functions of these organizations. For much of their history, NGOs were usually identified with relief and charity work. Although these roles continue to be at the core of the work done by many NGOs, in recent years NGOs have expanded their roles to include work in areas such as economic and social development, advocacy, agenda setting, public education, monitoring of international agreements, interacting with intergovernmental organizations, etc.[1]

RELIEF

The International Committee of the Red Cross as well as some of the most widely known NGOs grew out of war. Save the Children was founded in 1920 as a result of the dislocations caused by World War I. Foster Parents Plan was created during the Spanish Civil War. Oxfam and the Cooperative for American Relief Everywhere, commonly known as CARE, were created during or shortly after World War II. The consequences of conflict, war, and disasters are among the reasons why charity and relief remain most important to numerous NGOs. Awarding the Nobel Peace Prize in 1999 to Médecins Sans Frontièrs is a clear indication of the significance of this work to the present.[2]

NGOs have long been associated with humanitarian relief and emergency work. As a matter of fact, many NGOs were created to manage disasters and other conflict situations. NGOs have been involved in the distribution of resources in the form of food, clothing, shelter, and healthcare. "It became customary to think of humanitarian intervention by NGOs as concerned with natural disasters, such as cyclones or floods or sudden emergencies created by earthquakes or volcanoes, or with man-made disasters such as the creation of refugees or displaced persons following outbreak of armed conflict."[3]

One of the occasions that relief is crucial is during and after natural disasters. And, of course, there are multiple examples that could be cited. One such example is Bangladesh, a country that has been plagued by many calamities. The international community has played an important role in Bangladesh since the early 1970s in providing relief to disaster victims. After realizing widespread corruption and misuse of relief funds by the government of Bangladesh, foreign donors began to channel emergency assistance through NGOs. The government soon concluded that NGOs were usurping its authority over external disaster aid and looked for opportunities to demonstrate its ability to effectively deliver services to disaster victims. This opportunity came in July 1998 when Bangladesh experienced devasting floods.[4]

The government of Bangladesh, considering its limited resources, made an appeal to the international community in August 1998 for help to rebuild the country and to help the victims. The response was generous. By February 1998, the government had received about US $700 million of the requested US $850 million. "With foreign donor support, both the government of Bangladesh and 163 local, national, and international NGOs initiated massive relief and rehabilitation programs to remedy the extensive damage." One of the pleasant outcomes of this case was that both the government and the NGOs performed satisfactorily.[5]

In a related work, Ekhtekharul Islam examines the performance of governmental organizations (GOs) and NGOs in managing drinking water in coastal Bangladesh. UNICEF has described access to safe water as a human right, and access to safe water is listed as one of the development goals included in the UN Millennium Development Goals. In conjunction with this, the World Bank has revealed that Bangladesh is one of the top disaster-prone countries in the world. The World Bank has warned that during the next few years drinking water sources will shrink dramatically, and Bangladesh's coastal population will be greatly affected. Considering this, GOs and NGOs in Bangladesh have worked to develop disaster management plans.[6]

Islam is primarily interested in comparing the services provided and their effectiveness in terms of public perception and documentation.

Formation of social capital facilitates the participation and efficiency of the community people for any activity. Views on Government Organizations include [reluctance] to rely on official commitments and unwillingness to communicate with the government staffs which were literally pessimistic. All these acted as barriers to get access to institutional public services provided by the local government offices. These barriers ultimately resulted in reducing adaptive capacities among the affected people.... On the other hand, views on NGO activities include strong monitoring, including local people [in] the decision-making process, use of renewable energy in water supply activities, better social cohesion, direct economic gains or rewards, and long-term facilities. The NGOs were seen trying to improve their efficiency and accountability whereas the GOs were found less accountable and efficient.[7]

The services provided by NGOs in many countries show great continuity throughout the twentieth century. One such affected country, among many, was Japan from the beginning to the end of the twentieth century. During the early part of the twentieth century, NNGOs "acted as important conveyors of social technology to philanthropic Japanese organizations." And while some Buddhist organizations provided relief, Christian organizations did similar work as well. Among these organizations were YMCA groups, the Red Cross, the Foreign Auxiliary of the Women's Christian Temperance Union (WCTU), and HELP (which grew out of WCTU).[8]

NGOs could and do play a role in social protection to reduce vulnerability of poor and marginal groups. By doing so, NGOs help to promote social cohesion, integrate marginalized groups within communities, and enhance voting habits and regime stability. In more general terms, it is argued that social protection helps to extend the social contract between states and citizens, "in that it can help render states more legitimate in the eyes of citizens and, where participatory mechanisms are integrated in a more 'transformative' approach, it can help enhance the citizenship status and claim-making capacities of local communities."[9]

Badru Bukenya examined the role of an NGO in rural Uganda, the AIDS Support Organization (TASO), in protecting and promoting the rights of people living with HIV and AIDS (PLHIV) and noted that it empowered those involved as citizens and transformed the approach of the state, which then led to new social contract.[10] The author concludes by stating that

TASO used the [Mini TASO Project] MTP to "work both sides of the equation"; that is, on the one hand, to "civilize the state" and, on the other, to empower citizens to engage the state to improve service delivery. These effects were consistently deeper and more extensive where MTP had been implemented more fully. "State civilizing" attributes of MTP, such as health workers' shadowing, training, and financial facilitation, enhanced the ability as well as the commitment of government hospitals to deliver increased quantity of HIV/AIDS services.... On the part of PLHIV citizens, the MTP supplied resources in the form of training, ARV drugs, and actively enlisted their participation in service delivery.... Social protection programs with built-in accountability arrangements can therefore provide useful forms of state society linkage, offering opportunities through which marginal groups can start to build a sense of citizenship ...

Citizenship building works in a "snowballing" fashion here, whereby enhanced citizen engagement in one area strengthens the possibilities of successful engagement in other areas. In MTPs, citizen action, whether through contentious action, MDD (music, dance, and drama) activities, or engaging in coproduction, left behind transferable skills that some PLHIV used to engage in other activities, such as direct politics....

Lastly, notwithstanding the vagaries of NGO financing and short lifespan of their projects, it is worth noting that such actors can also play a role in helping states to see marginal groups as rights-bearing citizens in need of protection, and so help at least to some extent to reveal a pathway through which more progressive forms of social contracts can be promoted.[11]

It is noteworthy to mention the need for NGO involvement to help refugees in resettlement, especially in recent decades because of the incredible number of people who for reasons beyond their control have been forced to leave their country of origin and become refugees. With resettlement needs growing and more and more refugees living outside of refugee camps, NGOs can better identify and interview refugees and play a greater role in refugee resettlement. Until recently, UNHCR was exclusively responsible for making referrals to countries willing to accept refugees. But as the number of refugees dramatically increased and as the number of refugees living outside of refugee camps has also increased, UNHRC and its partners have found it more difficult to identify and refer cases for resettlement.[12]

Despite increased demand for referrals, direct NGO referral programs have not increased proportionally. Not only should the number of qualified NGOs in referral cases increase for reasons mentioned above, but other benefits could be derived by expanding NGO referral programs.

First is the establishment of parallel pathways for resettlement. For example, if UNHCR must focus on one specific country for one reason or another, NGOs could assist in filling the gap.

Second, referrals from NGOs could alleviate some of the pressure on UNHCR to produce referrals.

Third, direct referrals increase access for vulnerable people.

Fourth, NGO direct referrals are cost efficient.[13]

While expanding the role of NGOs in identification and referral is seen as positive by UNHCR and resettlement countries, the NGOs' role in the referral process has its critics.

> Critics argue that this model can cause refugees to perceive direct referral NGOs as gateways to resettlement countries. To mitigate this, NGOs should only submit cases that are referred to them by external partners. If they deem a client to need resettlement (a so-called internal referral), the case should be referred to UNHCR or to another agency approved to submit cases directly....

Resettlement countries that have employed surges readily admit that the associated costs are unsustainable and that the speed with which cases are processed led to integration difficulties and increased anxiety among refugees and caseworkers, and was one of many contributing factors to high dropout rates prior to departure. The most easily accessible vulnerable cases were identified for submission, which is not the same as prioritizing cases based solely on vulnerability. In effect, the surges, while producing larger numbers of people for resettlement, have taken resources from more protracted caseloads, exacerbated tensions between refugee populations and created an imbalance between addressing vulnerable cases and achieving targets.[14]

Melonee Douglas et al. argue that a new model is necessary as related to the direct referral system. NGOs must play a greater role in helping UNHCR to achieve growth while at the same time prioritizing vulnerability. And for this to effectively happen, the following must be put in place:

Approve more NGOs to conduct referrals.
Train NGOs to conduct direct referrals.
Increase the number of resettlement countries that accept direct referrals from NGOs.
Provide more funding for direct referrals.
Strategically use NGO referral agencies to expand resettlement in specific locations.[15]

Since the end of the Cold War, the UN and donor governments have been heavily involved in efforts to end civil wars and to build sustainable peace. Such developments have led to a greater engagement of NGOs as implementing partners of donor governments and various kinds of organizations. The focus on post-conflict peacebuilding efforts in order to put in place the foundation for sustainable peace has led to an even more important role for international NGOs regarding addressing civil conflicts. "Their presence at the local level ... their knowledge of specific local conditions, and their expertise in social and economic development mean that they can make an important contribution to peacebuilding, in particular when other actors, such as UN organizations or regional arrangements, lack the required human and financial resources."[16]

The functions of NGOs during the after civil wars can be divided into four broad categories: humanitarian aid and providing basic public services; post-conflict reconstruction and development; mediation and conflict resolution; and monitoring and advocacy.

HUMANITARIAN AID AND PROVISION OF BASIC SERVICES

One of the most important functions of NGOs during civil wars is providing humanitarian relief and basic services such as healthcare, education, and drinkable water. Humanitarian assistance is a multibillion-dollar industry funded by individuals, governments, and multilateral organizations such as UNHCR, WFP, and the EU. The civil wars in Bosnia and Herzegovina and in southern Sudan are examples of the importance of aid in societies suffering from civil wars. "In 1989, UNCEF, the WFP, and 35 NGOs started Operation Lifeline Sudan (OLS), providing humanitarian aid in southern Sudan after a famine induced by drought and civil war. At its height it distributed more than 10,000 tons of food every month, feeding up to 1.3 million people." In the case of Bosnia and Herzegovina, between 1992 and 1995, the UNCHR and about 250 NGOs provided food for approximately 2.7 million people and more than 950 metric tons of humanitarian assistance. In addition, NGOs become the providers of public services where effective government does not exist because of civil war.[17]

Muhammad Ammad Khan et al. make interesting comments about the role of NGOs in restoring health services in the Federally Administered Tribal Areas (FATA) of Pakistan. They begin by noting that armed conflict is a significant public health problem and that NGOs play an essential role in providing health services in complex emergencies. NGOs provide these services during the conflict as well as after the cessation of hostilities.[18]

When the immediate crisis facing people confronted with conflict is addressed,

> the next phase of assistance shifts to designing a cost-effective package of basic services, setting priorities … and establishing delivery mechanisms. NGOs also play a role here, and an increasingly popular approach is for donors and country health ministries to contract jointly with NGOs for provision of a basic package of health services.…

In many countries, good health governance … was weak prior to the emergence of conflict. Thus, rehabilitation often means creating new elements of the health system, not restoring something that existed previously but was damaged during the conflict. The public health system, as a component of the state, needs to develop legitimacy in the eyes of citizens and be seen as effective, responsive, and accountable. This rehabilitation phase puts premium on capacity building of the health system to enable public health actors to prepare budgets and plans, administer grants and contracts, manage human resources and facilities, handle medicine and equipment logistics, and so on.

For example, in postwar Ethiopia, donor willingness to channel rehabilitation resources for essential drugs through the health ministry helped the new government establish its legitimacy, as well as facilitating a quick return to basic services provision through local health facilities.[19]

RECONSTRUCTION AND DEVELOPMENT

Large INGOs such as Oxfam, in addition to providing humanitarian aid, are involved in social and economic development during the fighting and especially after the civil wars are over. In Bosnia and Herzegovina and in Kosovo, NGOs built houses, schools, and hospitals, they encouraged refugees to return home, and they provided funding to returnees to enable them to become self-sufficient. "In Kosovo, donors spent more than 143 [million] euros on the reconstruction of housing in 2000 and 2001 alone, much through NGOs. In Angola, NGOs ran the demobilization and reintegration program for former soldiers, funded by the US government."[20]

MEDIATION AND CONFLICT RESOLUTION

The serious divisions within countries during civil wars make it difficult for other governments to mediate between conflicting parties. Governments are reluctant to become involved because such an involvement might imply official recognition of rebel groups. Also, if a government maintains relations with one of the parties to the conflict, the other side will not trust it. Especially in countries where government has collapsed completely, "NGOs might be the only institutions with any authority across the different parties."[21]

Organizations like the Carter Center, the Berghof Center, and the Conflict and Analysis Center have, along with international organizations and governments, much contributed to mediating and ending conflicts. But there are limitations to how much NGOs can do in this respect because of their close "connection with local groups [which] can shape and distort their perception of the conflict." In addition, "their autonomy and their local focus makes coordination between NGOs inherently difficult, as they might see conflict only from the perspective of the particular groups they are dealing with and fail to take into account wider national developments and dynamics. ..." Furthermore, NGOs place emphasis "on their reputations as neutral and without a stake in a particular conflict to encourage negotiations between conflict parties," and as a result they "have a 'muscle' to coerce parties to reach an agreement."[22]

HUMAN RIGHTS MONITORING AND ADVOCACY

Because NGOs tend to be on the ground even before conflicts begin, they can warn governments and international institutions of an upcoming conflict and can behave "as monitors of major human rights violations, war crimes, and crimes against humanity." By being there, NGOs can bring the matter to the attention of the international community, and in at least some cases, minimize atrocities and human rights abuses. "For many NGOs, the 'early warning' or advocacy role has come as a consequence of their development and humanitarian activities, which brought them into countries affected by civil conflict, but some NGOs, like the International Crisis Group (ICG), have actively sought to develop into a monitoring and 'early warning' organization, with a presence in many conflict territories, and regular reports and recommendations to the wider international community, in particular western governments."[23]

As more and more countries, developed as well as developing, are faced with the challenge of aging populations, NGOs in this situation could and often do play an important role. An interesting example is the work of DeBrenna LaFa Agbenyiga and Lihua Huang, which considers the impact of the organizational network of HelpAge Ghana about elderly care in Ghana. "By defining aging issues as developmental issues, HelpAge Ghana actively changes the quality of life of older people and elderly care infrastructure through the passage of national healthcare policies, in pursuit of national policy on aging, raising awareness of rights of older people, and empowerment."[24]

HelpAge Ghana successfully established an organizational network consisting of governmental agencies, international NGOs, national and local NGOs and for-profit organizations, individual donors and volunteers, and older people. This network has allowed HelpAge Ghana to gain recognition and resources as the first NGO in Ghana to provide services to the elderly. It has also aided HelpAge Ghana to gain "independent standing to pursue the best interest of older people." Agbenyiga and Huang conclude by stating the following: "First, aging has gradually been recognized as a human rights issue as well as a social service issue in Ghana. HelpAge Ghana and its selected network played a key role in promoting aging and inclusion in national public policy awareness on aging.... Secondly, there is an emerging Third Sector that addresses diverse needs of older people in Ghana in general and in urban Ghana in particular. In the last 20 years, HelpAge Ghana has established its reputation as the leading service NGO for older people.... Finally, HelpAge Ghana has mobilized all possible resources to establish, extend, and redefine its boundaries. Although HelpAge International and the governmental agencies have been key supporters of the organization,

HelpAge Ghana has established its free standing by using homophily and diversity as two principles of alliance selection. The principle of diversity created HelpAge Ghana's new paths to new sets of partners within communities associated with eldercare in its particular cultural, demographic, and policy context."[25]

In providing relief, NGOs do not always get it right. In fact, often NGOs contribute to the miseries afflicting people facing crises. An example is refugee protection. Since the end of the Cold War, NGOs became even more concerned about the treatment of refugees than previously. Because of conflicts or other kinds of challenges more and more people find themselves crossing borders. Therefore, many NGOs were established with the encouragement of the international community or by citizens recognizing the scope of the problem. Today, it is a rare to find a country not affected by the refugee issue; and "yet there is not a single government that gets refugee protection right all the time."[26]

Eve Lester, in examining the role of NGOs during the annual meetings of the UNHCR in Geneva, argues that even though they bring a reality check to these gatherings, they can do much more beyond the confines of Geneva.

> There has been much — and often just — criticism of the talk fests that are held at the international level where policies are discussed between government representatives, UNHCR and other international agencies, and NGOs, and sometimes (but too rarely) refugees themselves.... It is easy to feel disillusioned by Geneva talk fests where discussions appear to bear little resemblance to realities on the ground.
>
> However, the work of NGOs will only be effective if it is rigorous in those discussions as it is on the ground. Thus, the human rights squalor of refugee camps and urban slums, the complex and angst-ridden realities of navigating one's way through refugee status determination procedures, and the emptiness, boredom, and brutality of life day in day out in detention centers must be brought to the "sterile" environment of Geneva [meetings] and the outcomes of those meeting brought back again to those places.
>
> Finally, the old medical mantra of "*First, do no harm*" is as important in Geneva as it is on the ground, precisely because those that do deals in Geneva do not necessarily bear witness to the "*Realprotectionvoid*" implications of what they are doing. It is the responsibility of NGOs to safeguard this standard, as an absolute minimum, in those otherwise bland corridors of power along the shores of Lake Geneva, where peacocks roam in the gardens — however far away from reality it may all seem.[27]

Walden Bello, in an examination of relief and reconstruction, offers some useful insights to what the author refers to as the relief and reconstruction complex (RRC). Bello notes that for a long time, relief and reconstruction efforts were dominated by UN agencies and the Red Cross. These agencies and organizations provided physical relief to victims, and tried to reduce social dislocation, restore social organizations, and repair physical infrastructure. In recent years, though, much has changed and has become more complex. "Strategic considerations have become more prevalent in military-led disaster relief operations. Post-disaster and post-conflict reconstruction planning and implementation are increasingly influenced by neoliberal market economics. A new militant humanitarianism infuses not only post-conflict reconstruction work but, in a number of cases, has itself helped to precipitate conflicts." With this new paradigm, relief and reconstruction have become more and more intertwined. "This is all the more true since the same set of actors now dominate both arenas: the US military-political command, the World Bank, corporate contractors and humanitarian and development NGOs. Efforts once led by the UN and the Red Cross have become things of the past, even though these organizations continue to participate in relief and reconstruction work."[28]

Bello questions the superiority of the new paradigm over the traditional arrangements for relief and reconstruction and makes the following recommendations to reverse the tide:

First, "in a major disaster it is important to immediately establish a rescue and recovery command center under the auspices of the UN, the Red Cross and affected governments that will supervise relief efforts ..."

Second, "direct military-to-military entanglements must be discouraged except for operational purposes. Key decisions for relief activities within a country should be cleared and approved by civilian authorities."

Third, "medium-term and long-term relief and recovery should be managed by a consortium led by UN agencies, with the role and programs of the World Bank set by this grouping. Affected governments, other than multilateral bodies and INGOs should be included in this aid consortium, which would take the lead in terms of determining from the governments."

Fourth, when it comes to post-conflict reconstruction, participation in such efforts should be undertaken only when no violation of the principles of national sovereignty have taken place. In situations where these principles have been observed, the role of external participants should fall under a reconstruction consortium led by the UN and the affected government. While there should be sufficient flexibility, NGO efforts should be coordinated with the host government and NGO support must not lead to activities that displace government services. If anything, these efforts should facilitate the development and independence of local service providers."

Finally, "participants in post-conflict reconstruction must scrupulously observe neutrality when it comes to dealing with target groups and political groupings within the country."[29]

In an examination of the experiences of children during the 1990s in Yugoslavia, Constantine Danopoulos et al. assert that relief agencies, including NGOs, "are effective in providing food, medical care and other forms of assistance to those affected during combat or in emergency situations, such as famine or forced movement of people. Pressing needs elsewhere, shortage of funds and personnel prompt relief-providing organizations to leave the scene once formal hostilities come to an end and the mass media spotlight has been eclipsed. NGO involvement tends to be of short duration and reach, and tends to suffer from lack of coordination and long-term perspective. Yet, what the Yugoslav situation makes abundantly clear is that war-affected children are as much in need of help after the fighting stops as they are during combat."[30]

The Yugoslav experience leads the authors to conclude that NGOs ought to put more emphasis "on post-conflict relief and rehabilitation. While food and emergency care become less pressing once the guns go silent, those affected need help to acquire the skills that would allow them to fend for themselves." NGOs can help by promoting capacity building, that is "to reinforce or to create strengths upon which communities can draw to offset disaster-relief vulnerability." Capacity building is not easy; it requires sustained effort and a close working relationship between government and NGOs.[31]

SOCIAL AND ECONOMIC DEVELOPMENT

NGOs have come to realize that relief and charitable work address primarily short-term needs and do not do much to deal with long-term development issues. The effect of this is for more NGOs to place greater emphasis on how to rehabilitate communities in the long run. Others have focused their efforts on social and economic development in developing countries as a means of addressing long-term matters related to poverty and inequality. Some NGOs provide technical support to encourage development and some operate their own development programs.[32]

A significant, at times controversial, service provided by NGOs is education of young children. Elizabeth Ross, in her article about small NGOs in Uganda, discusses such an issue. According to her, Uganda, a nation of 35 million, is the youngest country in the world with 52 percent of the people under the age of 15. And with a fast-growing population, the challenges facing the Ugandan government will become even more severe.[33]

Ross and the Kasiisi Primary School principal, Lydia Kasenene, established in the late 1980s the Kasiisi Project, an NGO with two main goals. The first was to manage the great dropout rate, and the second was to provide good education. On both fronts the Kasiisi Project, despite many obstacles, has proven successful. Teacher and staff presence have increased. And not surprisingly, there is correlation between teacher and staff attendance and student attendance. As for academic standards, in the Kasiisi Project schools' exam scores improved by 29 percent, 25 percent higher than other similar schools. Also, the girls are doing as well, if not better than, the boys.[34]

Sunhyuk Kim notes that the kind of role NGOs play in South Korea, Thailand, and Indonesia depends on "the existence/absence of political pluralism/democracy, the existence/absence of a developmental welfare state, and the nature of historical development of civil society. Influenced by these factors, NGOs in the three countries have concentrated on either indirect pressure or direct provision."[35]

Sunhyuk Kim concludes that in South Korea, where there is a consolidated democracy and "tradition of a strong developmental welfare state," pressure seems to be the chief role of NGOs in social protection. In Thailand, with its fragile democracy and the immature developmental welfare state, NGOs "have been active in both direct provision of social protection and indirect pressure vis-à-vis the state to pay greater heed to welfare issues." And in Indonesia, where civil society is strong and the developmental welfare state is not developed, "NGOs focus mostly on the direct provision of social protection to the population in need, rather than challenging and pressuring the government."[36]

Pertinent to the discussion of social and economic development is the role of NGOs in relationship to women and their place in society especially in developing nations. Pranab Kumar Panday and Shelly Feldman examine the role of NGOs in mainstreaming gender in politics in Bangladesh. The authors state that large NGOs such as the Bangladesh Rural Advancement Committee (BRAC) and Grameen Bank as well as smaller ones have paid much attention to women in Bangladesh. Overall, the position of Bangladeshi women has improved, and NGOs have made a significant contribution.[37]

Panday and Feldman conclude that NGOs have failed to enhance women's participation in politics through the formal law-making process ("a situation where different political actors, including the government interact in making new laws") that continues to be dominated by bureaucrats and members of the political elite. But if this is the case, how do NGOs play a role in strengthening women's political participation? They suggest three mechanisms used by NGOs:

> First, NGOs publish research reports and organize press and media conferences and human chains to attract government attention. In addition, they submit memoranda to the responsible authorities to draw attention to their research. NGOs also respond to government invitations to express their opinion on any particular issues....
> Second, NGOs through providing micro-credit are trying to empower women

economically since economic independence is perceived as a precondition for women's empowerment. It is generally assumed that women vie for other aspects of empowerment (political and social) when they will achieve economic self-dependence....

Third, awareness development programs are another important channel that has arisen within the wide focus of Bangladeshi NGOs since [the] late 1980s. These programs were carried out with an expectation that women would develop with a degree of consciousness about their civil and political rights that would ultimately help them to raise their voices against any sort of discrimination in the society....[38]

BRAC and Grameen Bank are not the only NGOs that have contributed to women's awareness development programs. Among other Bangladeshi NGOs that have made significant contributions are Nijera Kori, Proshika, Steps Towards Development, Caritas, and others. Why have these large and small NGOs have played such an important role? Panday and Feldman have identified four reasons:

First, due to the absence of the state in the rural economy NGOs have captured the economy from rural credit to telecommunications to primary [education]. Second, a giant share of NGO loans (more than two-thirds) is channeled through in rural areas.... Third, the scarcity of job opportunities for the young population in the public sector has established NGOs as a major source of employment.... Fourth, by providing consultancies to a larger number of university teachers, NGOs have become successful in not speaking out against [NGO] credit programs.[39]

To many scholars, related to social and economic development is population growth and family planning in developing countries. An example is Ethiopia. With a population of 87 million in 2012, Ethiopia is the second most populous country in Africa and the fourteenth largest in the world. The Ethiopian government was determined to slow these trends and introduced an ambitious CPR (contraceptive prevalence rate) target of 66 percent by 2015. The determination of the country's government but also the significant cooperation and support of donors, LNGOs, and INGOs very much contributed to the success of the program.[40]

Ethiopia's experience provides other African countries with lessons learned. Among them are:

1. There must be political commitment to the program at every level. Only then "money, community mobilization, NGOs, and public-private partnerships all flow more easily when political will is strong."
2. "The Ethiopian government has sometimes been overly wary of civil society, including national and international NGOs, the private sector,

universities, research institutions, churches, and faith-based organizations. Its government and other African governments must overcome their distrust of these critical partners and create an environment that is conducive for NGOs and others to contribute to family planning."[41]

Sarah A. Blue, in her work on the need to include women in development, discusses the role played by Mama Maquin, a Mexican refugee women's NGO formed in 1990, in Mexico and Guatemala by taking into consideration the local political, economic, and geographic environment. She notes that "[recent] years have witnessed an important shift in the administration of development aid away from large government programs to the smaller projects of NGOs and widespread recognition of the general failure of governmental programs to include women in development.... [Large] government-administered development projects ... failed to take local realities into account."[42]

Blue "investigates the impact of different sociopolitical environments and the agendas of different kinds of NGOs on women's empowerment in Mexican refugee camps and in Guatemalan returned-refugee communities." By focusing on two different sociopolitical contexts, the author shows how the development philosophies of NGOs have an impact on women's participation and women's equality.[43]

> The implementation of an agenda of women's empowerment in the Mexican refugee camps addressed women's subordination at a structural level, allowing the women to negotiate local political barriers. By addressing barriers to participation such as illiteracy and the depreciation of women's contributions to the community, Mama Maquin . . . and UNHCR successfully addressed structural constraints to women's participation. The refugee women were able to overcome the resistance of male community leaders to a change in women's traditional roles by accessing a support structure and funding independent of local politics. Mama Maquin received support at a regional level that it could use to convince its political opponents at home and ultimately increase women's literacy and community participation.[44]

The experience of women in Guatemala was very different. They did not receive the structural support in continuing work in empowering women.

> The technical support provided by NGOs for practical women's projects in return communities did not incorporate women's strategic goals of equal rights and equal participation in community affairs. The Guatemalan NGOs, with their predesigned economic projects, failed to address the structural barriers that prevent women from fully participating in development projects. Further, they failed to support the repatriated refugee women in their own empowerment

projects (i.e., reaching out to surrounding communities with women's literacy, human rights, and women's rights workshops). Without an outside source of ideological support, the women of Mama Maquin were considerably constrained in the continuation of their work. Moreover, by failing to adjust to and incorporate a new set of structural constraints into their empowerment work, Mama Maquin effectively limited itself in obtaining local support for its progressive goals.[45]

NGOs involved in microfinancing have played a critical role in supporting individuals around the world and particularly in developing countries. Serena Cosgrove presents an interesting study on levels of empowerment by examining the role of microenterprise-lending NGOs in El Salvador. She notes that high population density, a large informal economy, and declining foreign aid have made El Salvador a good candidate for microenterprise-lending programs. After examining microcredit NGOs and microentrepreneurs between 1994 and 1997, she concluded that microenterprise-lending led to the empowerment not only of the recipients of loans but also the empowerment of the NGOs as well as local municipalities.[46]

Being able to get small loans is essential to urban marketers struggling for survival because of structural adjustment policies, cuts in subsidies provided by the state, limited development aid, and social unrest, especially in urban centers. "For many marketers, microcredit means the chance to break out of the vicious circle of debt that borrowing from loan sharks entails." Much of the research on microcredit NGOs moves between two opposites. Some view these NGOs as the answer to all problems of development, while others see them as "sell-outs to neoliberal political agendas." Cosgrove proposes a more complex analysis of the activities of NGOs and a broader definition of empowerment.[47]

Empowerment could be achieved on many levels. Cosgrove's analysis of two NGOs in El Salvador — FUSAI and PROCOMES — shows that other players were empowered beyond the intended clients. FUSAI benefited from income earned from interest charged on loans to clients, which then guaranteed the financial stability of the NGO and allowed it to set its own priorities. As for PROCOMES, its successful microcredit program in the municipality of Nejapa greatly enhanced the effectiveness of the local mayor. As this case study demonstrates, NGOs can gain financial autonomy, and as FUSAI shows, clients receive needed loans, and active clients can promote "participative municipal development as in the case of PROCOMES in Nejapa."[48]

Rie Makita discusses empowerment of the poor by considering the case of a Bangladesh NGO, the Institute of Integrated Rural Development (IIRD), and its efforts to eradicate poverty in rural Bangladesh since 1987. By examining two programs, broiler rearing and silk production, the author explored the "role an NGO can play as intermediary in business development for the poor with focus on the relations between the NGO and local elites. In theory, as market demand for a product or service increases, it attracts more interest from local elites or wealthier competitors; all the benefits tend to go to local elites in the end." But that did not prove to be the case in this instance. Some of the benefits went to he poor as well. IIRD, by acting as an intermediary, not only convinced local elites to cooperate but also convinced the elites to allow the poor to receive some of the benefits in an elite-controlled local economy.[49]

The case of IIRD also shows that the cooperative relationship between an NGO and local elites has limited life.

> Local elites may fear the empowerment of the intermediary NGO as a new patron for poor clients. Furthermore, even if a market for the poor is secured away from general competitive markets, the special market will be merged in other markets over time. Therefore, efforts should be concentrated on enabling the poor to make the most of the new NGO-elite relations in the short term. It is particularly reasonable to use a market intermediary in order to help the chronically indebted poor reduce their debt and to help the moderate poor become self-supporting. While economic growth is indispensable for poverty reduction, economic growth is not automatically open to the poor. To enable the poor to take advantage of economic growth is the role of NGOs as intermediaries. Both donors and policymakers have to be prepared to bear higher costs to support such intermediary NGOs who need to provide more personnel and commitment than in implementing a conventional microcredit scheme.[50]

A somewhat similar work was done by David Forkuor and Seth Agymang as related to fighting urban poverty and empowerment. The authors examined the role of NGOs in urban Ghana and found that they provide "social intervention and livelihood empowerment programs to the extremely poor who were mostly migrants to the city." Women and young people were the primary beneficiaries. "However, the efforts of the NGOs in reducing poverty were found to be short term rather than long term." Furkuor and Agymang give three reasons for this outcome. First, the supposed beneficiaries were not included "in the choice, design, and implementation of the poverty reduction programs." Second, "the NGOs were faced with endogenous challenges that limited the extent of their impact in touching the lives of the poor." For example, the NGO programs provided education to the poor in an effort to move them out of poverty. But the education provided is limited to the secondary level, which "does not adequately resource the individual to have a [decent] livelihood in the future." Third, there was limited collaboration between the NGOs and the government in fighting poverty.[51]

It is argued by many scholars that effectively fighting poverty depends on the bureaucratic capacity of states. And the question often asked is whether development INGOs weaken or strengthen state capacity. To some, INGOs weaken state capacity by delivering services that the government is supposed to provide. Others note that "by increasing a country's domestic demand for improved human rights, development INGOs improve a government's capacity to fulfill them." Susanna Campbell et al. argue that "the effect of development INGOs on state capacity depends on whether a state is democratic or nondemocratic."[52]

To Campbell et al., many INGOs attempt to alleviate poverty by improving state capacity to provide services needed by the population. And they try to accomplish this task in both democratic and nondemocratic countries. But the authors conclude that INGOs are more likely to affect the capacity of democratic states. Efforts by INGOs to empower people are well received by democratic governments, unlike nondemocratic ones, which are not as "responsive to their [citizen's] demands."[53]

Scholarship on development assistance has placed much emphasis on the necessity to improve the bureaucratic capacity of states, especially "in fragile and conflict-affected countries where the state is relatively weak. Because the political institutions in many of these countries are weak, INGOs "are unlikely to fully achieve their poverty-reduction goals ... Although the work of development INGOs could still alleviate poverty and provide social services, development INGOs working in nondemocracies are unlikely to strengthen the state's capacity to provide these services themselves."[54]

Jovo Ateljevic, in a fascinating study of the region between Bosnia-Herzegovina and Serbia, examines how an INGO (Social Solutions) engages "in activities of social and institutional entrepreneurship in developing capabilities at different levels: social, human, economic and institutional." The author takes into consideration the political and historical context of the area, including the civil war in the 1990s as well as the parochial thinking combined with a legacy of corruption and poor local economies. "Creating new practice and institutional infrastructure is essentially an example of institutional and social entrepreneurship as it relates to alteration of existing practices in order to add economic and social values to the local communities through tourism development."[55]

Before the involvement of Social Solutions, the focus was the state as the major mover and the weak private community sectors were the recipient of resources and not the movers in the decision-making process. It was up to an INGO to act as the catalyst for the process to succeed. An NGO that was neutral with no political affiliation and "an NGO which keeps the social aspects to the fore whilst, at the same time, encouraging local initiatives, especially those of local entrepreneurs." From the experiences u to date, an NGO like Social Solutions was essential given "the political context and the potential for power imbalances. However, it must be said that the prevailing entitlement attitudes, the power of the local state and the virtual non-existence of relevant LNGOs presented a high potential for failure. But consistent efforts towards maximum participation and transparency have borne some fruit and the process continues quite successfully even though ... was a mistake and will be rectified in the future, that is, more inclusivity."[56]

Local ownership, a popular Western development model, is yet another way to encourage economic development. Theoretically, allowing local ownership "involves giving more effective control of the design and implementation of development aid to local actors in aid-receiving countries." But after examining the case of a Tajikistan NGO, Change, Karolina Kluczewska says that "despite a constant use of the rhetoric of local ownership, financial power relations, bureaucratic management practices and complicated project frameworks allow donors to discipline NGOs and subordinate their everyday work to the donors' own vision of development work."[57]

However, Kluczewska also asserts that local NGOs, as in the case of Change, "posses a subaltern agency" and could use it in relation to donors, "even within the most rigid frameworks of development aid." Change managed to accomplish this by completing the following steps: First, for its fundraising, Change decided to "rely on foreign interns to write high-quality project proposals" and on networking with foreign donors. Second, instead of competing with other local NGOs for scarce funding, Change chose to cooperate with them. Third, rather than applying for all available grants, Change focused on grants closely related to its own interests. Finally, "when writing project proposals, the NGO employees attempted to propose their own activities, while making them resonate with donors' priorities. While some of these practices ... although not illicit, are ethically questionable. They are, however, revealing of several features of donors' behavior towards local partners, including a limited scope of the actual ownership given to local NGOs by donors, in contrast with the discursive ownership."[58]

ADVOCACY AND LOBBYING

Advocacy networks bring together hundreds of NGOs to consider global issues. Such advocacy networks engage in the following: information politics, in which networks provide information on issues under consideration; symbolic politics, in which networks use symbols to raise awareness about specific issues; leverage politics, in which networks attempt to gain leverage over powerful actors; and accountability politics, in which networks try to hold states accountable. Lobbying is a related important activity for NGOs. It should not be of surprise to anyone that NGOs attempt to influence their government, other governments, and different organizations and institutions.[59]

Cornelia Beyer states that an important power of NGOs is their "Decisional power." Such power can be "exerted on the political process at every level: at agenda-setting, at policy formulation, at implementation and at monitoring stages. In many cases, NGOs seem to have more decisional power than political influence, as they are especially active and successful in influencing agenda-setting and monitoring, and less so in actual decision-making, which is still the domain of state actors. Forms of exertion of decisional power are lobbying, advocacy, monitoring, protest and participation."[60]

Krista Masonis El-Gawhary offers a different point of view. She says that NGOs "have been touted as a cure for almost every malady afflicting developing societies. Western governments, international organizations, and regional activists expect NGOs to help fill the gap left by underfunded, ineffective state bureaucracies. NGOs are viewed as antidotes to authoritarian and corrupt rule and considered more efficient providers of social services than beleaguered governments. In the Middle East, NGOs are also thought to be potential catalysts for significant social and political change in the region, hastening its transition to democracy."[61]

El-Gawhary continues by noting that despite Egyptian NGO efforts, their impact as far as human rights and development is concerned has been limited. "The general lack [of] popular support for the advocacy NGOs' mission has led activists to seek solace in international organizations. Yet this alliance has diverted their focus away from working with and for 'the people's priorities' while further compromising their legitimacy by the simple fact that they work with foreign organizations."[62]

Christoph Schnellbach offers an interesting perspective related to the role of NGOs in promoting, albeit with limited success, minority rights in the EU, specifically the rights of the Roma people and special minority rights such as those of Russians in the Baltic states, Hungarians in Slovakia, etc. As noted previously, for the longest time international organizations have reflected their member states' priorities. But in recent years, NGOs have attracted serious attention in international institutions. "Although state actors still seem to be the main players in the field of minority protection, issues concerning Roma are increasingly pushed forward by intermediary actors. In an effort to co-ordinate governmental policy on Roma, an unique initiative is presented by the *Decade of Roma Inclusion* (2005-2015), which involves not only governments (the 12 participating countries are Albania, Bosnia and Herzegovina, Bulgaria, Croatia, Czech Republic, Hungary, Macedonia, Montenegro, Romania, Serbia, Slovakia and Spain) and international organizations, but also NGOs."[63]

The limited interactions between Roma communities and international organizations has led to doubtful results for the Roma. The EU's report in 2004, *Roma Situation in an Enlarged Europe,* concluded that the Roma are confronted with many problems in comparison to the rest of the population in the areas of education, employment, housing, and health. "There is a vast gap between the policy level and the operational reality through the relative absence of Romani grass-root and stalagmite mobilization in the transnational political context. Thus, it is hard to detect shared interests as there is hardly a 'legitimate' Romani voice in international organizations."[64]

The very narrow representation of Romani interests in international organizations has contributed to the founding of NGOs whose purpose is to erase such a gap. For instance, the European Roma Rights Center (ERRC) has consultative status with the Council of Europe and ECOSOC of the UN. The activities and publications of the ERRC attempt to promote the most relevant interests of the Romani. "One leading NGO in the area, the Budapest-based ERRC, was established in 1996 as an international public interest law organization focusing exclusively on the human rights situation of the Roma. In the context of EU enlargement, the ERRC has conducted research on the human rights of Roma and produced several reports on behalf of European institutions … In combining legal and political activities with advocacy on all levels, the ERRC has been especially engaged in inducing domestic political actors to uphold international norms." The European Roma Information Office (ERIO) is yet another NGO that was established to advance the cause of the Roma communities. ERIO has contributed to the development of an *EU Strategy on the Roma Inclusion.*[65]

Regarding special minority rights, NGO advocacy influence is more difficult to ascertain. Even though significant legal improvements have taken place in relationship to minority rights at the EU level, when it comes to special minority rights, which go beyond equal treatment and nondiscrimination, the EU has had limited leverage "in areas of weak EU competence such as special minority rights." And although NGOs have demanded the promotion of special minority rights including political representation, individual governments, such as the Hungarian government, have decided not to take on the issue. "Opportunity structures for NGOs seem to be limited, as EU leverage is minimal in the area of political participation, which belongs to collective minority rights."[66]

What then has been the effect of NGO advocacy in the EU policy process? Despite the attention brought by NGOs to the cause of the Roma and despite some improvements in their lives, Roma still suffer from discrimination and marginalization in EU member states. As for special minority rights, the situation is even worse. "Member states can undermine NGO advocacy for minorities in intergovernmental institutions. Moreover, collective minority rights are mostly directional issues and can touch upon very sensitive questions of state organization. It is therefore not surprising that in the mid-term perspective, advocacy group influence remains rather low in that specific area."[67]

An interesting study on the Roma is presented by Monique Frey and Gerhard Meili in their work on social inclusion of Roma communities in Southeastern Europe. The authors examine the role of the Swiss NGO Caritas in promoting the rights of Roma in Kosovo and Bosnia and Herzegovina. About 35,000 Roma live in Kosovo. Caritas has worked with two Roma communities in Prizren and Gjakove. "Since 2005 a Caritas project called Minority Assistance and Returnees (MAAR) has aimed at social integration of the entire Roma community, community building, improved community infrastructure, and inter-ethnic cooperation at the municipality level." A significant step was taken when the government of Kosovo in 2008 approved a strategy for Roma integration in the fields of infrastructure, education, employment, gender, and political participation. As for Bosnia and Herzegovina, the Roma are the largest minority there. Despite this fact, the Roma were not mentioned in the Treaty of Dayton, which is considered the constitution of the country. As a result, they lack rights corresponding to a national minority. There are approximately 50,000 to 80,000 Roma in Bosnia and Herzegovina.[68]

Caritas has cooperated in Kosovo with three Roma NGOs as well as the municipality. The three NGOs are

Initiative 6, which focuses on pedagogic and social integration and has a strategy of integration through the official education system

Durmish Aslano, which focuses on cultivating Roma tradition and values, literature, music, dances, and media work

Foleja, a women's NGO, which focuses on building health awareness and health training

Caritas also cooperates with the multiethnic women's organization Dora Dores and the multiethnic youth organization Fisniket.

Caritas has worked in Bosnia and Herzegovina primarily with two local organizations: Roma NGO and Budi moj prijatelj. The first implements projects in Sarajevo and the second pays much attention to research, education, community building, and capacity building.[69]

Despite some successes, many challenges remain working with or for Roma communities in Kosovo and Bosnia and Herzegovina. Some of the challenges related to Kosovo include limited skills, limited management resources, difficulties implementing a systematic gender approach (the NGOs are dominated by men), and high unemployment among the Roma. The challenges in Bosnia and Herzegovina include the lack of responsible project managers, lack of organization and skills, structural discrimination against Roma, and that the Roma have little representation and power.[70]

As in the case of Roma and even though developed and developing countries are signatories of the United Nations Refugee Convention, many of them, including the United States, Japan, European states, and others, take actions related to refugees that do not meet their obligations under the Refugee Convention. NGOs and international organizations could play an important role in socializing states. Through the activities of these groups, states could learn how to act appropriately. The domestic and international contexts are important in achieving greater compliance with the Refugee Convention. "Compliance signals an identification of states with the norms codified in international law. Identification with international norms is not easily attained, but NGOs and international organizations play key roles in imparting the social learning necessary for states to improve compliance."[71]

An even more striking argument about NGOs and advocacy, especially as related to Africa, is made by Warren Nyamugarisa. The author notes that many NGOs have intensified their advocacy efforts to overcome the limitations put on them by the global powers — both political and economic — to better represent the interests of the poor. NGOs have come to the realization that even though they have had some limited successes, "the systems and structures that determine power and resource allocations — locally, nationally, and globally — remain largely intact. Therefore, they need to find ways to 'scale up' their influence upon these determinants, so that their small-scale successes have greater and more lasting impact."[72]

Nyamugarisa asserts that Africa "is not part of the global agenda-setting mechanism.... It has no authentic advocates.... There is no distinct African voice in global forums. 'Representatives' for Africa either sing the tune of global elite or simply occupy space at the table." NGOs, governments, and global institutions must change the way they represent Africa's interests. "There is a real challenge in a world that is seemingly indifferent to the continent's future."[73]

The absence of the African perspective is not the creation or the fault of NGOs, but one might wonder if they have done any better than governments. Have NGOs challenged the status quo enough? NGOs need self-examination. For organizations that claim they speak truth to power, they are often "unable to speak the truth to themselves. By obstructing such essential feedback, NGOs prove how big is the gap between rhetoric and reality." In addition, NGOs must follow some of what those who are promoting global economic liberalization are doing. NGOs must be as assertive, competitive, and dynamic in representing the interests of the poor. They cannot develop successful strategies by holding "[onto] the 'protectionism' of the past; old forms of propping up NGOs in the South need to be re-examined and transformed."

Furthermore, the poor must be empowered to behave as their own advocates. For this to happen, global institutions must provide the poor with resources to create their own wealth. The business community must be convinced to pay the poor decent wages, and to also facilitate the poor to produce quality products. The poor must find their own niche in global trade and must appreciate the need to save in order to invest. "It is such activities that NGOs should be investing [in] to make the poor more dynamic, aggressive, and competitive.... This is what will make it possible to break the vicious cycle of poverty.... In supporting them, economic advocacy perhaps must take precedence over political advocacy on the NGO agenda. Otherwise the poor, and perhaps NGOs along with them, will continue to be marginalized in the emerging dynamic of the global economy."[74]

In considering the role of NGOs in Africa in promoting land rights, Nazneen Kanji et al. argue that even though NGOs have contributed to the development and dissemination of new land laws, when it came to their implementation the process was fraught with difficulties. Despite the obstacles, the authors argue, NGOs should keep the following in mind: "Trade-offs may sometimes have to be made between seizing opportunities for advocacy and lobbying in policy and slower-paced work with grassroots organizations, but there will be more pro-poor policy gains in the longer term if NGOs promote advocacy capacity of representative organizations of less powerful groups."[75]

Do NGOs have the skills for advocacy work, or should they focus on innovation in development interventions at the community level? Kanji et al. contend that

> [just] as policy development and implementation are not as dichotomous as they seem, the division between community level work and policy advocacy may also be artificial. [In their work], NGOs tended to combine these roles. Service delivery is often important, not only in itself, but as a way of gaining legitimacy and as an entry point for advocacy. The current shifts in donor support for NGOs to work upstream on policy development risk undermining the legitimacy of NGOs and their important role in building sustainable policy influence from the grassroots. There is, however, room for NGOs to functionally specialize, so that some may devote themselves to service provision, including providing information and resources to other NGOs.... Certainly, it is not being suggested that all NGOs must claim "the people" as their constituency, but those that do, need to maintain close links with communities.[76]

NGOs have played a significant role in highlighting the many issues facing indigenous peoples related to the environment. Indigenous peoples did not attract much attention until the 1970s when LNGOs and INGOs attempted to promote their concerns. But it was not until the 1990s when INGOs began to focus on indigenous peoples' environmental issues. "This internationalization of indigenous peoples' environmental concerns could take place due to the advocacy role of INGOs such as IUCN (International Union for Conservation of Nature and Natural Resources), WWF, Friends of the Earth, Greenpeace International, and Conservation International." An example is the deforestation matter in Brazil. The "Amazon Alliance" in Brazil was established by a small group of LNGOs and along with INGOs such as Conservation International, Oxfam International, and Sierra Club generated an international campaign. By doing so, this network of NGOs produced a series of norms and declarations and helped to gain an international audience, which had not been the case before the involvement of these NGOs.[77]

The expertise of INGOs on this matter enabled them to play an important role in the "preparatory meetings of United Nations Conference on Environment and Development (UNCED, or Earth Summit) in 1992." During this conference, Greenpeace and IUCN very much influenced the agenda under consideration. "In fact, it is due to the advocacy by INGOs about the negative impact environmental degradation could have on indigenous peoples, the UNCED for the first time formally recognized the important role indigenous peoples could play in the conservation of the environment and sustainable management of natural resources."[78]

In addition, "because of "IUCN's efforts, the … UNEP formulated drafts for adoption of a global convention concerned with conservation of biodiversity. This convention also has important provision for the role of indigenous peoples in the management of biodiversity … Provisions on indigenous peoples were included after these NGOs lobbied countries, mobilized local victim interests, issued oral statements, publications, and organized conferences…. Another important document adopted at the Earth Summit, with possible repercussions on indigenous peoples was the 'Forest Principles.' The problem of deforestation became a global issue as early as the 1980s, but the inability of states to deal with the issue … made way for the NGOs to come into the picture…. Here the INGOs were credited for 'framing' the agenda in such a way to get the interest of the international audience."[79]

PUBLIC EDUCATION AND CONSCIOUSNESS RAISING

Public education and consciousness raising might be two of the most important activities of NGOs. Lacking the resources available to states, multinational corporations and other important actors, NGOs more and more frequently become involved in the area of political socialization. NGOs participate in outreach activities in order to educate local, national, or international governments and organizations. For example, Greenpeace tries to bring to the attention of people environmental abuse by disseminating information through television, radio, and newspaper stories.[80]

Baogang He and Hannah Murphy make a noteworthy statement when they say that "a global-level set of contracts between citizens and international organizations remains conspicuously absent." As such, INGOs through protests against the economic policies of the World Trade Organization (WTO) endeavor to formulate "a global social contract or a series of global social contracts involving civil society, governments and international organizations."[81] This is a matter that has become more urgent with the latest phase of globalization with its many perils including the social, political, and economic effects of neoliberal policies, the gap between the wealthy and the poor, the lack of widespread labor standards, the environmental degradation, etc.

He and Murphy examined two NGO campaigns against the WTO. The first was enforceable labor standards linked to economic liberalization and the second was Trade Related Intellectual Property Rights (TRIPS) to increase access to medicines in developing countries at affordable prices. INGOs have had limited success in relation to the first campaign and greater success about the second.[82]

After considering these two campaigns, He and Murphy concluded that the ability of NGOs to develop global social contracts depends on several factors.

"[The] extent of NGO links with governmental power; the institutional structure of the intergovernmental arena in which the original contract was developed; the level of consensus and solidarity within the international NGO campaign network; and the power of the NGOs to frame debates and define the concepts at stake."

Links with governmental power

In the TRIPS case, the NGOs played a vital role in supporting developing countries to clarify the use of the TRIPS safeguards at the WTO. The NGOs provided these governments with legal and technical expertise, financial resources and moral support. They also worked to mobilize international public opinion in support of the right of developing country citizens to affordable medicines. In the labor standards campaign, domestic and international lobbying by trade unions and other NGOs resulted in backing from the US and several Europeans governments for a discussion about core labor standards at the WTO.

Surprisingly, however, even with the support of the most powerful nation-states … NGOs failed to realize their key campaign goal at the WTO with respect to universal labor standards. In contrast, the TRIPS and generic medicines case reveals that less powerful nation-states in alliance with NGOs can attain success, despite strong opposition from the US government.

Consensus and the Solidarity of International NGO Alliances

In regards to labor standards, despite the fact there was general agreement between trade unions on the need for enforceable international labor standards, "several NGOs disagreed with the trade unions' view that the WTO was the appropriate venue for such an agreement. In comparison, the TRIPS case involved a powerful, transnational alliance of international NGOs and nation-based NGOs working towards the common goal of clarifying the TRIPS safeguard rules."

Power to Frame Debates and Define Concepts

> The TRIPS case had the benefit of being a relatively clear-cut issue, ... [It] was essentially a campaign about life and death ... In comparison, the attempt to frame international labor standards as a human rights issue was impeded by the competing economic development frame put forward by developing country NGOs and their governments, which successfully argued that an international labor agreement would affect the economic advancement of developing nations.[83]

He and Murphy conclude by noting that NGOs can be successful in transforming international economic agreements into global social contracts by engaging with states and businesses. The cases examined demonstrate that NGOs could significantly affect the WTO agenda, which in turn makes them significant actors in the development a of global social contract at the WTO. While there are limitations to NGOs speaking on behalf of the voiceless, the moderate success of TRIPS and access to medicines campaign "challenges the pessimism about the emergence of global social contracts encountered in the literature ..."[84]

Other multiple examples of NGOs involved in the education of the public could be cited. One such example is the role of NGOs involved in environmental education in Southeastern Europe (SEE), which began to emerge in the 1980s. Albania is representative of the pattern of development across the region. Most environmental NGOs (ENGOs) were founded in Tirana and their members were limited to people involved in the environmental sciences. But later their membership was transformed to include students and members of the general public. Most of these groups are small with limited financial resources and inexperienced management. Because government funding is not significant, there is much dependence on foreign donors. Serbia is on the same level as Albania.[85]

In spite of the problems associated with NGOs in Greece, Greek ENGOs have been in operation for a longer period. They receive funding from the government as well as from the EU and private citizens. In addition to the presence of large global organizations such as Greenpeace and Worldwide Fund for Nature, there are dozens of ENGOs in Greece. Among them are Mediterranean SOS, HELMEPA (for the protection of the seas and marine life), Arcturus (for the protection of the brown bear), the Hellenic Society for the Protection of the Environment and Cultural Heritage, the GAIA Center for Environmental Education, etc.[86]

Some other examples of ENGO activity in SEE are Albamont, the Green Foundation, and the Bosnian Environmental Association (BETA):

> Albamont — the ecological and mountain tourism club in Alba Iulia, Romania — seeks to raise public awareness with regard to the urban fabric (e.g. preserving Europe's largest Vauban fortress), rural development in the Apuseni Mountains and control of pollution through both mining ... and wood processing which generates large quantities of sawdust. Education with the aim of raising awareness and training of facilitators ... is clearly important ... Across Transylvania there is much concern over water quality and endangered species ... Elsewhere, industrial pollution is still a threat from mercury contamination at Vlora (Albania) linked with a now-abandoned caustic soda factory...
>
> Nuclear issues have arisen in connection with Bulgaria's reactors, but Serbia and Montenegro have to find a permanent storage for spent fuel still lying within a research reactor at the Vinca Institute of Nuclear Sciences near Belgrade ...
>
> Examples of ENGO activity in environmental education include Albamont with its guidebooks for open air activities as well as its course manuals and reserve guides. In western Romania, the Green Foundation runs camps in addition to its Nature in School program. The Bosnian Environmental Association BETA runs a summer camp for students on Mount Vranica.[87]

The limited financial resources available to ENGOs across SEE make the establishment of extensive networks very difficult. As such, there is great need for umbrella groups like Bosnia's Sarajevo-based Eco organization, and Serbia's "Green Table" to coordinate activities. ENGOs in SEE are also supported by the Western governments. For example, the Green Foundation gets funding from the Precious Planet project run by the French Embassy in Bucharest, the Romanian Carpathian Foundation gets support from Belgium's King Baudouin Foundation, and USAID is developing a "Dialogue" project in many Romanian cities. USAID has significant presence in Bulgaria through its Biodiversity Conservation and Economic Growth Project. And the Regional Environmental Center for Central and Eastern Europe (REC), an international nonprofit organization founded in 1990 with help from the United States and the EU, has the aim of rebuilding NGOs and civil society in SEE.[88]

National and international campaigns run by NGOs are an important way to promote public education and to raise public consciousness on a particular issue. Jennifer Chapman and Thomas Fisher examine the effectiveness of two NGO-run campaigns: one to promote breastfeeding in Ghana and the other against the use of child labor in the carpet industry in India.[89]

The breastfeeding campaign in Ghana began in 1987 when a Ghanaian doctor discovered negative effects of free samples of infant formula given to health clinics. He founded the Ghanaian Infant Nutrition Action Network (GINAN) and put pressure on the government to take corrective action. The promotion of breastfeeding received more attention when health workers were trained, and Ghana became involved in UNICEF's Baby Friendly Hospital Initiative and in the celebration of World Breastfeeding Week started by the World Alliance on Breastfeeding Action (WABA).[90]

Although problems remain, the breastfeeding campaign has led to numerous achievements. Among them "[The] Ministry of Health and many health workers are now aware of the issue and breastfeeding is included in the plan of action for health ...current marketing practices are being monitored and violations reported internationally; and there are [numerous] mother-to-mother support groups." Such developments have led to a significant increase in breastfeeding rates. "Most importantly, although direct links are hard to establish, and many other factors have played a part, infant mortality has fallen from 82 deaths/1,000 live births in 1978 to 66 deaths/1,000 live births in 1993. ... Diarrhea among children under two years of age has also dropped from 36 percent in 1988 to 22 percent in 1993..."[91]

The campaign against the use of child labor in the carpet industry in India was primarily started by Indian NGOs, although NNGOs, consumers, and importers played an important role as well. The campaign first focused on bonded laborers and then on bonded child laborers in the carpet industry. The narrower focus helped in attracting the attention of international media. After this initial success, the campaign became wider to encompass all children working illegally in the carpet industry, and then to call for universal primary education. The campaign utilized many strategies. It started with raids to free bonded children. It was followed by a consumer campaign, which attempted to educate consumers about the predicament of child laborers in this specific industry. Concurrently, the Harkin Bill was considered in the US, "threatening to legislate against the import of goods made with child labor. These two pressures prompted talk of a labelling system."[92]

As these actions were taking place, LNGOs, which until then were focusing on social welfare and education in the carpet-weaving area, also began to pay greater attention to child labor in the carpet industry. These grassroots efforts included mobilizing the public against child labor and demand for schools.

Since 1983, an enormous amount has been achieved. NGOs have worked with the judiciary and government officials to enforce existing laws; they have been able to threaten export markets sufficiently to bring about some changes in industry without actually implementing a boycott; they established the labelling scheme (Rugmark) as a constructive outcome for the consumer campaign; and they have also had a significant impact at the grassroots level and on the emergence of civil society. Above all, there is some evidence of a reduction in child labor in the specific industries and areas targeted, although it is debatable whether there has been a reduction in child labor overall.[93]

AGENDA SETTING

Public education, advocacy, and lobbying are activities utilized by NGOs to influence the political agenda before decision makers, at the local, national, and international level. Influencing the political agenda means advocating for certain issues so that policymakers pay attention to them. Framing the issue is an important NGO public education activity. NGOs have had success in regards to many issues when they were able to convince the public, governments, and members of IGOs such as the International Monetary Fund (IMF), the World Bank, and the WTO that there was a better way to view persistent problems.

Greenpeace is a good example of an NGO involved in issue framing. Since the whole world is vulnerable to environmental consequences, Greenpeace tries to persuade people and governments to pursue policies that protect the environment. And the result has been millions of people and many governments around the world taking actions to protect the earth. Activist NGOs like Greenpeace are complemented in their activities by think-tank NGOs whose focus is the collection of information through research for public education and advocacy. Two such NGOs are the Institute for Agriculture and Trade Policy and the Rural Advancement Foundation International.[94]

Adam Fagan and Indraneel Sircar, in examining the role of foreign donors, especially the European Commission, note that they have influenced the issue agendas of civil society members in post-socialist countries that have recently joined the EU. In Central and Eastern Europe, foreign donor emphasis on building the capacity of recipient ENGOs to "participate in policy-making procedures has served to institutionalize 'green' civil society networks. It may also have generated improved environmental governance, or, at least laid the foundations for multi-level interaction among investors, state, non-state and technical actors in new member states."[95]

But after considering the case of Bosnia-Herzegovina, the authors argue that while some Bosnian ENGOs have become more professionalized and have improved their project management capacity, these NGOs do not seem to be significantly involved in environmental impact assessments. Among the reasons for this outcome is the fact that they are mostly involved in short-term donor-funded projects and that they do not have the technical and scientific expertise to engage in such assessments.[96]

> Multi-and bi-lateral foreign donors invariably frame their assistance for NGOs in terms of "capacity building" and augmenting the voice of civil society in new deliberative forums. Our research suggests that building democratic deliberation and good governance within processes of multilateral interaction in post-conflict transitional states is a complex process. From the perspective of ENGO involvement in EIAs [environmental impact assessments] it would appear that success is dependent not only just on the capacity of local ENGOs to engage communities and to manage short-term projects but also on the ability of non-state actors to be able to mobilize appropriate scientific and technical expertise. Relating our findings more generally to the issue of E.U. compliance and the development of environmental governance, the EIA optic reveals the extent to which the existence of legal and formal compliance is not necessarily triggering changes in the interaction between state and non-state actors.[97]

In the Westphalian system, states were the most important actors and, of course, at the center of the security discourse in developing (as well as developed) societies. But in a post-Westphalian system, actors once considered insignificant are now at the center of this conversation. Such actors are NGOs and the children they try to represent.[98] Children are part of the discourse on security. The matter of children has been given much more attention in recent decades because they are greatly affected by conflict.

> Thus, given that children are disproportionally affected by conflict, it is increasingly considered to be essential to focus on the younger generation to regenerate those societies that are in the process of transition from a conflict to (relative) peace. ... Many children are charged with significant societal roles at a local level. The forces that act against their assuming such significance at an international level are often revealed to be those same forces that preclude active consideration of other marginalized actors in the international system. Moving away from the bias of the "powerful" toward a consideration of the "knowledgeable" may thus lead to a more rounded consideration of standard security discourses.[99]

Briana Nichols et al. in "Transnational Information Politics and the 'Child Migration Crisis': Guatemalan NGOs Respond to Youth Migration" present data related to how Guatemalan NGOs responded to the 2014 child migration "crisis" and thus helped to set the agenda on the issue. The authors note that Guatemalan NGOs selectively espoused and were critical of how youth migration from Guatemala to the US was depicted. While they adopted some of the opinions emanating from the media and governments, they disputed others including "the very notion of a child migration 'crisis.'"[100]

Guatemalan NGOs pointed out that child migration was not a new phenomenon but something that was happening for a long time and as such they questioned the changes in immigration enforcement measures that led to the declaration of a "crisis." These NGOs viewed the use of the label "crisis" as having political rather than humanitarian causes.

> Our NGO stakeholders felt that youth migration was both costly and embarrassing to the USA, thus labeling youth migration as a "crisis" legitimated US pressure on Guatemala to reduce migration flows and served as an advantageous political strategy for the US government. Similarly, some of our NGO participants also took issue with the label of youth migrants as "children," articulating the position that the legalistic definition of who is a child employed by US immigration authorities is not shared by all populations and subcultures south of the border, and neglects the varied roles that youth occupy within Guatemalan family and community structures.... Focusing on the youth migrants as children legitimated a strong US response to a problem that perhaps would not have occurred had the migrants been viewed as adults and agentive actors.[101]

Criticizing the US and Guatemalan governments for the reasons related to youth migration was another area contested by Guatemalan NGOs. "Many interlocutors reflected the widespread Guatemalan public opinion blaming the USA for the push and pull factors associated with migration. [US free market politics which hurt Guatemalans the most]. Others linked the spate of Guatemalan governmental resignations in 2015 to political pressure from the USA after the Guatemalan government paid inadequate attention to youth migration issues.... It was the production of a 'crisis' in the USA that forced the Guatemalan government to enact policies to appease the USA," though most NGOs interviewed did not believe that the Guatemalan government had the ability to introduce the necessary changes to actually reduce youth migration.[102]

Perhaps nothing was more evident in the media and government discussions than the "root causes" of the youth migration "crisis." The US government and the Inter-American Development Bank focused on poverty, low educational levels and employment opportunities, and insecurity as the main reasons for youth migration. Even though Guatemalan NGOs did not disagree that these causes contributed to youth migration, "they did push back against the facile notion that addressing them piecemeal would staunch the northward movement of Guatemalan youth." They argued that the reasons for youth migration were too complex to be "eradicated by a checklist approach."[103]

While blaming both the US and Guatemalan governments and trying to promote the rights of migrant youth, Guatemalan NGOs "also expressed varying degrees of moral evaluation on families and migrant youth." Guatemalan families and youth were presented as naïve, willing to risk everything while pursuing the illusion of the American dream. "Here we see a contradiction or even frustration on the part of some of the NGO stakeholders: the Guatemalan government is to blame for creating a political and economic environment that youths desire to leave; the US government is to blame for how youths are treated once they migrate; but the youths and their families are simultaneously victims of these broad socioeconomic systems and to blame for their decisions to migrate, both brave and foolish for attempting such life-changing action.... Ultimately, many Guatemalan NGO stakeholders felt that both the ability to migrate, especially as a life-saving measure, and the ability to make a productive life in your home country, should be considered human rights."[104]

Even an organization like Médecins Sans Frontières, which is committed to neutrality, impartiality, and independence, can affect the policy agenda of another organization or government by becoming highly political and confrontational. That was the case during the height of the EU refugee crisis between April 2015 and June 2016. The severity of the crisis and the organization's independence made it possible for MSF to follow the path it chose in this case. And it chose this path despite its close ties with national and international elites, and the expectation that humanitarian NGOs are "generally cooperative and, ultimately, depoliticizing agents in global governance."[105]

By openly criticizing the EU and specific European governments, MSF successfully mobilized "European societies by bearing witness from search and rescue vessels in the Mediterranean Sea. In direct opposition to the EU-Turkey deal, MSF withdrew from refugee camps in Greece and rejected significant EU funds. Finally, the NGO reached out to more political organizations within wider civil society, at least partially and on an ad hoc basis.... [These] strategies were particularly outspoken and confrontational behaviors by MSF which aimed to increase public awareness and mobilize societies about refugee issues, and to put pressure on national and EU decision-makers to change their policies."[106]

There are many ways NGOs attempt to influence the agenda of governments, multilateral institutions, and other kinds of organizations. One of those ways is campaigning. Even though campaigning is not a new phenomenon, NGOs have in recent years have rediscovered it as an effective tool to be used . Some of the reasons for this trend are "the need for NGOs to find new roles, as Southern NGOs take over project work; the recognition that projects will have limited effects without structural changes; an increasing call by Southern organizations for Northern NGOs to do more campaign and policy work; and the desire among NGOs for public profile. The latter has two distinct aspects: the belief that media coverage is crucial for policy change, and the somewhat sounder assumption that it helps fundraising."[107]

To many scholars, one of the most crucial goals of development NGOs is "to achieve a fair global economic system. Campaigns alone cannot achieve this objective, but they can make an important contribution. They can raise awareness and create symbols of the problem." They can mobilize people and they can create coalitions of organizations around the world. "They can raise and win arguments about defining what is fair and what is patently unjust. They can create a new narrative for development."[108]

MONITORING OTHER TRANSNATIONAL ACTORS

NGOs monitor the behavior of governments as well as the behavior of multinational corporations and intergovernmental organizations to ensure that states and organizations comply with laws and international treaties. In addition, NGOs have formed advocacy networks to pressure international financial institutions such as the World Bank and the International Monetary Fund for greater accountability and transparency.[109]

There has been increased acceptance of NGOs by states and international organizations (IOs). As already mentioned, IOs, including the United Nations, have permitted the participation of NGOs in deliberations. They are accredited with the Economic and Social Council (ECOSOC) and have some rights. The World Trade Organization has recently given "a number of participatory rights for NGOs." Such participation increases the legitimacy of NGOs as well as that of IOs by making both sets of actors more representative.[110] NGO presence in IO's, it could be argued, extends participatory democracy and makes it easier for NGOs to monitor transnational actors.

Beginning in the early 1990s, NGOs became involved in the formulation as well as implementation of laws. By participating at conferences and negotiation processes, NGOs can influence government representatives or representatives of other kinds of organizations and institutions. As related to human rights, NGOs have greatly contributed to the advancement of such rights. For example, representatives of Amnesty International participated in the establishment and writing of the *Convention of the Abolition of Torture* and the drafting of the *Convention of the Rights of the Child*.[111] "[The] claim on the universality of human rights is increasingly supported by a much stronger legal, political, social and cultural global rooting. NGOs deserve credit for having contributed to this global culture of human rights."[112] Success in promoting human rights does not mean that there have been no failures. There have been many. For example, in examining the Arab Spring Gerald Steinberg notes that by the end of 2011, after the overthrow of the dictatorial regimes in Tunisia, Libya, Egypt, Yemen, Syria, and Bahrain "the hopes for significant and lasting human rights reforms in these countries and in the regions had receded." The UN Human Rights Council (UNHRC), the Office of the High Commissioner for Human Rights (OHCHR), and many NGOs that are so instrumental in promoting human rights failed in these cases to devote attention and significant resources.[113]

Yet another example of NGOs playing a role in monitoring other transnational actors is the case of the WTO, which claims to advance the interests of citizens through trade liberalization. Lin Zhengling, in his work on NGOs in the WTO, notes how many oppose NGO participation because their presence will lead to distortion of the decision-making process, to inefficiency, and "special interest manipulation." But the proponents of NGO engagement say otherwise. Instead, they say that the WTO will benefit for the following reasons: 1. NGOs "can serve as resource enhancers." NGOs often have information and expertise that governments do not. 2. Governments are not perfect operations and they do not always have the best ideas. 3. "NGOs also provide an additional oversight and audit mechanism. Well-informed citizen groups can act as watchdogs of national governments and report on whether they are fulfilling their obligations under international economic law." 4. "[The] participation of NGOs provides the WTO not only with a mechanism to hear views beyond governmental ones, but also with a means for sharing information about what is happening within the international trading system."[114]

As discussed previously, in the area of the environment NGOs have played a significant role in informing the public and holding various actors accountable. There is a long list of environment-related NGOs, among them are the Earth Island Institute, Rainforest Action Network, and of course Greenpeace. The first of these NGOs "develops and supports projects that counteract threats to the biological and cultural diversity that sustains the environment. Through education, these projects promote the conservation, preservation and restoration of the Earth." The second NGO "educates thousands of elementary school students about rainforest protection issues, 'informs and mobilizes' an international network of grassroots activists, provides grants to 'indigenous forest communities' and NGOs in rainforest countries, holds conferences and seminars, publishes reports and other informational materials, and conducts what it describes as 'hard-hitting campaigns that work to bring corporate and governmental policies into alignment with popular support for rainforest conservation." And the third NGO "is essentially a network of national and regional offices committed to a philosophy of nonviolence and a strategy of 'bearing witness.'" Greenpeace attempts to draw "attention to an abuse of the environment through an unwavering presence at the scene, whatever the risk."[115]

Civil society organizations have played a crucial role in promoting and implementing the Arms Trade Treaty (ATT) initiative; the treaty entered into force in 2014, and it is expected for NGOs to continue monitoring the implementation of the ATT to prevent illicit and irresponsible arms transfers. Specific non-governmental monitoring includes "(a) gathering information on states' arms transfers, (b) uncovering illegal or illicit arms transfers, (c) assessing the extent to which states are complying with criteria of an ATT, and (d) evaluating whether states' transfer control systems allow them to implement an ATT effectively. Such monitoring would therefore be comparable to the work carried out by the Landmine and Cluster Munition Monitor in overseeing states' implementation of the APM Convention on Cluster Munitions, by European NGOs to assess arms exports from EU member states against the criteria of the EU Common Position, or a number of international NGOs in highlighting arms transfers used in the commission of human rights abuses or violations of international humanitarian law."[116]

Numerous NGOs, especially in Europe, try to assess the arms export policies of European countries. In most cases, the NGO reports concern the state in which they are based. At times, NGOs produce reports about other states or groups of states and how they carry out arms export controls. "The reports are usually based on date on arms export licenses and arms exports that is produced by the government's national licensing authority and include assessments of the appropriateness of particular exports. For example, since 1998 Project Ploughshares has published regular reports on the Canadian Government's annual reports on the export of military goods."[117]

Many NGOs have also paid close attention to the application of the eight criteria of the EU Common Position related to arms export licensing decisions. Most NGO reports have attempted to determine the extent to which these "criteria are being interpreted in a consistent and uniform manner by EU member states. Most studies highlight examples of lax and conflicting interpretations of the common criteria on the part of different EU member states. Other studies have analyzed data from either the Comtrade Database or SIPRI [First Conference of States Parties] Arms Transfers Database to measure trends in EU member states' exports to particular types of destination, such as those engaged in armed conflict or where systematic violations of human rights have been reported."[118]

ONLINE RESOURCE NETWORKS

As the Internet becomes even more important in the lives of people in developed and developing nations, NGOs help to further fuel this change. Among the NGOs that have played a role in this arena are the Institute for Global Communications and OneWorld. Both of these NGOs are online resource networks that function as a common Internet gateway to NGOs focusing on human rights and development; offer Internet-based tools and services to their members; provide means for members to communicate with each other; and serve as an information resource for the public.[119]

The Institute for Global Communications was launched in Palo Alto, California, and went on to have thousands of clients all over the world. It is a nonprofit and interested in peace. Even though the institute "maintains a physical presence in the Presidio [San Francisco], for all practical purposes the organization is a 'virtual' entity built around four networks." Each of these networks (PeaceNet, EcoNet, WomensNet, and Anti-RacismNet) offers "issue-specific feature stories, headlines, action alerts, and discussion forums, as well as commonly shared search engine, members directory, and other resources."[120]

OneWorld was founded in England by Peter Armstrong who for years worked as a producer for the BBC. Despite his professional experience as a member of the media, he did not believe that they were the right "fit" for what interested him the most — sustainable global development or global justice. "OneWorld began as the Internet arm of the OneWorld Broadcasting Trust ... a small but influential UK based charity that aims to encourage effective use of the media ... to promote a clear and balanced awareness of human rights and global development issues." OneWorld has become "the world's leading portal on global justice and a gateway to over 700 NGOs worldwide."[121]

Through the formation of online networks NGOs not only provide access to information to other NGOs, they also provide information and expertise to governments and various other organizations and institutions to promote a certain agenda or to accomplish a certain task. The work of Heather L. Wipfli et al. on global tobacco control diffusion provides a good example of such an online network, GLOBALink.

The authors note that in response to the impact of tobacco smoking, in 1999, the members of WHO began negotiations on an international treaty in order to reduce tobacco consumption. The intergovernmental negotiating team met several times in Geneva between 2000 and 2003. More than 170 countries sent representatives to attend the negotiations. Scientific experts and advocacy networks also participated in these negotiations to provide information and to hold seminars on technical issues. As mentioned above, one such advocacy network was GLOBALink, internationally recognized for facilitating communications between tobacco control advocates.[122]

In May 2003, the 56th World Health Assembly adopted the WHO Framework Convention on Tobacco Control (FCTC). "The institutionalization of tobacco control within the WHO and the subsequent ratification of the FCTC ... provides an opportunity to analyze the system and network dynamics that facilitate global tobacco control diffusion. Diffusion refers to the process by which an innovation is communicated through certain channels over time among members of a social system.... Given studies of diffusion in other contexts, we hypothesized that the global diffusion of the FCTC has been partly driven by interpersonal communication and networking developed throughout the negotiation of the FCTC and facilitated through the existing global tobacco control networks."[123]

It is of interest to note again that NGOs' "instrumental collective action networks exist to produce [often but not always] public goods. Moreover, these organizations' hyperlinks function to express tangible collective identity.... [Offline behavior, like engaging in a common social issue, financial ties, membership ties, collaborative ties, and instrumental action leading to media visibility, are associated with hyperlink patterns.... NGO hyperlinks are expressive forms of collective action. Hyperlinks do so by providing a low-cost way for NGOs to publicly express a collective identity. Moreover, the results of the research suggest that instrumental collective action activities are related to NGO hyperlinking behavior. These results add to previous research showing the impact [of] offline characteristics on hyperlinks. As a result, for NGOs, hyperlinks act as extensions of such prior offline relationships."[124]

It is to be expected that other organizations, including development organizations, beyond NGOs, use online networks to raise the quality of their activities, their outputs, to enhance "a collective learning process, and to contribute to a 'shifting up' of development activities to an international audience." Among the development organizations that is extensively utilizing online networks is the World Bank. According to the World Bank, these networks are essential for the following reasons:

They promote learning among bank staff and "outside practitioners who share similar goals, interests, problems, and approaches."

They make it easier to respond to questions from bank members and bank clients.

They develop and transfer best practices by sharing knowledge.

They contribute to better development outcomes by promoting informed dialogue.

They connect diverse groups from very different disciplines.

They promote innovative approaches to deal with development challenges.[125]

These networks not only benefit the World Bank, they also benefit NGOs that work with the Bank or just by having access to information they can gather from the networks. Another development organization that is using online networks is the International Institute for Sustainable Development (IISD) in Canada. "IISD is researching the functioning of the 'formal knowledge networks' with which it is involved." Another example is the International Institute for Communication and Development (IICD) in the Netherlands, "which uses thematic networks as the main way to disseminate sector-specific lessons, news, and ideas. Working with these networks, or forming something new when it is needed, each network supports IICD's local partners by bringing expertise and knowledge to them; and by providing a platform where their experiences can be shared more widely."[126]

A further illustration of the great usage of networks is the creation of

Dgroups (www.dgroups.org), a platform of collaborative tools and services. By December 2005, Dgroups supported 1,537 virtual communities, made up of 47,242 members. Partners in Dgroups include Bellanet, the UK Department for International Development, the International Council on Archives, IICD, OneWorld, the Joint United Nations Program on HIV/AIDS (UNAIDS), and the World Bank. Such examples are dominated by online networks set up by Northern development institutions, because these institutions were the first to be in a position to support them. Given its recent emergence, most of the evidence in this field is anecdotal. An increasing number of Southern networks are now working effectively. One such example is C3NET, the Community Content Creation Network. C3NET aims to facilitate the exchange of information among members from Southern countries.[127]

C3NET put much emphasis on improving the lives of people living in rural areas.

Of course, as with much of everything done by NGOs, there are scholars who point toward some serious problems with NGO networks and network-ing. It is often argued that networks allow for the voices of the weak and the poor to be heard at policy-making gatherings. It is also argued that networking allows for greater flexibility, strength, and efficiency. But INGOs and LNGOs may have different expectations with networking. While LNGOs might be more interested in community service projects, INGOs might be more interested in greater visibility and a platform to influence policy. "Hence, a network that consists of participants with different backgrounds must define its language, methods, and priorities according to the needs of its weakest partner. Often it appears to be the other way around, with aims and methods defined in a top-down manner. Most 'lower-order' organizations depend on 'higher-order' organizations (and ultimately on donors) for financial resources.... The result often is a one-way dissemination of information."[128]

In addition, NGOs are not a homogeneous group "and there are good reasons to doubt that NGOs represent some kind of alternative development. Since there are so many ideologies, strategies, and objectives represented among NGOs, one might ask whether there really is so much to network about."[129]

OTHER NGO FUNCTIONS

NGOs perform many more functions related to and overlapping with the previously discussed NGO roles. Among them are the following: create new standards, enhance transparency, provide expertise and information, and diminish the North-South division.

NGOs at times play a role in the "formation of international institutions and reinforce the norms promoted by these institutions through public education as well as through organized attempts at holding states accountable to these, and enhance institutional effectiveness by reducing the implementation costs associated with international institutions." NGOs also promote norm application by exerting pressure upon "target actors to adopt new policies, and by monitoring compliance with international standards."[130]

NGOs often and significantly contribute to transparency. "The role of NGOs for the democratization or re-democratization of international politics or foreign policy decision-making processes, respectively, is seen in the creation of transparency through information and education of the public about these processes." NGOs contribute to democratization through "the conduct of publicly effective campaigns against illegal, dangerous or unethical practices, for example, and they again and again [provide] information and education [to] the public about political decisions ... and the implementation of internationally agreed upon measures."[131] Even though one might question the mission and purpose of WikiLeaks, exposing the misdeeds of individuals and institutions is one of their functions.

The role of NGOs in the Ottawa Process to Ban Landmines is an example of NGOs democratizing foreign policy. In 1997, 122 countries met in Ottawa to sign the Convention on the Prohibition of the Use, Stockpiling, Production and Transfer of Anti-Personnel Mines and their Destruction, a major accomplishment celebrated in many quarters. Beyond the signing of this major convention, the process followed to bring about the treaty is regarded as a model for cooperation between governments and NGOs. "Indeed, some academics have called the Ottawa Process 'a stunning example of a new form of diplomacy.'"[132]

Are these claims valid? NGOs were successful in this case because they accessed to the Ottawa Process by having a patron government and the support of other governments. But what if the agenda promoted by governments does not coincide with that of NGOs? What if governments and NGOs do not agree with each other? Obviously, NGOs would not be as impactful. And does NGO involvement in international negotiation democratize foreign policy?

> The participation of NGOs in many respects was narrow and centralized. Furthermore, NGOs themselves were not globally representative. A survey at the Ottawa Treaty Signing NGO Forum found that only 20 percent of the NGOs were non-European or non-North American....
> The funding of the Ottawa Process suggests that it might be difficult to replicate. It benefited from the strong support of a very few funders. These sources of funding were in large part governmental. Much of the rest came from the Open Society Institute, an element of the Soros Foundation network... Can NGOs be said to represent the interests of civil society [to be defined below] if they need the support of a few powerful entities?
> ... It should be reiterated that the [Ottawa] Process has taken significant, tangible steps to confront a profound humanitarian crisis that traditional diplomatic channels had proven unable to address meaningfully.... There may be potential in the Ottawa Process model to confront other humanitarian crises that conform to the parameters raised above. However, the limitations of such an approach and the claims it may make about democracy and participation should be rigorously examined as the Ottawa Process is discussed vis-à-vis new problems.[133]

NGOs, because of their proximity to problems and issues as well as their proximity to the affected people, could be of service to governments and international institutions. In addition, the leaders of these NGOs become specialists; they gain specialist knowledge thT could be of great value. And they become "professionals in the use of information ... [and] should often be regarded as being more reliable in presenting information than either journalists or government officials."[134]

The work of Jungin Kim provides a noteworthy example of how NGOs could provide services to governments. Kim focuses on the US government, by examining the roles of NGOs in relation to the human rights of North Korean refugees. Kim states that despite the attempts by the US government to improve the human rights of North Korean refugees, their plight does not seem to improve. Among the plethora of reasons for this situation is the lack of information about the situation of these refugees and the difficulty of obtaining information from the North Korean government so that the US government can proceed with the required checks to resettle North Korean applicants.[135]

Kim chose four NGOs for this study: Human Rights First in the US, Citizen's Alliance for North Korean Human Rights in South Korea, Life Funds for North Korean Refugees in Japan, and World Vision International. All four have worked hard to improve the human rights of North Korean refugees by forming networks with other NGOs in order to share information and rescue refugees. Additionally, these NGOs have published annual reports and they have tried to make the human rights of refugees part of the policy agendas considered by governments and other organizations and institutions at the domestic and international levels.[136]

Kim concludes by saying that NGOs have influenced policies related to the human rights of North Korean refugees "by acting as information sources and establishing coalitions among other NGOs, the private sector, and governments. Also, NGOs can play a positive role in dealing with politically sensitive issues through people-to-people diplomacy for dealing with refugees' human rights issues in international society." But at the same time, Kim recognizes that NGOs working in this area face a few difficulties. One of the frequently cited problem is that NGOs compete for limited resources and recognition. "In light of the problem of limited resources, one of the most important questions that concerns NGOs is that of their independence. That is, whether NGOs can maintain their independence ... and resist becoming either agents of government or free-charging private consultancy firms remains unclear."[137]

Another problem is that NGOs have difficulties protecting their staff. Many individuals, for instance, working for North Koreans' human rights have been in danger since the UN, individual governments, [and NGOs themselves] cannot always protect them. For example, many NGO personnel have been threatened with arrest and prosecution in China [and elsewhere in the world, astonishingly in both democratic and nondemocratic societies]. An additional problem is "cultural conflicts caused by overemphasizing a westernized point of view toward human rights might be a limitation on the NGOs' activities for supporting North Korean refugees. Since North Korea is a closed society, North Korean refugees are not familiar with westernized programs or with the aid provided by some NGOs. Often, they tend to have strong dislike of western values and do not want to be 'defectors' or 'refugees.' Rather, they want to maintain self-respect by considering themselves 'immigrants for economic motives.'"[138]

NGOs, as relatively new actors in international politics, bring a new and different perspective to international politics. Also, "[by] having a foot in the North and a foot in the South, NGOs are in a good position to link the micro and the macro levels, using their experience in the South to inform their advocacy and policy work in the North. They can contribute to strengthen southern voices and thus diminish the North-South division."[139] By performing the

Chapter 2

functions NGOs perform, they have contributed to the expansion of civil society at the domestic level and to an emerging global civil society.

John Burroughs and Jacqueline Cabasso, in their work on the role of NGOs in nuclear weapons related negotiations, make some similar arguments about the effectiveness and democratizing role of NGOs. The authors examine the role of NGOs regarding negotiations in the 1990s about the Partial Test Ban Treaty (PTBT), the Comprehensive Test Ban Treaty (CTBT), the Nuclear Non-Proliferation Treaty (NPT), and the Statute of the International Criminal Court (ICC). "Such negotiations have been an occasion for NGOs to voice public aspirations for an end to the nuclear threat and in this way to help stimulate some progress, but generally not to influence substantially the terms of the instruments under negotiation."[140]

Burroughs and Cabasso state that a state-centered global system is being undermined by globalization, which is undermining the sovereign states and is providing a greater role for players such as corporations, banks, and other kinds of international institutions. The sovereignty of states is also undercut by "transnational networks of citizens and NGOs based upon normative commitments and access to information networks which may be more effective and satisfying role of democratic political participation than electoral politics and the dynamics of representative democracy at the level of the state." Even though NGOs tend to play an important role when it comes to human rights and environmental matters, in respect to nuclear weapons NGOs are not as influential because of the states' insistence on having exclusive control over military and security policy. "The centrality of secrecy, the quasi-theological and allegedly subtle doctrines of nuclear 'deterrence,' the technical complexity and sheer scale of the nuclear enterprise, the unimaginable power and horror of the weapons, all reinforce the nuclear weapon states' extremely strong resistance to any significant role for the public and NGOs in nuclear weapons related negotiations." Despite the difficulties present, NGOs must "articulate and promote a vision of a nuclear weapon free world and a program for its achievement ..." They must mobilize public opinion and create coalitions with social movements advancing issues related to the environment, social justice, and democratization, and with non-nuclear states.[141]

CIVIL SOCIETY

Jean Grugel defines civil society as "the arena of associations and of individual and community agency. The term is used to designate the sphere of activity between the individual and the state."[142] Lewis and Kanji provide a lengthier and more detailed definition. To them "[civil] society is usually taken to mean a realm or space in which there exists a set of organizational actors which are not a part of the household, the state or the market. These organizations form a wide-ranging group which include associations, people's movements, citizens' groups, consumer associations, small producer associations, women's organizations, indigenous peoples' organizations — and of course NGOs."[143]

Jo Crotty describes civil society as "the sphere situated between the state and the market which can serve as a promoter of democratic values, provide models of active citizenship and temper the power of the state. This sphere is made up of autonomous freely chosen, intermediary organizations."[144] Lina Suleiman states the following about civil society:

> The concept is diffuse, hard to define, empirically imprecise, ideologically laden and not consistently useful as an analytical tool. The term "civil society" still lacks a generic classification or a universal definition. However, scholars have mainly defined civil society as being comprised of groups, a social space and the vision of a common moral dimension. There are, however, differences amongst scholars about which groups comprise civil society, what is the institutional boundary of civil society as a social space, and whether civil society should describe the society we have or the society to which we aspire — one that is associated with positive social virtues such as the common good, altruism, liberty, social justice and equity, democracy, tolerance and civility. In the context of developing countries, civil society is mainly equated with NGOs.[145]

Beginning in the 1980s, civil society was often discussed in relation to development policy, and "debates about politics and democratization, public participation and improved service delivery — as well as in connection with NGO campaigning and advocacy work at the international level." Even though civil society is today closely linked to NGOs, the idea of civil society goes at least as far back the Scottish Enlightenment thinkers such as David Hume and Adam Ferguson, and the German thinker G.W. F. Hegel in the nineteenth century. The French thinker Alexis de Tocqueville expressed his admiration for Americans and their desire to join associations. He considered the desire for "associational life in the United States ... as a source of democratic strength and economic power." The Italian theorist Antonio Gramsci viewed civil society "as the site into which state power was projected and consolidated in capitalist societies, but also as a location where contestation and resistance to hegemonic power was possible." All these thinkers essentially represent two approaches to civil society, the liberal (Hume, Ferguson, de Tocqueville, etc.) and the radical (Gramsci).[146] Irrespective of the approach scholars adopt, in examining civil society they must consider the role of NGOs.

Before the role of NGOs in civil society is considered, it is important to refer to the following themes identified with civil society since the eighteenth century:

The first is the emergence of the individual as a self-determining actor in society, as the ties of family and other kin diminish under early capitalist development.... The second was the importance of ideas about "civility" as a distinguishing mark between Europeans and "other" societies encountered during the travels of overseas merchants and, later, colonialists.... Third was the idea that political virtue, or the idea of a common good, which the ancient Greeks had identified as an essential component of civilization ... Fourth was the emergence of a new public space in which there could be a broader debate around rules, laws and policies, since power was no longer the sole preserve of the absolutist monarchs. Voice was now being demanded by the new bourgeoisie, whose interests needed to be served within the political order.... Fifth was the need to find ways to reconcile the tensions between the particular and the universal in society ... Finally, a sixth perspective arises from the long-standing sociological debates about the shift from pre-capitalist to modern social orders in the work of Durkheim and others ...[147]

What is distinct about the above given definitions of civil society is that they are confined to the borders of states. There is something new about the concept of civil society especially since the late 1980s, globalization and an emerging of a global civil society. According to Mary Kaldor, there are five meanings of global civil society.

Societas civilis. This is what "could be described as the original version of the term — civil society as a rule of law and a political community, a peaceful order based on implicit or explicit consent of individuals, a zone of 'civility.' Civility is defined not just as 'good manners' or 'polite society' but as a situation where violence has been minimized as a way of organizing social relations."

Bourgeois society. "For [F.] Hegel and [K.] Marx, civil society was the arena of ethical life in between the state and the family. It was a historically produced phenomenon linked to the emergence of capitalism.... Civil society was, for the first time, contrasted with the state."

The activist version. This "perspective is probably closest to the version of civil society that emerged from the opposition in Central Europe in the 1970s and 1980s.... It is a definition that presupposes a state or rule of law but insists not only on restraints on state power but on a redistribution of power. It is a radicalization of democracy and an extension of participation and autonomy. On this definition, civil society refers to active citizenship, to growing self-organization outside the formal political circles, and expanded space in which individual citizens can influence the conditions in which they live ..."

The neoliberal version. "According to this definition, civil society consists of associational life — a non-profit, voluntary 'third sector' — that not only [restrains] state power but also actually provides a substitute for many of the functions performed by the state."

The postmodern version. In this perspective, civil society is "an arena of pluralism and contestation, a source of incivility as well as civility."[148]

Why did NGOs, organizations that are especially interested in alleviating poverty and promoting economic development, become so enamored with the idea of civil society? According to Grugel, at least as related to European NGOs in Latin America, they began to focus on civil society for the following reasons:

> First, the term is increasingly used throughout Europe to express commitment to political and social change based on the resurrection of the values of community, social associations, and individual rights. Second, the changes in the mode of delivery of European aid have made NGOs more sensitive to the demands of international donors. Third, NGOs assign growing importance to the concept of international civil society, the activities of non-state actors and transnational activism. Finally, civil society has emerged as a project for democratic empowerment in Latin America. NGOs have been influenced by a sense that civil society is the term that captures the complex reality and current state of development of Latin America's popular movements.[149]

It is noted by numerous scholars that a vibrant civil society contributes to democratic governance. Larry Diamond asserts the following: "In sum, it is widely argued that civil society can contribute to democratic governance and that civil society and the state can create synergy in democratic governance. However, this argument raises an important question: under what circumstances can this positive relationship be achieved?" Diamond also says that there are thirteen democratic functions of civil society:

> The first and most basic democratic function of civil society is to provide the basis for the limitation of state power....
>
> A second democracy-building function of civil society is to supplement the role of political parties in stimulating political participation, increasing the political efficacy and skill of democratic citizens, and promoting an appreciation of the obligations as well as rights of democratic citizenship.
>
> Third ... education for democracy has become an explicit project of civil society organizations in new democracies and also an international cause.
>
> A fourth way in which civil society may serve democracy is by structuring multiple channels, beyond the political party, for articulating, aggregating, and representing interests.
>
> A fifth way is by effecting transition from clientelism to citizenship at the local level.
>
> Sixth, a rich and pluralistic civil society ... tends to generate a wide range of interests that may cross-cut, and so mitigate, the principal polarities of political conflict.
>
> A seventh function ... is recruiting and training new political leaders.

Eighth, many civic society organizations have explicit democracy-building purposes, beyond leadership training.

Ninth ... civil society widely disseminates information and so empowers citizens in the collective pursuit and defense of their interests and values.

The mobilization of new information and understanding are essential to the achievement of economic reform in a democracy, and this is the tenth function that civil society can play.

Eleventh, a growing number of civil society organizations are developing techniques for conflict mediation and resolution and offering these services.

Twelfth, a vigorous civil society can strengthen the social foundations of democracy even when its activities focus on community development and have no explicit connection to or concern with political democracy per se.

Thirteenth, by enhancing the accountability, responsiveness, inclusiveness, effectiveness, and hence legitimacy of the political system, a vigorous civil society gives citizens respect for the state and positive engagement with it. In the end, this improves the ability of the state to govern and to command voluntary obedience from its citizens.[150]

Diamond goes even further than what was stated above when he says that "[by] enhancing the accountability, responsiveness, effectiveness, and hence legitimacy of the political system, a vigorous civil society gives citizens respect for the state and a positive engagement with it. In the end, this improves the ability of the state to govern and to command voluntary obedience from its citizens. In addition, a rich associational life may also multiply the capacities of groups to improve their own welfare, independently of the state. Effective grassroots development efforts may thus help to relieve the burdens of expectation fixed on the state, and so lower the stakes of politics, especially at the national level."[151]

It is not an easy task to foster a vibrant civil society as described by Diamond and others. Even in mature democracies, important civil society actors find it difficult to have the significant effect they are expected to have. One among many other examples is France. For many decades, NGOs and other civil society organizations (CSOs) occupied an ambivalent status regarding the policy-making process. This was the result of two main reasons: "First, forms of decision-making and state-society relationships in the context of the Fifth Republic offered little opportunities for non-state actors to shape policy-making. CSOs and NGOs were primarily considered as service providers at policy implementation stage, by contrast with the formal role granted to workers' unions and professional organizations in the policy process after World War II. Second, the French neo-corporatist model of policy-making favored the participation of a limited number of organized CSOs to policy formulation ..."[152]

Following the 1982 laws, also known as Gaston Defferre Laws of 1982 and which are about policy decentralization, the role of non-state actors was strengthened "in development of policy offer and the provision of public services at the local level. Yet the formulation of public policies themselves, and the production of policy analysis, remained concentrated at the national level and in the hands of higher civil servants and professionals. As a result, until recently, the relationship between NGOs and policy analysis was characterized either by mutual lack of interest or by strong distrust."[153]

Despite the recently growing interest in the work done by NGOs and CSOs related to knowledge production and expertise, as well as their more formal inclusion into government-led consultation processes, their role in the policy-making process should not be overexaggerated. This kind of statement is caused by the following: NGOs and CSOs depend upon "formal recognition procedures and public subsidies. As such, only a few NGOs and CSOs are able to gain more autonomy.... Second ... the development of an actor-centered approach to public policy confirms ... the critical role played by classic veto-players (for example *Grands Corps*, professional interest groups) in the French ... tradition in relegating NGOs and CSOs to acting as watchdogs, service providers or in some rare cases as external consultants during policy-making."[154]

An interesting example of the role of NGOs and civil society is Bosnia-Herzegovina. The number of NGOs in Bosnia-Herzegovina grew substantially in the 1990s with assistance from international actors. Their primary concern at first was humanitarian relief and social services. But after the Dayton Peace Accords (1995), which ended the war in Bosnia-Herzegovina, NGOs played an important role "in peace-building, postwar trauma and the reintegration of the country. Nowadays, NGOs take an active role in the monitoring of political leadership, political participation and elections, advocating anti-corruption awareness, values of tolerance and understanding, civic education and human rights, and promoting of public issues."[155]

In examining the role of women's NGOs in Bosnia-Herzegovina, Muhidin Mulalic states that such NGOs have been "in particular active in the protection function during and after the war. NGOs such as Women to Women, La Strata, the International Forum of Solidarity, Lara, Medica Zenica and the Future were helping [women] victims by providing shelter, healthcare services, counseling and legal assistance. Besides, their activities have also been aimed at the establishment of a stable multiethnic state of Bosnia-Herzegovina. Women were the first to cross the ethnic boundaries and contributed to reconciliation of ethno-national groups.... The war in Bosnia-Herzegovina and the subsequent process of democratization created profound social, political and economic changes. In this regard, the Muslim women NGOs contributed significantly toward the construction and the development of the civil society."[156]

Before the Bosnian war in the 1990s, Muslim women in Bosnia-Herzegovina were excluded from participating in civil society for several reasons including perceptions of them as backward, uneducated, provincial, and not modern. But with the end of the war, newly founded NGOs significantly changed views about Muslim women, and they became much more active civil society members. They could be found working in schools, universities, government, and private industry. Despite these developments and because they were religious, Muslim women's NGOs did target western NGOs. Western NGOs also were hesitant to support religious NGOs thinking that they were "exclusive and against [the] multiethnic state of Bosnia-Herzegovina. As a result, Muslim women's NGOs attempt to develop ways of self-sustenance through NGO membership and offering services for the public at a minimal cost."[157]

Among the most influential Muslim women's NGOs are the Nahla Education Center for women and Kewser-Zehra Association of Muslim Women. These two NGOs as well as others, by emphasizing gender-related issues within a Muslim society, attempt to enhance the role of women as active and autonomous members of society. And in the process, they try to promote tolerance and understanding andcivil education, and to foster civil society.[158]

Panday and Feldman, in their study of gender politics in Bangladesh, argue that NGOs and civil society can enhance equality for women through the use of various means. "[Despite] having no formal access to the policy process, NGOs augment participation of women in the political process through informal means as is exemplified by their training programs that enhance women's social and economic status." NGOs helped in passing the Act of 1997, which has reserved a number of legislative seats for women. Even though this was a critical step, creating more opportunities for women through institutional means may not be sufficient.[159]

Panday and Feldman assert that "there is a need to complement institutional reform with the creation of new opportunities for women through education, social recognition, and a changing social context." The authors also suggest that NGOs can play a role in expanding women's participation in electoral politics. In fact, NGOs "have helped women to engage in community-based activities that in turn enhances their bargaining position in the society and increases the likelihood that they will choose to stand for election and engage directly in local politics."[160]

One of the authors' significant findings is that NGOs, through their microcredit initiatives and development programs, have made it more possible for women "to participate in the democratization process in general and local government politics in particular by encouraging them to contest local government elections as well as casting votes in favor of candidates belonging to their groups." But encouraging anyone, women included, to vote for a specific candidate has positive as well as negative outcomes. A positive outcome is that women, by contesting elections and exercising their right to vote, contribute to the "consolidation of democratic practices. From a negative perspective there is fear that these women can be used to serve the interests of others through casting their vote in favor of NGO-supported candidates. In this case, women's freedom of choice will be overridden by the choice of NGOs. If that happens, it would make them dependent on others in terms of exercising their voting rights which is not at all desirable in the process of mainstreaming gender politics. Thus, there is an urgency to make women knowledgeable about their rights and duties so that they could decide whom to vote for."[161]

Apart from playing a role in promoting moderate civil society by encouraging voting, NGOs in Bolivia [as well as in many other countries, especially in countries where democracy is not on a strong footing and institutions are viewed with mistrust] "also play a more controversial role by mobilizing protest activities.... Instead [of] acting as training grounds for the type of citizenship we associate with developed democracies, NGOs may be invoking much less stable and predictable forms of participation. Protest may well be a necessary and vital part of democratic participation, but it [is] rarely what advocates of civil society have in mind when they advocate for NGOs.... Protest ... carries the connotation of violence and political instability, but in some circumstances may be a vital mechanism for making voices heard that would be obscured through more traditional procedures of participation."[162] Having even a rudimentary civil society is not a precondition for successful transition to democracy. But a strong civil society is fundamental for [the] consolidation of democracy .

Yianna Lambrou makes an important contribution to our understanding of NGOs and civil society by examining the changing role of NGOs in southern Chile. She chooses to focus on one NGO (OPDECH) before and after 1973, during the dictatorship under Pinochet and after the return of democracy. During the years of the Pinochet regime, NGOs "maintained a critical distance from the government by creating a niche for opposition researchers and activists. They provided a possibility of economic survival for professionals whilst working on alternative proposals to address the socio-economic needs of the poor majority." External donors provided necessary funding, but at the same time it led to the creation of "a culture of reliance and clientilistic middle class of professionals." OPDECH became the center for resistance and "expertise on regional development by safekeeping democratic tradition and providing a range of solutions to local development problems." When

democracy was restored, NGOs "exchanged their altruism for a more prag-
matic, opportunistic and, in some cases, more efficient role as executors of
government programs."[163]

NGOs in Chile have undergone significant changes since the return of
democracy. "From intermediary, non-profit organizations working for economic and social development, in 1973, they abruptly changed to being
defenders of democracy and agents of local development in the cities and the
countryside." They provided safety to those working on social change. They
learned how to work without support from the government, how to oppose the
government, and how to collaborate with it "in a democratic climate." They
learned how to attract foreign funding and use it to promote local growth.
"Yet they also learned the perils of excessive funding and corruption. Their
biggest contribution has been their commitment to the grassroots communities, the [campesinos], the poor, and their capacity to interpret their needs to
more distant agencies and governments." NGOs have helped to shape domestic policies as well as international development aid policies.[164]

In rediscovering the strength of civil society in Eastern Europe, Tsveta
Petrova focuses on Bulgaria. The author notes that after the collapse of the
socialist regimes in Central and Eastern Europe there was desire to prevent
the socialist elite from setting goals and controlling the agenda. This became
the focal point for mobilizing opposition to state socialism and for supporting
democratization. Since the collapse of the socialist regimes, scholars, politicians, and activists placed much attention on issues such as accountability,
legitimacy, popular representation, and responsiveness of governments to
citizen demands at the center of discussions about democratization.[165]

More specifically, Petrova concentrates on the impact of citizen participation in local government. The author's study shows that

> despite the passivity of local government in many municipalities, and their pref-
> erence for working primarily with political actors, there has been widespread
> and diverse, if weakly institutionalized, cooperation between local authorities
> and societal actors. Moreover, it seems that in the Bulgarian case, but perhaps
> throughout the region as well, the problem-solving capacity of municipalities
> grows with the increasing involvement of social and economic actors in the
> policy-making process. This improved government efficacy is most likely a
> result of the professionalization and organizational strength of the [civil soci-
> ety]. Although the politicization of the local state has undermined its capacity,
> many municipalities have been able not only to reconstitute some of their
> authority but also to improve the output and the quality of their policy-making
> by employing the expertise and support of major local civic organizations.[166]

Japan represents an interesting instance of a mature democracy where civil
society is small, yet influential, in comparison to other Asian democracies.

For example, in relation to overstayed foreigners, Japanese citizens are organizing to protect them because of the absence of government programs to help unskilled Asian workers. "[Small], issue-oriented groups, rather than large, identity-reproducing ethnic associations ... are increasingly having an impact on policy and on advancing democracy in Japan. The APFS [Asian People's Friendship Society], with assistance from the epistemic communities, has successfully pressured the government to grant certain overstayed foreigners with 'special residence permission,' while others have challenged the government to extend NHI [National Health Insurance] to certain unqualified foreigners."[167]

Even though few foreigner support NGOs have achieved a nonprofit organization [NPO] status, the Japanese NOP law favors the inclusion of women's groups as well as medical NGOs, groups that offer social welfare services "and whose agenda supports government interests. But rather than being a passive partner or co-opted by the state, these groups are pushing local governments to accept broader responsibilities in caring for their foreign residents." Often local governments are establishing partnerships with these NGOs and asking them for new, innovative ideas and ways to implement them. "Instead of the state molding the civil society, civil society organizations are shaping the role of the state in actively redefining membership rules and the boundaries of state responsibilities to *residents*, as distinct from citizens."[168]

Volkhart Finn Heinrich provides interesting insights regarding the role of NGOs in strengthening South African democracy. When democracy was first installed in South Africa in 1994, many scholars were pessimistic about a successful transition to democracy. Despite the many remaining problems with democracy in South Africa, the country successfully moved toward a consolidated democracy and South African NGOs played an important role in that. While numerous studies on the role of NGOs and democratization focus on NGOs as watchdogs and providing services to black communities, Heinrich focuses on the following ways NGOs strengthen democracy in South Africa: "(1) as 'schools of democracy,' (2) in mitigating societal conflicts, and (3) as effective channels of interest representation for the poor." Heinrich concludes by saying that in spite of the obstacles presented by the nonresponsiveness of the political parties and the problems related to "mass political behavior and attitudes," South African NGOs counteracted the obstacles "by taking over from political parties the task of representing relevant societal interests in the political process, and through educating citizens in democratic practices and promoting tolerance toward others.... However, the state and other external actors play crucial roles ..."[169]

Timothy D. Sisk, in examining the role of domestic and international actors, makes a related argument about South Africa's transition from apartheid to democracy. He concludes by stating that

International engagement in support of democratic transition took both hard (or coercive) and soft (or incentive-oriented) approaches. Through coercive measures, outsiders contributed to the demise of the authoritarian regime and the onset of talks. Thereafter, engagement was primarily seen in terms of reassurance and persuasion, direct financial support to critical social organizations, technical assistance to key institutions, and repeated election monitoring. In terms of learning, South Africa also represents an example in which domestic actors absorbed and adapted a wide range of experiences from abroad: from deliberations on constitutional models, to negotiation and bargaining concepts and approaches, to the institutional borrowing of the truth-and-reconciliation approach to transitional justice. In the final phase, too, international support to civil society took the form of financial support and capacity development in the critical areas of parliamentary processes, election management, rule of law and judicial strengthening, and support to institutions and processes of local democracy.

... [While] external engagement was critical in specific turning points or moments, the principal drivers of democratization were domestic. Thus, in this case, international influences are best described as "enabling" of liberation of the black majority from apartheid ... and of reinforcing the fundamentally internal dynamics that determined the pathway from apartheid to democracy.[170]

Balaji Ogunseye makes a somewhat different assertion about the role of African NGOs as members of civil society. Ogunseye says that "[if] civil society covers the 'space' existing outside the state, there is little evidence on the ground that African NGOs loom sufficiently large in that space to be declared its most significant advocate. As indicated ... in virtually all of Africa, the voluntary sector comes a distant fourth in order of development impact, behind the state, formal business, and the informal economic sector. It is clear that Africa's service NGOs lack the capacity and influence to represent, advocate for, or effectively engage with the formal private sector, organized professional classes, or the informal sector."[171]

It is imperative for African NGOs to play a greater role in strengthening civil society to "articulate and implement strategies for their own self-development as a sector, and to define more clearly the nature of their actual and potential collaboration with all important actors in African development." Some important questions that need to be asked are:

What are some of the elements of development that are best performed by the state and what role could members of civil society play in "influencing such state-dominated functions in sustainable development?"

What elements of sustainable development are best performed by a collaboration between the state and other members of civil society, especially NGOs?

What roles of development could be left to the private sector with little interference by the state?

"[How] can NGOs effectively influence the pervasive hand of the state, and the enormous market power of the business sector towards redistributive and equity-enhancing goals, which are supportive of the self-transforming efforts of the poor and marginalized, and which promote sound environmental practices?"[172]

By examining the impact of Chinese-built dams — an important segment of economic growth — in Africa, Matthew Todd Bradley articulates interesting arguments about the role of African NGOs and civil society in general. The author notes that hydropower can become the vehicle to instigate economic development. But at what price and at whose expense — the rural poor's? And what role should NGOs play? "Coupled with external forces and actors like the World Bank, vigorous Chinese investors, and the Chinese government, civil society's tasks are even more challenging. This momentum hinders the ability of civil society to question the choices being made for Africa's energy future.... [There] is a mixed level of NGO involvement in hydropower economic development in Africa." It seems that NGOs are minimally involved in politically and economically unstable African countries. This is significant because civil society organizations tend to flourish in more stable countries with mature institutions of government.[173]

In addition, "autonomy and independence are relative." That is, African NGOs do not have the ability to make a significant difference from start to finish. Hence, as globalization and economic development are on the increase, "the richness of Africa's political liberalization efforts at the village and local levels may continue to be the catalyst for nurturing civil rights/liberties. Unlike Western democratic models of governance where power is divided among branches of government at different levels, "power is being garnered and sustained at the grassroots levels in Africa, and perhaps African NGOs may be at the vanguard."[174]

In considering the case of Cambodia and the prospects for democratic consolidation, Kheang Un asserts that after the 1993 transition to democracy efforts at consolidation have faltered because of the prevailing domestic circumstances. After the introduction of democracy, "Cambodian elites continued to employ patronage and corruption" for the purpose of promoting their interests and maintaining their privileged position. The employment of these elements makes consolidation difficult because "consolidation requires both the establishment of vertical and horizontal accountability institutions. Without those institutions, elites will continue to employ traditional means, i.e., patrimonialism, to serve their interests."[175]

New members of civil society and especially NGOs are attempting to change "the imbalance in the relationship between state and society. However, their efforts have been an uphill struggle, given the unequal power configuration. The state appears to be strong, in that it can silence and oppress government opponents; however, the state apparatus is apparently weak in providing services and ensuring the rule of law. Such weakness is the byproduct of a state built on a patrimonial foundation rather than on rational Weberian institutions. Under this system, elites tolerate elements of a weak state, such as a politically dependent and corrupt judiciary. With weak institutions, the state ... can use 'legitimate, legal procedures' to silence and oppress NGOs, the press, trade unions and oppositional leaders, further undermining the relatively weak civil society organizations."[176]

The reality according to Un is that civil society cannot significantly contribute to the consolidation of democracy unless Cambodia expands its urban educated population, enlarges its middle class, has greater experience "with the idea of non-political 'secondary associations' and to generate 'norms of reciprocity' that deviate from standard patronage networks."[177]

Carew E. Boulding and Jami Nelson-Nuñez make more nuanced comments about civil society and democracy in their examination of Bolivia. They note that membership in civil society groups reinforces support for the political system, even in a country like Bolivia while facing political crisis and poor government performance. "More important, [the authors found] that membership is associated with more supportive attitudes even among those who have recently protested against the government." Being members of civil society organizations does not prevent people from criticizing their government or expressing distrust of it. "But membership is associated with high levels of general system support."[178]

The relationship between civil society and support for the political system does not seem to be affected by who joins civil society groups, that is people "with greater resources or more politically conservative views.... In fact, in Bolivia, those with fewer resources and lower levels of education and those who are indigenous are slightly more likely to join. Moreover, the relationship between civil society membership and support for the political system cannot be attributed to more supportive people joining civil society organizations." Membership in such organizations strengthens support for the political system even among those who are protesting the government. To put it differently, membership enhances support among those who are satisfied with the political system as well as among those who are not.[179]

Boulding and Nelson-Nuñez conclude their study with an optimistic note about the future of democracies during crises. Even though civil society can present a challenge to the status quo through the articulation of interests, civil society can also be a stabilizing force by erecting support for democracy. "At first this may seem like a profound contradiction, but in the context of highly unequal societies, it is possible that both roles are necessary for democracy to succeed. Engaging new voices into [an] elite-dominated political system is unlikely to be easy, but it is more likely to be successful if there is strong consensus over the rules of the game. At least in the case of Bolivia, it appears that civil society assists with both the articulation of new interests and the building of support for a democratic political system."[180]

Consolidation of democracy is difficult, if not impossible, without a strong and independent judiciary capable of becoming an agent of/for justice. For example, in the 1990s, in Latin America, judicial decisions overturning "amnesty laws, declaring the non-applicability of statutory limitations, or sentencing [politicians and military officers for human rights violations] were few and far between." The situation changed after 2000 because Latin American judges decided "to put an end to an era of judicial acquiescence, characterized by the presence of seemingly impenetrable impunity regimes."[181] Why did this change happen at this juncture?

According to Ezequiel Gonzales Ocantos there are many approaches as to why. But most of these approaches consider the judiciary as a secondary actor. Ocantos argues that "the expectation is that judges behave as agents of political actors.... Departing from these approaches, the central contention ... is that to become vehicles of justice, judicial bureaucracies must be made aware of, and come to understand and endorse, international legal standards that allow them to nullify amnesty laws or ignore statutory limitations. Enhanced technical skills and new legal visions embolden judicial actors to defy anti-transitional justice governing coalitions; the absence of these changes leads to pro-transitional justice political pressures to [fall] in an empty sack. Via skillful pedagogical interventions and personnel replacement strategies, NGOs are the engine behind the diffusion of new technical skills and legal visions."[182]

Building a strong civil society is not an easy task, especially in near nondemocratic or nondemocratic states. Crotty notes that numerous studies have been done across Russia since the collapse of the Soviet Union in order to determine the role of NGOs in relation to the development of civil society. These studies have concluded that "the structure of NGOs is inappropriate for civil society building; that overseas funding has been inadequate or insufficiently grounded in the Russian context to contribute to civil society building; and that the groups themselves often lack the will or ability...to actively participate in civil society."[183]

In his own study, Crotty examines the capacity of the environmental movement, probably the most promising actor of civil society in Russia, and its impact on the development of civil society within the country. After considering numerous environmental NGOs, Crotty notes that only three, the Cottage People, I2, and Friends, made some contributions to the development of civil society. Even though all three had initial success engaging the people and acting as a counterweight to the state, at the end the Cottage People and I2 failed to broaden the scope of their organizations. Friends was the exception by successfully using overseas funding to build an organization based on volunteers who were able to raise even more funding, and "thus effecting sustained and successful campaigning, in their case within the area of the National Park. Thus, Friends was the only group in this study ... teaching citizens the 'norms and values' of democracy and acting as a counterweight to the state ..." Many factors are responsible for this outcome including the Soviet legacy, the absence of trust in democratic institutions, "nostalgia for the past" resulting from the disappointing "outcome of the transition process," and the more recent limitations placed by the government upon NGOs.[184]

The Soviet past continues to influence the structure of Russian society and the inclination of individuals to join civil society organizations.

> In this context the Soviet Union's approach to civic activity remains a topic of debate ... with some scholars viewing Soviet civil society as 'historically weak' or "oppressed" and actively removed from society. Others contend that Soviet civil society was not weak, but "institutionalized." As the state provided institutions where individuals could interact outside the home — such as sports clubs, social clubs and creches — the membership of these state-sponsored organizations was not voluntary but assumed. This assumed membership represented an institutionalization of Soviet civil space rather than its outright removal. The institutionalized civil space, alongside the active state suppression of spontaneous, autonomous voluntary associations, led individuals to rely on their network of friends, family and individual connections inside the home. These networks nurtured a mistrust of elites and so put distance between the individual and the state. ... The forced voluntarism and assumed membership of state-run organizations of the past has fostered a rejection of such in the present.[185]

During the period Yeltsin was in power, the law On Public Associations was passed in 1999, which required all public organizations registered under a previous 1995 law to reregister. The new law led to the disappearance from the list of official groups. Some of these groups failed to reregister or their reregistration was denied. Putin, even before his election in 1994, was even more determined than Yeltsin to control NGOs. Even though NGOs and other social groups were invited to participate in public forums with the government, it was the government that determined the agenda and the outcomes. In addition, participation in forums was connected to a social tax on nonprofit organizations. This was an effort not only to limit the activities of trade unions but also to limit participation in the civil forum process.[186]

After his reelection in 2004, Putin endeavored to completely control civil society organizations in the Russian Federation. He tried to ruin the reputations of many of these organizations by referring to them as treasonous because of their connections to donors from outside Russia. This was followed by passing legislation to restrict the activities of NGOs and other social movements in response to the role played by INGOs in the "Color Revolutions" in former Soviet republics. Furthermore, through a new NGO Law, Putin "sought to restrict the activity of advocacy groups that threatened the sovereignty of Russia, its national independence, territorial integrity, unity or originality, its cultural heritage or national interests." The new law also limited the funds Russian NGOs could receive from foreign donors and complicated even more the bureaucratic obstacles they had to overcome.[187]

In a related article, Olga Oleinikova considers the new laws and restrictive amendments to legislation and their effect on the operations of foreign-funded NGOs in Russia, Belarus, and Ukraine. Oleinikova argues that "the restrictive legislation creates new barriers to NGOs' operations ... and damages the potential for NGOs to organize mutual aid and provide support for democratic efforts to a young unstable democracy. Furthermore, this new legislation is argued to affect the marketization of the NGO sector ... pushing NGOs to adopt the approaches and values of the private market, which risks harming the fragile democracy and fails to create and maintain a strong civil society."[188]

Olga Beznosova and Lisa McIntosh Sundstrom attempt to analyze the relationship between NGOs and local governments as related to democracy promotion in two different regions of Russia, Velikii Novgorod and Khabarovsk. Throughout the 1990s, scholars have noticed that Novgorod was a region where Western aid programs could lead to greater democratic governance because of long-lasting autonomy from Moscow and because of a degree of democratic tradition. Unlike Novgorod, Khabarovsk has had a history of being ruled by Moscow-controlled politicians who had had little if any use for civil society.[189]

During the 1990s, Novgorod was a place with a seemingly vibrant civil society and a strong NGO sector. These NGOs were the recipients of significant Western aid for economic and democratic development. In Khabarovsk, NGOs tried to organize and maintain themselves while also receiving important assistance from Western donors, but they were weak relative to organizational structure and their ability to influence policy. "However, upon re-examination in 2006, after more than a decade of aid programs, the NGO community in Novgorod seems fragmented, diffuse, and quite dependent on the regional government. By contrast, although civil society in Khabarovsk is not extremely vibrant, it seems to be somewhat more organized and has learned new ways to pressure government."[190]

Why the Different Outcomes?

The diverging trajectories of state-society relations in the two cities may have something to do with the arrangement of local state-society relations in each region combined with the intervening factor of Western aid to promote civil

society development. Where there is a linkage between the state and civil society, and the state is the dominant actor, civil society can become dependent on
the state rather than grow stronger through inclusion in policy deliberations.
Meanwhile, where a divide exists between state and civil society, aid to civil
society can encourage the development of horizontally networked and independent minded civic groups. Western aid programs can play a role — if the
devoted resources are large enough — by supporting and strengthening the
mobilizational capabilities of either the state or civil society in local contexts.
Moreover, donors can encourage civil society and state actors to interact with
one another. Throughout the post-Soviet period, donors have used different
approaches in different contexts, but generally the trend among major donors
has been to encourage more institutionalized dialogue between state and society
over time, in a manner that has shifted from a pluralist model of state-society
relations to a more corporatist one.

   While such a shift may be warranted in some contexts, it has inherent dangers in contexts where a model of authoritarian corporatism dominated until the
recent past.[191]

Edward Aspinall and Marcus Mietzner in their work on Indonesia present
some interesting material related to the role of domestic and external factors
contributing to the transition from an authoritarian system to a democratic
one. The Asian financial crisis of 1997 and 1998 caused the collapse of the
status quo and the resignation of Suharto. The intervention of the IMF to
bolster the Indonesian economy proved to be a failure and instead of helping the economy it caused even greater damage. The pressure generated by
these factors was compounded by pressure from a growing international civil
society that provided support to Indonesian NGOs.[192]

   It is significant to note that most foreign donors including NGOs were
not necessarily interested in helping to topple the Suharto regime. Instead,
they were more preoccupied with the gradual opening-up of civil society.
"Consequently, foreign-funded NGOs did not play a leading role in the
anti-regime mobilizations of 1998. Led by a small intellectual elite that
lacked organized links to the bulk of the population, NGOs were ill-equipped
to pose a direct political threat to the regime.... Nevertheless, the foreign
funding of critical NGOs since the 1980s had not been without effects on
Indonesian society. These groups had helped to delegitimize [Suharto's
regime] and disseminate important ideas about human rights, political reform,
and individual liberties in Indonesia, contributing to a climate in which the
student movement could successfully mobilize against the government."[193]

   Dimitri A. Sotiropoulos provides intriguing insights related to the role of
civil society in Greece in the wake of the financial crisis. He notes that in a
democratic setting civil society must be autonomous from the government
and political parties so that it can counterbalance the state. If civil society

does not operate freely, citizen's participation is limited, and the quality of democracy could be challenged. "[Civil] society makes democracy work." He also says that an aspect of civil society is "uncivil society," which consists of groups averse to civil society's values of pluralism and diversity.[194]

More important, Sotiropoulos at first discusses civil society after 1974 and the transition to democracy. He states that from 1974 to 2012, governments in Greece were stable, in contrast to the governments in countries which became democratic after 1974. But apart from a few members of Greek civil society consisting primarily of well-organized professions, most other members besides the student and labor movements and including NGOs were not well-developed. A major reason for this was the dominance of the political parties, which then stifled "any autonomous collective action.... Such under-development had a negative impact on the quality of democracy, particularly with regard to accountability, transparency and representation."[195]

The state-society relations are not the only reason for the limitations of Greek civil society. The internal problems of NGOs account for this situation. These problems include the fact that many Greek NGOs have not become modern organizations, they often consisted of groups of close friends with few connections to INGOs, they lacked the management and organizational structures, decisions were not always transparent, and many suffered from corruption. But in the late 1980s and early 1990s, changes began to occur in favor of a healthier civil society. Support for political parties and labor unions started to decline, which left "space for the development of civil society."[196]

In the 2000s, NGOs helped to transform Greek civil society in the following ways:

1. The unprecedented rise of migration to Greece led to a crisis and the state proved incapable of managing the situation. This gave birth to numerous NGOs that then stepped in to help.
2. The greater sensitivity exhibited by many Greeks with regards to the environment has led to the founding of hundreds of ENGOs.
3. As Greece faced default in 2010–2013, Greek citizens became acutely aware of the corruption among the political elites and they formed "watch dog" groups to expose and fight corruption.
4. Since 2010, when Greece resorted to the European Commission, the European Central Bank, and the International Monetary Fund, civil society was mobilized even more because of the inability of the major political parties to deal with the crisis.[197]

Finally, Sotiropoulos analyzes the role of NGOs after 2010 in providing food, clothes, shelter, health care and education, as well as supporting and organizing social protests, which very much affected the political system.

He concludes by asserting that "even though since 2010 there have been out-bursts of violent social conflict and racial discrimination, overall civil society mobilization has contributed to the deepening of democracy and social cohesion. It remains to be seen whether these developments will outlast the crisis in Greece."[198]

Nikolaos Tzifakis et al. also offer important commentary on the impact of the economic crisis on NGOs. To them, the economic environment has had a "mixed" impact on the sector. Because of the crisis, small donations from individuals were affected as well as funding from the state. In addition, financial resources from corporations were cut down. Simultaneously, though, the crisis led to some positive developments. More citizens became engaged, new organizations were founded and old ones became more active in providing services to Greek citizens and migrants. Moreover, "informal social networks and self-help groups emerged and became more active in the exchange and distribution of goods and services, healthcare, education, food and shelter provision ... Importantly, the new forms of activism and engagement that are on the rise are not linked to the state. There is probably for the first time — a discernibly autonomous from traditional political authority (...) civil society."[199]

The crisis has also led Greek NGOs to improve their resilience by restructuring and diversifying themselves. The crisis has also given rise to new sources of funding including private foundations. But while dependence on the Greek state and the EU has been lessened, Greek NGOs are relying more and more on private foundations. "In some respects, this privatization of donations is a positive step — since it means a more autonomous civil society, much less dependent on political connections and clientilistic networks. However, at the same time, this privatization of funds creates another type of dependency. Greek NGOs continue to look for funding at the 'top' rather than at the grassroots bases."[200]

Brazil, like Greece and numerous other countries, has gone through a transition from dictatorship to democracy. And as with these other states, the role of NGOs in Brazil has changed. Brazil has had dictatorial government through the 1960s, 1970s, and half of the 1980s. During the years of dictatorship, an important group of civil society organizations emerged based on the ideals of democracy and citizen participation. Many of these organizations were supported and were inspired by Liberation Theology. Most of these civil society groups "believed in local popular knowledge as a way of disseminating their political and socio-economic policies to the poor and to local communities."[201]

In the 1980s, organizations began to appear in Brazilian civil society that were staffed by professionals who were specialists in popular mobilization. This was the time when NGOs emerged in Brazil. During this period, the NGOs had a confrontational relationship with the government because they were opposed to the dictatorship and were supported by INGOs such as Amnesty International. After the dictatorship ended, many NGOs gained greater significance "because they are potential partners of ... governments, due to their professional ability and structure.... [One] of the reasons for NGOs being perceived as potential partners is because neoliberal discourse presupposes the withdrawal of the state from a number of activities and the primacy of the market."[202]

During the more recent past, the role of NGOs in Brazil has changed. Even though they "continue to work for the poor ... [they] are now focusing on providing professional, technical, and managerial support to the disadvantaged members of society on issues regarding public policy and public management as well as on the preparation and implementation of policies that result in better living conditions for the population.... [These] activities have highlighted the position that NGOs hold within the matrix of the state, market, and civil society. The partnership approach is based on an assumption that NGOs can produce better and more useful knowledge and solutions to the social problems than the state and, in many cases, that even the academic world fails to address. So, partnerships with civil society organizations could bring more effective technical and social solutions to these problems."[203]

It is important to note that for the past few years, NGOs and other grass-roots organizations have been under pressure because of the "War on Terror," the "securitization of aid," and the "backlash on civil society." Because of the fear of terrorism, many donors have become risk-averse and NGOs find it difficult to locate funders. During the Cold War years as well as since September 11, 2001, "development aid is increasingly linked to geopolitical or security concerns of donating countries.... Donor policies are thus increasingly driven by security concerns at home. This is particularly the case in war zones, where countries like the United States, the United Kingdom, or the Netherlands [and other countries] have integrated their military and diplomatic interventions with development assistance. In those situations, civil society as inherently harmonious and working for the common good has been replaced by a more chaotic and often conflictive picture of self-interested, co-opted, or misguided entities. Various actors, including governments, local communities, and international organizations have become suspicious of NGOs and started to question whether these actors actually represent the legitimate interests of society, as they claim to do."[204]

Related arguments are made by many other authors including Jonas Wolff and Annika Elena Poppe in their study on the closing of spaces in which NGOs operate. They note that even though the 2011 raid on NGOs in Egypt and the harassment of so-called "foreign agents" in Russia attracted some global attention, this treatment of NGOs is much broader. According to a

report of the Carnegie Endowment for International Peace, multiple governments in Asia, Africa, Latin America, the Middle East, and the former Soviet
Union have taken actions to limit external support for democracy and human
rights. From 1993 to 2012, 45 countries have introduced laws to restrict
LNGOs and INGOs, through which governments "constrain the space, the
capacity and/or the autonomy of civil society groups."[205] The civil society
revolution that took place beginning in the 1980s has been succeeded by a
civil society counterrevolution.[206]

The extent of the closing of spaces is not only about dictators who try
to prevent any democratic challenges to their power. The list of countries
included in the 2014 Carnegie report includes many relatively democratic
countries such as Bangladesh, Bolivia, Ecuador, Honduras, India, Indonesia,
Kenya, etc. What is even more disturbing is that these restrictions are not limited to developing countries. "Since one of the drivers behind the trend is the
so-called War on Terror, the U.S. and its European allies are very much impli-
cated, either by supporting restrictive policies in the name of counterterrorism
or by, themselves, introducing restrictive laws and regulations at home."[207]

As noted above, India is one among numerous examples where the closing of civic space is happening. "Civic space has been adversely impacted
by a combination of the broad concept of national security influenced by the
nationalist rhetoric and the promulgation of vaguely worded counterterrorism legislation." Such developments have given the Indian government the
power to try to silence NGOs and activists. "The current discourse has created
an intolerant public sphere, where organizations working on human rights
and holding the government accountable are construed as a serious threat to
national interest." The government has been able to maintain support from
segments of Indian society and "polarize Indians along national versus antin-
ational lines. The government ignores the fact that by alienating civil society
actors, it harms India's security and hinders economic development."[208]

Despite the efforts undertaken by the Indian government to undermine
NGOs and other civil society actors, a significant number of Indians believe
that human rights organizations protect the rights of Indians and they have
constructive influence on the country. "The society still relies on CSOs [civil
society organizations] to uphold human rights principles and standards,
the rule of law, and good governance, as well as provide much-needed
services."[209]

What are some of the measures introduced by governments to restrict the
space, the capacity, and/or autonomy of civil society organizations? They
include restrictions on the right to associate and establish NGOs, obstacles
that make difficult the registration process, regulations to increase the super-
visory capacity of government officials and enable them to interfere in the

internal affairs of these associations, constraints to limit foreign funding, and harassment or prosecution of civil society activists.[210]

The efforts to restrict civil society are referred to by some as backlash against civil society that became more and more evident after the September 11, 2001, attacks and the War on Terror that followed. Since then there has been "systematic repression of civil society in authoritarian states and 'managed democracies,' at one end, to a more general querying of the probity of ... CSOs, especially NGOs at the other." Assertions that NGOs are representative organizations, effective, democratic, and close to constituents are being challenged by governments as well as social movements and CSOs that do not see themselves as NGOs. Meanwhile, donor agencies are attempting to "tidy-up" their relations with NGOs, and the UN is "promoting disciplined networks to improve its response to the cacophony of diverse and sometimes conflicting voices of civil society."[211]

The questioning of civil society and the enactment of anti-terror legislation are causing a "chill factor", which then leads to NGOs trying to censor themselves, "conservatism, regulation, and oversight from donors." Oversight and regulation are to be expected, but too much of it "threatens debate" and other behaviors that are "antithetical to democratic governance." These dangers have led members of civil society to pay close attention and they have begun to take actions to limit the negative impacts of the backlash. "Such organized civil-society initiatives are crucial, both symbolically and politically, if civil societies are to maintain their emancipatory potential and widen the spaces for public discussion and deliberation."[212]

Thomas Carothers of the Carnegie Endowment for International Peace provides a detailed analysis of the problem of the closing spaces all over the globe. He notes that some of the crucial features of the closing space phenomenon include:

The attacks on foreign funding [of] civil society are often the leading edge of greater crackdowns on civil society.

Countries engaging in closing spaces have different political systems ranging from authoritarian to semi-authoritarian to democratic.

Multiple factors lead to this problem — overconfidence of those in power, the insecurity of others, rising nationalism, migration movements, etc.

Counterterrorism policies continue to contribute to the problem as well.

Many aid providers try to respond to the closing spaces problem by:

Paying greater attention to the problem.

Operating remotely when needed.

Developing better communication strategies.

Engaging in greater risk analysis.

Attempting to enhance cooperation with local funding partners.

Aid providers are changing what they do by:

Scaling back to avoid triggering local sensitivities.

Increasing the availability of emergency funds for grantees in trouble.

Expanding protective assistance.

Searching for alternative assistance.

Aid providers are also increasing efforts to head off or limit closing spaces actions by:

Pushing back against restrictive measures.

Starting campaigns to block or change problematic new NGO laws.

Strengthening engagement by multilateral organizations.

Exploring new partnerships with international business actors.

Lastly, despite of the above listed actions and efforts, weaknesses and divisions remain. Among them are:

US v. European perspectives. At times, Europeans prefer a softer approach to the matter. More important, in recent years the US does not seem to be interested when it comes to the problem of closing spaces.

Private v. public. Private funders are at times reluctant to work closely with their own governments to forge a common response.

Developmental v. political. Developmentally oriented funders are often wary of joining forces with politically oriented funders.

Us v. them. One more division is a division existing as much within funders as between them.[213]

It is true that civil society organizations are always important to domestic administrative regulations. It is, after all, the government that makes possible the space called civil society. It is also common for governments, including mature democratic ones, to enact rules and regulations related to the treatment of foreign organizations and foreign funding. Lastly, it is no surprise that autocratic governments such as in North Korea and Saudi Arabia strictly limit the space of civil society groups at home and of the foreign players that attempt to support them. "Still, the observation that in recent years between 40 and 50 countries have significantly intensified such restrictions signals that we are confronted here with a different situation. From the perspective of those external actors that engage in civil society support this is particularly palpable because many of the countries that are now closing their space had previously allowed or even welcomed democracy and rights support activities inside their borders."[214]

As this chapter indicates, NGOs perform a plethora of functions. Some of them concentrate on activities within a country or a small number of them while others operate across the globe.

NOTES

1. Ahmed and Potter, 37.

2. Ibid., 38–39.

3. David Lewis and Nazneen Kanji, *Non-Governmental Organizations and Development* (New York: Routledge, 2009), 186–187.

4. Bimal Kanti Paul, "Relief Assistance to 1998 Flood Victims: A Comparison of the Performance of the Government and NGOs," *The Geographical Journal* 169, no. 1 (March 2003): 75.

5. Ibid., 75–76.

6. Ekhtekharul Islam, "Governmental Organizations and Non-Governmental Organizations Involvement in Managing Drinking Water: Disaster Affected Coastal Rural Area of Bangladesh," *The Global Studies Journal* 6 (2014): 45–46.

7. Ibid., 51.

8. Ahmed and Potter, 39.

9. Badru Bukenya, "From Social Accountability to a New Social Contract? The Role of NGOs in Protecting and Empowering PLHIV in Uganda," *The Journal of Development Studies* 52, no. 8 (2016): 1162.

10. Ibid., 1163.

11. Ibid., 1173.

12. Melonee Douglas et al., "Expanding the Role of NGOs in Resettlement," *Forced Migration Review,* issue 54 (February 2017): 34.

13. Ibid., 35.

14. Ibid., 36.

15. Ibid., 36–37.

16. Dominik Zaum, "International Non-Governmental Organizations and Civil Wars," *Civil Wars* 11, no. 1 (March 2009): 22.

17. Ibid., 23–24.

18. Muhammad Ammad Khan et al., "Armed Conflict in the Federally Administered Tribal Areas of Pakistan and the Role of NGOs in Restoring Health Services," *Social Work in Public Health* 31, no. 4 (2016): 215.

19. Ibid., 216.

20. Zaum, 24.

21. Ibid., 25

22. Ibid., 25–26.

23. Ibid., 26–27.

24. DeBrenna LaFa Agbenyiga and Lihua Huang, "Impact of the Organizational Networks on the Roles of NGOs in Eldercare: Perspectives from HelpAge Ghana Day Centres," *Ageing International* 37 (2012): 338.

25. Ibid., 351–352.

26. Eve Lester, "A Place at the Table: The Role of NGOs in Refugee Protection: International Advocacy and Policy-Making," *Refugee Survey Quarterly* 24, no. 2 (2005): 125.

27. Ibid., 138–139.

28. Walden Bello, "The Rise of the Relief-And-Reconstruction Complex," *Journal of International Affairs* 59, no. 2 (Spring/Summer 2006): 281.

29. Ibid., 293–294.

30. Constantine P. Danopoulos et al., "Children and Armed Conflict: The Yugoslav Experience," *Journal of Balkan and Near Eastern Studies* 14, no. 1 (March 2012): 160–161.

31. Ibid., 161.

32. Ahmed and Potter, 40.

33. Elizabeth Ross, "The Role of Small NGOs: Building Quality International Education," *Harvard International Review*, (Summer 2013): 41.

34. Ibid., 40–41.

35. Sunhyuk Kim, "NGOs and Social Protection in East Asia: Korea, Thailand and Indonesia," *Asian Journal of Political Science* 23, no. 1 (2015): 40. Sunhyuk Kim defines developmental welfare states, social protection, provision, and pressure as follows: Developmental welfare states "see social policy as an instrument for economic development and rely to a great extent on the family as the site for social welfare and service delivery.... Social protection is defined as the policies and programs that enable vulnerable groups to prevent, reduce, or cope with risks that: 1. Fall outside the preview of other development sectors such as education, health, and rural/community development and 2. Involve direct transfers, whether in cash or kind, to beneficiaries.... Provision means generating and delivering social protection directly, either replacing or complementing the state.... Pressure means influencing the state indirectly through social advocacy movements to better provide social protection," (pp. 24–28).

36. Kim, 40.

37. Pranab Kumar Panday and Shelley Feldman, "Mainstreaming Gender in Politics in Bangladesh: Role of NGOs," *Asian Journal of Political Science* 23, no. 3 (2015): 302.

38. Ibid., 311–313.

39. Ibid., 315–316.

40. David J. Olson and Andrew Piller, "Ethiopia: An Emerging Family Planning Success Story," *Studies in Family Planning* 44, no. 4 (December 2013): 457.

41. Ibid., 437.

42. Sarah A. Blue, "Including Women in Development: Guatemalan Refugees and Local NGOs," *Latin American Perspectives* 32, no. 5 (September 2005): 101.

43. Ibid., 102, 114.

44. Ibid., 114.

45. Ibid., 114.

46. Serena Cosgrove, "Levels of Empowerment: Marketers and Microenterprise-Lending NGOs in Apopa and Nejapa, El Salvador," *Latin American Perspectives* 29, no. 5 (September 2002): 48.

47. Ibid., 48, 62.

48. Ibid., 62; FUSAI and PROCOMES were founded in the late 1980s during the civil war in El Salvador to work with the vulnerable and disenfranchised sectors of the population.

49. Rie Makita, "New NGO-Elite Relations in Business Development for the Poor in Rural Bangladesh," *Voluntas: International Journal of Voluntary and Nonprofit Organizations* 20, no. 1 (March 2009): 67.

50. Ibid., 67.

51. David Forkuor and Seth Agyemang, "Fighting Urban Poverty in Ghana: The Role of Non-Governmental Organizations," *Urban Forum* 29 (2018): 127, 143.

52. Susanna Campbell et al., "International Development NGOs and Bureaucratic Capacity: Facilitator or Destroyer?," *Political Research Quarterly* 72, no. 1 (2019): 3.

53. Ibid., 14.

54. Ibid., 14.

55. Jovo Ateljevic, "Building Institutional, Economic and Social Capacities through Discourse: The Role of NGOs in the Context of Bosnia-Herzegovina and Serbia," *Journal of Southern Europe and the Balkans* 10, no. 3 (December 2008): 347–348.

56. Ibid., 361–362.

57. Karolina Kluczewska, "Questioning Local Ownership: Insights from Donor-Funded NGOs in Tajikistan," *Journal of Civil Society* 15, no. 4 (2019): 367.

58. Ibid., 367.

59. Ahmed and Potter, 43–44.

60. Beyer, 515–516.

61. Krista Masonis El-Gawhary, "Egyptian Advocacy NGOs: Catalysts for Social and Political Change?," *Middle East Report*, no. 214 (Spring 2000): 38, http://www.jstor.org/stable/1520194 .

62. El-Gawhary, 41.

63. Christoph Schnellbach, "The Role of NGOs in Promoting Minority Rights in the Enlarged European Union," *Perspectives on European Politics and Society* 13, no. 4 (December 2012): 505.

64. Ibid., 506.

65. Ibid., 506–507.

66. Ibid., 508.

67. Ibid., 510.

68. Monique Frey and Gerhard Meili, "Social Inclusion and Cultural Identity of Roma Communities in South-Eastern Europe," *Swisspeace* (2011): 50–51.

69. Ibid., 51–52.

70. Ibid., 55–56.

71. Petrice R. Flowers, "Failure to Protect Refugees? Domestic Institutions, International Organizations, and Civil Society in Japan," *Journal of Japanese Studies* 34, no. 2 (Summer 2008): 334, 359.

72. Warren Nyamugasira, *Development and Social Action* (London: Oxfam GB, 1999), 104.

73. Ibid., 116–117.

74. Ibid., 117–119.

75. Nazneen Kanji et al., "Promoting Land Rights in Africa: How Do NGOs Make a Difference," *International Institute for Environment and Development* (2002): 32.

76. Ibid., 33.

77. Smriti Sabbarwal, "Indigenous Peoples' Concerns for Environment: Examining the Role of Non-Governmental Organizations," *Fourth World Journal* (Winter 2017): 33.

78. Ibid., 33–34.

79. Ibid., 34–35.

80. Ahmed and Potter, 46–47.

81. Baogang He and Hannah Murphy, "Global Social Justice at the WTO? The Role of NGOs in Constructing Global Social Contracts," *International Affairs* 83, no. 4 (2007): 707.

82. Ibid., 708.

83. Ibid., 724–725.

84. Ibid., 727.

85. David Turnock, "The Role of NGOs in Environmental Education in South-Eastern Europe," *International Research in Geographical and Environmental Education* 13, no. 1 (2004):104)

86. Ibid., 104–105.

87. Ibid., 105–106.

88. Ibid., 106–107.

89. Jennifer Chapman and Thomas Fisher, "The Effectiveness of NGO Campaigning: Lessons from Practice," *Development in Practice* 10, no. 2 (May 2000): 151–152.

90. Ibid., 152.

91. Ibid., 153.

92. Ibid., 153.

93. Ibid., 154.

94. Ahmed and Potter, 48–49.

95. Adam Fagan and Indraneel Sircar, "Compliance without Governance: The Role of NGOs in Environmental Impact Assessment Processes in Bosnia-Herzegovina," *Environmental Politics* 19, no. 4 (July 2010): 599–600.

96. Ibid., 613.

97. Ibid., 614.

98. Alison MS Watson, "Saving More Than the Children: The Role of Child-Focused NGOs in the Creation of Southern Security Norms," *Third World Quarterly* 27, no. 2 (2006): 235.

99. Ibid., 235.

100. Briana Nichols et al., "Transnational Information Politics and the 'Child Migration Crisis': Guatemalan NGOs Respond to Youth Migration," *Voluntas: International Journal of Voluntary and Nonprofit Organizations* 28 (2017): 1980.

101. Ibid., 1980.

102. Ibid., 1981.

103. Ibid., 1981.

104. Ibid., 1981–1982.

105. Charlotte Dany, "Exploring the Political Agency of Humanitarian NGOs: Médecins Sans Frontièrs," *Global Society: Journal of Interdisciplinary International Relations* 33, no. 2 (2019): 184.

106. Ibid., 198.

107. Gerd Leipold, "Campaigning: A Fashion or Best Way to Change the Global Agenda?" in *Development and Advocacy*, ed. Oxfam GB (London: Oxfam GB, 2002), 74.

108. Ibid., 82.

109. Ahmed and Potter, 50–52.

110. Beyer, 513–514.

111. Martens, 273.

112. Peter Van Tuijl, "Entering the Global Dealing Room: Reflections on a Rights-Based Framework for NGOs in International Development," *Third World Quarterly* 21, no. 4 (2000): 618.

113. Gerald M. Steinberg, "International NGOs, the Arab Upheaval, and Human Rights: Examining NGO Resource Allocation," *Northwestern Journal of International Human Rights* 11, no. 1 (2013): 124–125.

114. Lin Zhengling, "An Analysis of the Role of NGOs in the WTO," *Chinese Journal of International Law* 3, issue 2 (2004): 491–493.

115. Warkentin, 39–40, 52–53, 67.

116. Paul Holtom and Mark Bromley, "Non-Governmental Monitoring of International Arms Transfers," *Stockholm International Peace Research Institute* (2011): 26.

117. Ibid., 31.

118. Ibid., 31–32.

119. Warkentin, 143.

120. Ibid., 145–146.

121. Ibid., 156–157.

122. Heather L. Wipfli, et al., "Global Tobacco Control Diffusion: The Case of the Framework Convention on Tobacco Control," *American Journal of Public Health* 100, no. 7 (July 2010): 1260.

123. Ibid., 1260.

124. Andrew Pilny and Michelle Shumate, "Hyperlinks as Extensions of Offline Instrumental Collective Action," *Information, Communication & Society* 15, no. 2 (March 2012): 260, 280.

125. Sarah Cummings et al., "Knowledge and Learning in Online Networks in Development: A Social-Capital Perspective," *Development in Practice* 16, no. 6 (November 2006): 571–572.

126. Ibid., 572.

127. Ibid., 572.

128. Hans Holmen and Magnus Jistrom, "Look Who's Talking! Second Thoughts about NGOs as Representing Civil Society," *Journal of Asian and African Studies* 44, no. 4 (2009): 433.

129. Ibid., 434.

130. Beyer, 525.

131. Ibid., 524–525.

132. Nicola Short, "The Role of NGOs in the Ottawa Process to Ban Landmines," *International Negotiation* 4 (1999):481.

133. Ibid., 495–497.

134. Beyer, 522–523.

135. Jungin Kim, "A Study of the Roles of NGOs for North Korean Refugees' Human Rights," *Journal of Immigrant & Refugee Studies* 8 (2010): 76–78.

136. Ibid., 80.

137. Ibid., 84.

138. Ibid., 84–85.

139. Beyer, 521.

140. John Burroughs and Jacqueline Cabasso, "Confronting the Nuclear-Armed States in International Negotiation Forums: Lessons for NGOs," *International Negotiation* 4 (1999): 457.

141. Ibid., 474–477.

142. Jean Grugel, "Romancing Civil Society: European NGOs in Latin America," *Journal of Interamerican Studies and World Affairs* 42, no. 2 (Summer 2000): 89.

143. Lewis and Kanji, 121.

144. Jo Crotty, "Making a Difference? NGOs and Civil Society Development in Russia," *Europe-Asia Studies* 61, no. 1 (January 2009): 86.

145. Lina Suleiman, "The NGOs and the Grand Illusions of Development and Democracy," *ISTR* 24 (2013): 245.

146. Lewis and Kanji, 122–124, 127.

147. Ibid., 124–125.

148. Mary Kaldor, *Global Civil Society: An Answer to War* (Malden, MA: Polity Press, 2003), 69.

149. Grugel, 93–94.

150. Larry Diamond, *Developing Democracy: Toward Consolidation* (Baltimore: The Johns Hopkins University Press, 1999), 239–249.

151. Larry Diamond, "Toward Democratic Consolidation," in *The Global Resurgence of Democracy*, eds. L. Diamond and M. Plattner (Baltimore: The Johns Hopkins University Press, 1996), 234.

152. Laurie Boussaguet and Charlotte Halpern, "NGOs, Civil Society and Policy Analysis: From Mutual Disinterest to Reciprocal Investment," in *Policy Analysis in France*, ed. Charlotte Halpern et al. (Bristol, UK: Bristol University Press, Policy Press, 2018), 243.

153. Ibid., 243.

154. Ibid., 256.

155. Muhidin Mulalic, "Fostering of Civil Society by Muslim Women's NGOs in Bosnia and Herzegovina," *Journal of Muslim Minority Affairs* 34, no. 4 (2014): 440.

156. Ibid., 441.

157. Ibid., 441–442.

158. Ibid., 443–446.

159. Panday and Feldman, 301.

160. Ibid., 316.

161. Ibid., 316–317.

162. Carew E. Boulding, "NGOs and Political Participation in Weak Democracies: Subnational Evidence on Protest and Voter Turnout from Bolivia," *The Journal of Politics* 72, no. 2 (April 2010): 456, 465, 467.

163. Yianna Lambrou, "The Changing Role of NGOs in Rural Chile after Democracy," *Bulletin of Latin American Research* 16, no. 1 (1997): 107.

164. Ibid., 115–116.

165. Tsveta Petrova, "Citizen Participation in Local Governance in Eastern Europe: Rediscovering a Strength of Civil Society in Post-Socialist World?" *Europe-Asia Studies* 63, no. 5 (July 2011): 757.

166. Ibid., 758.

167. Apichai W. Shipper, "Foreigners and Civil Society in Japan," *Pacific Affairs* 79, no. 2 (Summer 2006): 288–289.

168. Ibid., 289.

169. Volkhart Finn Heinrich, "The Role of NGOs in Strengthening the Foundations of South African Democracy," *Voluntas: International Journal of Voluntary and Nonprofit Organizations* 12, no. 1 (2001): 1–2, 13; Larry Diamond in "Toward Democratic Consolidation" says that "[*consolidation*] is the process by which democracy becomes so broadly and profoundly legitimate among its citizens that it is very unlikely to break down. It involves behavioral and institutional changes that normalize democratic politics and narrow its uncertainty," (p. 238).

170. Timothy D. Sisk, "South Africa: Enabling Liberation," in *Transitions to Democracy: A Comparative Perspective*, eds. Kathryn Stoner and Michael McFaul (Baltimore: The Johns Hopkins University Press, 2013), 186–187.

171. Bolaji Ogunseye, "NGOs and Which 'Civil Society'?" *International Institute for Environment and Development* (1997): 12.

172. Ibid., 13.

173. Matthew Todd Bradley, "Chinese-Built Dams, Africa, and Economic Growth: Is There a Role for African NGOs?" *Journal of the Indiana Academy of the Social Sciences* 14, issue 1 (2010): 88, 95.

174. Ibid., 95.

175. Kheang Un, "State, Society and Democratic Consolidation: The Case of Cambodia," *Pacific Affairs* 79, no. 2 (Summer 2006): 244.

176. Ibid., 244.

177. Ibid., 245.

178. Carew E. Boulding and Jami Nelson-Nunez, "Civil Society and Support for the Political System in Times of Crisis," *Latin American Research Review* 49, no. 1 (2014): 150.

179. Ibid., 150

180. Ibid., 150.

181. Ezequiel Gonzales Ocantos, "Persuade Them or Oust Them: Crafting Judicial Change and Transitional Justice in Argentina," *Comparative Politics* 46, no. 4 (July 2014): 479.

182. Ibid., 480.

183. Crotty, 85.

184. Ibid., 85–86, 101.

185. Ibid., 87.

186. Ibid., 88.

187. Ibid., 89

188. Olga Oleinikova, "Foreign Funded NGOs in Russia, Belarus and Ukraine: Recent Restrictions and Implications," *Cosmopolitan Societies: An Interdisciplinary Journal* 9, no. 3 (2017): 86.

189. Olga Beznosova and Lisa McIntosh Sundstrom, "Western Aid and the State-Society Balance in Novgorod and Khabarovsk," *Problems of Post-Communism* 56, no. 6 (2009): 21.

190. Ibid., 21–22.

191. Ibid., 22.

192. Edward Aspinall and Marcus Mietzner, "Indonesia: Economic Crisis, Foreign Pressure, and Regime Change," in *Transitions to Democracy: A Comparative Perspective*, eds. Kathryn Stoner and Michael McFaul (Baltimore: The Johns Hopkins University Press, 2013), 152–156.

193. Ibid., 157.

194. Dimitri A. Sotiropoulos, "Civil Society in Greece in the Wake of the Economic Crisis," *ELIAMEP* (December 2017): 2–3 .

195. Ibid., 3.

196. Ibid., 4.

197. Ibid., 5.

198. Ibid., 6, 11.

199. Nikolaos Tzifakis et al., "The Impact of Economic Crises on NGOs: The Case of Greece," *Voluntas: International Journal of Voluntary and Nonprofit Organizations* 28, issue 5 (October 2017): 2194–2195.

200. Ibid., 2195–2196.

201. Junia Fatime do Carmo Guerra and Walter Mswaka, "Knowledge and Power of Civil Society: An empirical Study of Brazilian Professionals Working in NGOs," *Cosmopolitan Civil Societies Journal* 8, no. 1 (2016): 67–68.

202. Ibid., 68.

203. Ibid., 68–69.

204. Chris van der Borgh and Carolijn Terwindt, "Shrinking Operational Space of NGOs — A Framework of Analysis," *Development in Practice* 22, no. 8 (November 2012): 1067–1068.

205. Jonas Wolff and Annika Elena Poppe, *Civil Society, NGOs and Foreign Funding: An Overview* (Frankfurt: Peace Research Institute Frankfurt, 2015), 4.

206. Thomas Richter, "Reduced Scope for Action Worldwide for Civil Society," *German Institute of Global and Area Studies* (GIGA) (2018): 1, https://www.jstor.org/stable/resrep21176 .

207. Wolff and Poppe, 5.

208. Lana Baydas, "Civic Space in India between the National Security Hammer and the Counterterrorism Anvil," *Center for Strategic and International Studies* (CSIS) (2018): 71.

209. Ibid., 72.

210. Wolff and Poppe, 6.

211. Jude Howell et al., "The Backlash against Civil Society in the Wake of the Long War on Terror," *Development in Practice* 18, no. 1 (February 2008): 83.

212. Ibid., 90.

213. Thomas Carothers, "The Closing Space Challenge: How Are Funders Responding?" *Carnegie Endowment for International Peace* (2015): 9, 23–27.
   214. Wolff and Poppe, 7.

Chapter 3

Assessment of Non-governmental Organizations

A study of the roles of NGOs should be followed by an assessment of their performance to make apparent their strengths and weaknesses. As it has been discussed until now, NGOs do play a significant role in an era of civil wars, failed states, financial problems, demand of services, and need for someone to represent the interests of those needing assistance and the voiceless. The valuable positive role of NGOs, though, should not prevent one from critically looking at them. Many NGOs are a force for good but, as with most organizations, they also suffer from a few deficiencies.

As Beyer notes, the enhancement of global civil society not only improves the legitimacy of global governance, but it also contributes to the lessening of the democratic deficit that characterizes global governance. But at the same time, "[the] dark side of this feature is the lack of coordination between NGOs; such coordination would be the only way to concentrate resources and influence relevant political processes."[1] For NGO-initiated campaigns to succeed, NGOs must find ways to cooperate with other NGOs. They must campaign at different levels, which "often require very different attitudes, strategies, and skills." Such collaboration is complex and difficult. But, if achieved, it is very beneficial to those involved. "However, this can also lead to conflicts, and collaboration is particularly difficult among NGOs pursuing very different campaigning styles and strategies, something which can actually undermine the progress of the campaigning."[2]

Often NGOs are identified with civil society and are considered its most important members. But not everyone, of course, agrees with this assertion. The claim that NGOs "represent a humanitarian alternative, and that they can and do represent the poor and the marginalized, rests on a number of assumptions:

1. Decisions made and activities pursued by inter-governmental organizations will improve, be fairer and more effective if NGOs are part of the decision-making process.
2. NGOs do not act out of self-interest.
3. Governments and inter-governmental institutions are uncivilized whereas civil society is civilized, homogenous and in agreement.
4. It is possible to transmit demands and standpoints from below without distortions.
5. NGOs are immune to corruption whereas politicians and public employees are not."[3]

Holmen and Jirsrom assert that none of these assumptions about NGOs have been met, at least not on a general level. As a result, it is questionable to claim that NGOs strengthen civil society, let alone represent it. "Actually, NGOs do not represent civil society, they represent interest groups of varying size and often with quite specific agendas. Nevertheless, donors, scholars and international institutions have developed a habit of treating NGOs as if they were civil society. On many occasions, NGOs have seized the opportunity to exploit this attitude but have also been accused of 'monopolizing' civil society, diverting attention from other associations. NGOs, apparently, are merely a privileged sub-section of civil society that may not be representative at all."[4]

There is a substantial number of NGOs and many of them have been able to exert great influence. Is this good or is it bad? According to critics, much of the influence is based on naïve assumptions about NGOs. Furthermore, because of the growth of many NGOs, the number of activities they are involved in, and the number of lower-level NGOs they support, many of them, which previously relied on volunteers, are now in need of hiring professional staff and they will represent their members to a lesser degree than previously. It becomes more difficult, the critics say, to separate NGOs from the private sector.[5]

Even if in some cases NGOs have strengthened civil society, there are examples where NGOs have weakened civil society. "[It] is not uncommon for foreign NGOs to subsidize small businesses that they support in Third World countries, thereby unfairly competing with indigenous efforts to develop 'from below.' … For example, in Bangladesh, NGOs and NGO-supported economic activities enjoy unfair competitive advantages and they do not permit their staff to join trade unions, a type of organization that many would definitely include in 'civil society.'"[6]

Since the late twentieth century, Western scholars have argued that a healthy civil society is essential to democratization. But NGOs have not always played a positive role in this area. For example, Grugel, in examining NGOs and democratization in Latin America, argues that NGOs either have failed to improve the well-being of the people they attempt to help, or they have made a marginal difference in their lives. And many of the reasons for the absence of success or limited success are connected to inadequate consultation with the local communities. Grugel also puts much emphasis on how NGOs "can straddle two policy agendas: their own, based on a notion of civil society as people-centered development and democratization; and that of their funders, who use the term to mean capitalist modernization and liberalization."[7] Of these two agendas, the second could easily undermine social cohesion and cause social unrest.

Grugel also notes that assistance strategies aiming to build up civil societies bring along specific problems. He asserts that

> First, there are inevitable limitations to how far civil societies can be built from outside. If civil society is a set of social values as well as organizations, then those values need time to develop and flourish within communities. ... Second, European NGOs support projects only for a specified length of time. . . . This has frequently led to the collapse of the initiatives they have funded and sometimes to the disintegration of Latin American NGOs, which often depend on external funding to survive. ... Finally, there is the question of whether the kind of projects European NGOs support are "right" for building civil society. Many of the projects they fund ... are at best a fragile way to strengthen civil society and deepen democracy because they depend on individuals to transform their immediate environment. ... Therefore, gains in citizenship may not necessarily survive beyond the life of a project, and rarely challenge the system of social and political privilege that NGOs identify as the root impediment to democracy in Latin America.[8]

It is possible that NGOs are not always the best tools to use to effect change. In the past, some NGOs have not wisely used their resources in support of civil society and democratization. Joel Beinin says that NGOs and other organizations and institutions have failed to fulfill their assigned roles in Arab society since 2011. Among the factors mentioned for the failure are

> First, the claim that building civil society is a strategy for democracy promotion has been overstated. Freedom of association is undoubtedly an essential feature of a democratic polity. But not all associations embrace democratic values . . . and associational life has flourished in undemocratic societies. Second . . . Arab advocacy NGOs did succeed, to varying extents, in propagating the discourse of universal human rights. Yet those NGOs tend to be staffed by a predictable group of cosmopolitan, middle-class professionals socially distant from the majority of the population. . . . Third, international advocates of building civil society commonly also promoted neoliberal "Washington Consensus" economic policies. In the Arab region, international financial institutions backed by the US government targeted large public sectors, commodity subsidies, and subsidized

social services for elimination. Civil society organizations were hailed as institutions that would assume the responsibilities abandoned by shrinking states.[9]

Euiyoung Kim, in his work on the limits of NGO-government relations in
South Korea, considers not only the reasons for the enormous growth of
NGOs since the transition to democracy in 1987, but also sheds light on
important concerns about the state of this relationship. What then are the
reasons for the emergence and increasing influence of civic organizations?
First, the most important factor was the democratic transition itself. Citizens
were now able to claim basic civil and political rights that they were denied
in the past. Second, members of the middle who supported the democratic
movement rejected the radical positions of people's movements groups. They
were more concerned with matters related to corruption, the environment,
education, and welfare. In addition, the collapse of communism weakened
the appeal of people's groups. These developments enabled the more moderate civic organizations to gain strength. Third, the weakness of South Korea's
political parties and the National Assembly also contributed to the growth
of NGOs. Fourth, voluntarism was yet another factor in the emergence of
NGOs. Voluntarism provides the basis of civil society and NGO activities.
Fifth, "the government itself has affected the growth of the NGO sector. For
example, the divide-and-rule strategy of the Roh Tae Woo (1988–92) and
the Kim Young Sam (1993–97) governments facilitated the expansion of the
NGO sector vis-à-vis the people's movement sector. That is, government used
a two-pronged strategy in dealing with civil society by promoting and supporting moderate civic organizations while suppressing the radical people's
movement groups."[10]

NGOs have been a significant player in South Korea's democratic governance, and they have played important roles in cooperation with the government. "However… the status of these once prominent organizations is in clear
decline. [The reasons for their loss of influence and credibility are related]
to their structural weakness, over-politicization, and the limits of NGO-
government relations. Simply put, we may characterize the current stage as a
situation where South Korean NGOs are beset by lack of citizen participation
and a poor resource base, disgraced with the stigma of over-politicization,
and faced with the risk of potentially being coopted by the government."[11]

In examining the case of Georgia after the "Rose Revolution" in 2003,
Brian Grodsky makes a related argument to Kim's. After twelve years of ruling the country, Eduard Shevardnadze's regime collapsed and a peaceful transition to democracy was the outcome. This outcome appeared to be the result
of the decision by political elites to abandon Shevardnadze and the strengthening of NGOs supportive of democracy. It seemed that the billions of dollars
provided by the United States to aid democracy development was a success.

"However, if civil society development, one component of this democracy aid, is designed to have long-term consequences, then this prognosis was premature. Around the world, pro-democracy organizations have been drawn into newly democratizing states. The case of Georgia demonstrates that this can weaken rather than empower pro-democracy groups."[12]

The inclusion of NGOs in government has potential benefits, but the case of Georgia shows that there are inherent pitfalls in this. "Former NGO actors whose allegiance is now with the state must deal with new constituencies and adopt new objectives. These institutionally defined priorities are likely to create tension in the relationship between new state leaders and their former organizations. As each category of actors operates with the expectation that its former partner will continue to support it, they are likely to clash." This, of course, does not mean that the new political elites will refuse to cooperate with NGOs. "But those organizations that go beyond political elites' expectations of them to do research and provide expertise are unlikely to find sympathy within government circles."[13]

Even though it is difficult to attribute these negative developments to the relationship between NGOs and government, the case of Georgia proves that Western donors, especially the United States, were too optimistic at the beginning of the Rose Revolution. "The United States government's transfer of resources away from the organizations that helped bring democratic breakthrough may have served to further encourage the new government that, indeed, the role of a critical civil society had ended.... The difference is in the years since Georgia's Rose Revolution of 2003, few outside observers believe the country has moved closer to democratic consolidation. Instead, critics inside and outside the country wonder how to get Georgia back on [the] track it appeared to be on in late 2003."[14]

Orysia Lutsevych, in her work on civil society in the Black Sea Region, tends to reinforce some of the conclusions reached by Brian Grodsky. Lutsevych specifically examines Georgia, Ukraine, and Moldova and says that all three experienced "color" revolutions, which led to new leaderships who were entrusted to reform the post-Soviet system of government. Despite these developments, all three countries still face challenges in consolidating democracy. One of the reasons for this is the role of Western governments. "The West viewed the task of supporting civil society development through the narrow lens of NGOs by providing financial and technical support to locally registered groups in order to make them active in influencing the state. These local NGOs became synonymous with civil society and de facto monopolized civil society discourse, leaving wider society and other non-institutional forms of citizens' engagement behind."[15]

One of the factors for the weakness of civil society is that "citizens are not at the heart of formal engagement." In all three countries, citizens are kept on the sidelines of discussions about important matters because LNGOs "have little ability to help them formulate opinions and influence state policies that affect them." Another reason for the feeble state of civil society is that during the period of post-Soviet transitions "a rather elitist non-profit organization sector emerged, which focuses on professional consulting and service provision. With strong competition for Western funding, LNGOs remain organization-centered rather than joining forces in coalitions and networks around issues." Furthermore, the state of civil society is also the result of post-Soviet governments frequently "fake dialogue with their societies or [limiting] their role. Ruling elites … maneuver around public pressure and became skilled in the rhetoric of civil society while paying lip-service to it."[16]

One final observation Lutsevych makes is that in contrast to the Western understanding of civility in society "where citizens have broad respect for one another based on trust and security, societies in Georgia, Moldova, and Ukraine have 'uncivil' traits with instances of repression of citizens' will. Post-Soviet societies, exhausted by tiresome and incomplete democratic transition, suffer from modern violence such as dramatic wealth disparities, corruption, and extensive citizen reliance on informal clientelist networks to find their ways around the dysfunctional system."[17]

Pauline Jones Luong and Erica Weinthal, in examining another former Soviet Republic, Kazakhstan, ask the following question: Why do local environmental NGOs as well as Western NGOs adopt strategies that seem to undermine their importance and the broader development of civil society and the democratization process? The authors argue that both LNGOs and Western NGOs in Kazakhstan operate under the same domestic and international constraints. The domestic constraints include the Soviet legacy, the legal and political limitations placed upon NGOs by the government, the lack of funding, and the importance of the energy sector for economic growth in Kazakhstan. Among the important international constraints are the dependence of Western NGOs on external sources of funding, which have their own agenda in Kazakhstan, and the role international actors play in the energy sector. These constraints have shaped LNGOs and have hindered their development.[18]

The case of Kazakhstan manifests that international donors are undermining civil society rather than promoting it. Even though the number of LNGOs has increased, their membership and their influence have decreased. In addition, even though the energy sector is recognized as Kazakhstan's most important sector for its economic future, LNGOs and Western NGOs have paid little attention to the impact of the energy sector on the environment. Instead, they chose to concentrate on international issues that might grasp the attention of the international community, and in return allow them to receive more funding from abroad.[19]

For a vibrant civil society to exist there must be linkages between the government and its citizens. But in Kazakhstan

> the relationship between state and society ... appears tenuous at best. An indirect and asymmetrical relationship between the state and society is arising in which non-domestic actors, such as Western NGOs, act as a source of mediation. Environmental and societal interests are not mediated through domestic institutions, as in a democracy, but rather through international actors and organizations. In the short term, we are finding the emergence of numerous NGOs and environmental laws and regulations, but no direct link between the two. Rather, the initiative for environmental protection emanates from international pressures, and direct foreign intervention. There seems to be nothing connecting state policy with societal interests and demands, except the mutual benefit they derive from international actors' involvement in domestic politics and the economy.[20]

Fiona B. Adamson makes similar assertions about NGOs and democratization in Uzbekistan and Kyrgyzstan. Since 1991, foreign donors, including INGOs, have spent millions of dollars to promote democracy in the region. Most of the money is devoted to strengthening civil society, which then is expected to lead to democratic reforms or transition to democracy. But how successful have these efforts been? "Despite many individual success stories, and some promising trends, the overall effect of democracy assistance in the region has been largely limited to the development of an externally funded third sector and has not brought about large-scale political changes leading to greater democratization."[21]

Adamson notes that there is "disjunction between visions of democracy as promoted by many international actors in the region and the actual social, political, and economic conditions in Central Asia.... [International] actors often rely on fixed meanings of democracy, civil society, and NGOs that bear little relation to the realities of the local environment." Foreign donors must take into consideration the effect of informal processes and institutions on their strategies, and "pay much attention to these factors as to the formal institutional environment. These include patronage networks, ethnic cleavages, the local political culture, and informal networks."[22]

Creating Western-style institutions, rather than working with and strengthening existing institutions, has its limits. A foreign-funded "democracy sector" that has shallow roots in local society, and interacts sparingly with indigenous structures, "is in danger of exacerbating tensions between the small elite that is able to benefit from international assistance and the majority of the population, which is struggling for economic survival ..." If democracy promotion is to be context specific to the region, "this may mean less democracy assistance and a greater emphasis on grassroots economic and local community development projects.... Any effective strategy of democracy assistance in Central Asia must focus first and foremost on programs that promote human development and redress social and economic inequalities in the region."[23]

Wesley Longhofer et al. make a similar argument related to the role of domestic NGOs and INGOs in effecting pro-environmental policies. The authors take three different perspectives into consideration: 1. The bottom-up perspective, emphasizing the role of domestic NGOs; 2. The interaction perspective, emphasizing alliances or reinforcing pressures from domestic and INGOs; 3. The top-down perspective, focusing on the role of INGOs. After considering the adoption of three pro-environmental policy reforms from 1970 to 2010 (omnibus environmental laws, environmental impact assessment reporting requirements, and national environmental ministries), Longhofer et al. concluded that while "there are compelling historical examples of bottom-up and interaction processes, the broad pattern of environmental policy adoption across the world is better explained by global rather than domestic organizational dynamics. In short, [the] findings support the top-down model of social change by highlighting the exogenous sources of environmental reform."[24]

When the relationship between the state, society, and foreign donors is as described above, NGOs lack social capital. An examination of Chinese labor NGOs brings to view this point because their survival depends on funding from foreign donors and their relationship with the state, and their ability to effectively represent Chinese workers is questionable. Their connection to workers is controversial to say the least. "Given the uneven relationship with authorities, their capacity to exert significant influence on local and central policies is limited at best. At the same time, owing to their precarious legal status, they are unable to represent workers in sensitive situations such as strikes and labor stoppages."[25]

As is the case in many countries, Chinese labor NGOs are too "fragmented and disconnected from their supposed constituency [the workers] that it would be an overstatement to depict them as an important force contributing to legal reform and raising social demands for legal justice. Yet ... it is not possible to generalize. Each organization has its own features and some of them are doing excellent work guaranteeing migrant workers' access to justice and bringing the plight of Chinese workers to the attention of the media."[26]

Ruth Phillips and Susan Goodwin present a fascinating study on human service NGOs as central actors in present-day welfare states, with greater focus on Australia. The authors note that NGOs in Australia have expanded their role as providers of human services that are an essential part of the welfare state and as lobbyists or advocates and agents for social change. The greater role of human service NGOs is related to their involvement "in the production of social policy knowledge through policy research activities."

This development could be "understood as the 'opening up' or 'democratization' of social policy processes to include [NGOs]."[27]

But NGOs becoming such an integral part of the delivery of human services could also

> [be] understood as a reconfiguring of the democratic system of policy determination, one that could potentially result, for example, in large faith-based organizations essentially shaping the way the state responds to human need. It may also be one in which the NGOs become "experts" on citizens' needs through research practices that are fundamentally less, rather than more inclusive, of the subjects of social policy. The implications of a possible shift in power to influence and, in some cases, determine who gets what in the welfare state is of deep concern in relationship to future models of social protection and ultimately the redistributive and democratic processes of a nation state. ... [The] giving over of the production of social policy knowledge is at odds with the values and ideas of universal civic, political and social citizenship that underpin the concept of a welfare state and which appears to be the only reliable mechanism for countering the ill effects of the market. Although there can be little doubt that what human service NGOs have contributed up to now is by and large for the common good, will this always be the case? Can the common good be determined, accepted or rejected without a commitment to the formal democratic direction that can only occur through government?[28]

An affiliated difficulty associated with NGOs is that of internal legitimacy, that is internal composition of the NGOs themselves. The question often raised is "how their internal decision-making processes are organized and according to which standards collectively binding decisions are made."[29] Many large NGOs are criticized for not being internally democratic. "NGOs themselves are not necessarily democratic, which raises the question of who represents what to whom. Elections are hardly frequent occurrences within NGOs, which do not function in the way representative governments do. And the elites of large NGOs at the summit or even at lower levels of expenditures may hardly be different from those of IGOs or the governments that they supposedly confront."[30]

For all their strengths, most NGOs, especially developing country NGOs, are "part of their societies' elite.... The bureaucratic requirements of donors ... inevitably exclude those developing country organizations and nationals who do not possess the necessary language ... and required project skills ... Access to such skills in developing countries is limited by scarcity of both human and financial resources which are more available to members of the elite than the majority of the population." In addition, "[intermediary] NGOs ... form part of the modern sector of society, simply because of the necessity that these organizations operate within a framework which is externally determined. It seems equally likely that the very idea of an intermediary organization requires that it be part of a society's elite." Under these circumstances, who then benefits? At times, the benefits derived by the supposed beneficiaries are marginal as shown by some studies on the role of NGOs in Indonesia, the Philippines, South Africa, and Sri Lanka. There are occasions "when NGOs campaigning 'in defense of the poorest' are advancing or defending interests of other groups or, indeed, their own."[31]

Another factor that affects the legitimacy of NGOs is the inclination by some of them not to include grassroots people in their discussions with transnational corporations (TNCs) about corporate social responsibility (CSR). The fact that TNCs have made contributions toward development and at the same time have caused harm to many people and especially the poor has attracted the attention of development NGOs in CSR. A number of NGOs "have adopted a cooperative strategy thus far in the form of TNC's financial contribution and technical assistance with management tools. This results in donor-driven programs and business-like change of NGOs. In the name of CSR, NGOs have also promoted voluntary regulations." But voluntary regulations are not necessarily an effective tool to hold TNCs accountable. "The CSR-related activities of NGOs have been centered on philanthropy of corporations and raised awareness of Northern citizens. Serious problems lie in the neglect of local people's voice and agency. These problems also raise questions about the legitimacy of NGOs. Without representing and advocating vulnerable people in developing countries, NGOs work cannot be legitimized."[32]

NGOs must attempt to change the CSR discussion with human rights issues of concern to grassroots people in developing countries as the focal point. Grassroots people have played a role in changing the behavior of corporations by acting as laborers, consumers, and citizens. But the effect of these activities often proved to be "too localized and too narrowly designed for economic interests." Therefore, the outcome was limited and ephemeral. "The human rights framework can provide core values, principled process and strategies for grassroots social movements." Such emphasis will provide NGOs with opportunities at a time when their "identity and legitimacy have been questioned."[33]

At times, international advocacy NGOs not only do not include grassroots organizations in their discussions with various organizations about matters of concern to them, they misrepresent the interests of the people they are supposed to represent. Kristina Hahn and Anna Holzscheiter argue that "advocacy NGOs whose legitimacy and authority depend on their roles as representatives of marginalized and disenfranchised populations are in many cases prone to exploit discourses on vulnerability and victimhood in order to fortify their own identity as 'advocates.'" By examining two case studies on prostitution and child labor, the authors attempted to "demonstrate that the ascription of identities by NGOs to their beneficiaries is an empirically contested phenomenon. When the allegedly weak and 'voiceless' persons whom advocacy NGOs claim to represent start to defend their own interests and publicly contradict the positions advocated on their behalf, conflict between these groups arises. Child workers and prostitutes contest the way in which they are portrayed by their advocates in public discourse and especially resist the ascription of 'victim' identity."[34]

The plethora of NGOs often leads to unhealthy competition among them, overlapping and duplication of services, and waste. One of the reasons for such an outcome is intense competition for limited funding, which leads to lack of cooperation and the adoption of a balanced approach to the issue at hand. The role of some NGOs in Haiti is a good example of such misguided actions.

Francois Pierre-Louis in discussing the role of CARE says the following: CARE moved to northwest Haiti in 1966 to implement development activities through a program called Food for Work. The goal of the international community was lessening Haiti's dependence "on subsistence agriculture and cash crops." The government of Jean Claude Duvalier in cooperation with NGOs encouraged Haitians to move from the countryside to Port-au-Prince to find employment in industries being built. "The Food for Work program was a means of paying peasants for building roads and installing drinkable water systems in rural communities and then paid them through surplus food that was donated by the United States, Canada, and other countries. The impact of this program in the northwest of Haiti was a massive exodus of peasants from the countryside to urban areas. Peasants began to abandon their land since the surplus food that was dumped in the market was cheaper than the food locally produced. Since they were also attracted by the factory jobs in Port-au-Prince, they preferred to settle there instead of eking out a living off the land." Even though the Food for Work program seemed to be innovative during that time, "the truth was that after a while it could not employ all those who wanted a job. Land in the northwest was abandoned, and many peasants who could not make it to Port-au-Prince left the country by boat to the United States and other Caribbean islands."[35]

Pierre-Louis also argues that the boycott imposed on Haiti by the international community during the nineteenth and twentieth centuries, the internal conflict among members of the Haitian elite to control government, and the "weakening of state structures through the creation of [non-governmental] organizations have weakened the government's capacity to deal with major catastrophe and meet the needs of its citizens."[36]

More specifically and related to the role of NGOs in Haiti after the 2010 earthquake, Pierre-Louis notes that three days after the earthquake "[the] government of Rene Preval was unable to either communicate with the population or provide any form of assistance.... There was no emergency management system in place that could be rapidly activated. Port-au-Prince ... was an urban jungle where residents built homes wherever they wanted. Since 1971 with the neoliberal agenda imposed by foreign donors, the mantra has been 'less government is better.' Therefore, governmental agencies that used to supervise construction in the city have been stripped of their staff. Junior state employees take government jobs in order to gain enough experience to work for NGOs, which pay them better and provide material and career advancement.... The Haitian government, which was already experiencing a deficit of qualified employees, was further depleted of its manpower."[37]

Similar assertions about Haiti after the 2010 earthquake are made by Mark Schuller. The earthquake brought into the public spotlight the role of the international aid system. In addition to greater scrutiny, the earthquake "provided a teachable moment." At a congressional hearing in 2010, President Clinton apologized "for destroying Haitian rice production under his presidency through the delivery of USAID food aid, calling it a 'Devil's bargain.'" The representative for the Organization of American States, Ricardo Seitenfus of Brazil, said that Haiti "is the proof of the failure of international aid." He also said that Haiti "may well become the Waterloo of the NGO system." What accounts for such failure, despite the billions in aid given, NGO's efforts, and even some individual successes?[38]

It is true that the earthquake presented many challenges because it struck an urban area and the country's nerve center. Another reason was the delay in delivering the aid promised. "Of the $5.6 billion official development aid pledged for the period through the end of September 2011, only 37 percent was sent by January 2011." A further reason was structural problems even before the earthquake. Local participation was prevented, and frontline staff were silenced. An additional reason was that NGOs became instrumentalized.[39]

Kevin Edmonds is yet another scholar who agrees with the abovementioned scholars with regards to Haiti after the 2010 earthquake. He notes that despite the goodwill of the international community and the influx of countless NGOs, the reconstruction process proved to be lucrative for many private organizations and not for the Haitian people. "The Interim Haiti Reconstruction Committee, led by Bill Clinton, [sought] to entrench the same neoliberal policies which laid the foundation for much of the pre-earthquake poverty and dependency." Such outcomes raise questions about these organizations and whether they are there to benefit the people of Haiti or themselves.[40]

Without transforming the way NGOs operate, it is not realistic to expect real results in Haiti. "Haiti's failed reconstruction is a beacon that warns us that NGOs cannot replace the state, and that any attempt to do so is destructive and dangerous. The NGOs in Haiti have increased the dependency of the Haitian people through undemocratic and non-transparent projects which serve to entrench the neoliberal ideals of privatized governance, a reduced role for the state, and free mobility of both foreign capital and people — while Haitians stay trapped in the IDP [Internally Displaced Persons] camps."[41]

Chelsey L. Kivland makes approximate assertions about NGOs and Haiti but she strikes an even sharper tone. She says the democratic transition in Haiti (1986–present) has been accompanied by numerous UN peacekeeping missions and many more NGOs. Most of these actions were undertaken in the name of building state capacity. But at least according to the residents in a Port-au-Prince neighborhood affected by the presence of "diverse governance projects," the result has been perceptions and experiences of "statelessness. Taking the peacekeeping mission as an exemplar of global governance ... the mission's social effects promote the perception of statelessness [resulting] not only in the weakness of the government of Haiti but also [from] the impotence that comes from a political field occupied by excessive, disordered forms of governance. The acknowledgement of statehood therefore depends on embodied displays of authorized force in which both those who govern and those who are governed acknowledge sovereign agency, power, and responsibility."[42]

Philip Awekeya et al., in their study of access to water in rural Ghana, also address the issue of dependency. They note that ad hoc measures adopted by NGOs only temporarily relieve the situation for the people they attempt to help. They do not provide them with the necessary tools "that will enable them to let themselves off the hooks of dependency." Even though NGOs continue to be important in developing areas, "they need to forge a closer link between and among themselves on the one hand, and government ministries and development agencies on the other hand in order to ensure that their assistance projects build capacities and enhance capabilities for achieving lasting impacts."[43]

Awekeya and his colleagues show that a one-sided approach does not necessarily lead to success. Problems that need to be solved are too many. And failures not only waste time and resources, they also cause loss of credibility. Severe negative consequences may result "when systemic capacity building is neglected. The change for positive outcomes lies with consistent use of concepts that foster long-term transformative change. NGO activities can only contribute to long-term change of living conditions in underdeveloped areas if they deploy a holistic approach and strategic intent.... This multi-faceted approach can best be theoretically founded in the Multi-Level-Perspective framework which portrays how socio-technical transformation is effected bottom-up through activities on the level below the institutional regime."[44]

Many NGOs began as private voluntary organizations connected to faith-based communities that raised their own funds. These organizations were associated with each other, emphasized self-sacrifice, and had a shared mission. Even though there are still many grassroots organizations that raise most of their funds from members, the aid system significantly changed after the Cold War ended. Donors like USAID and the World Bank did not any longer need strong states to compete with the Soviet Union. "In fact, they discovered that states were too strong, centralized, corrupt, and removed from the people. So, they began directly financing NGOs instead," and their budgets exploded.[45]

NGOs became more powerful, and many were corrupted by the process, which in turn affected participation. Decision-making became more central-ized and NGOs were "rewarded for a 'bean counting' approach that reduces people to statistics." Reporting requirements cut off intra-NGO communica-tion and led to the creation of top-heavy NGOs with bloated administrations. Also, the donors' relationships with NGOs discourages them from working together. In fact, they become competitors with one another and the Haitian government as well. And because of the "donors' systematic undermining of the state's oversight and coordination capacity, only a fraction of NGOs in Haiti submits the bare minimum, annual reports, to the Haitian government. In many cases, donors' policies encourage NGOs to disregard the authority of the state."[46]

NGOs are viewed by many as representing the best of people trying to deal with global inequities. "But behind the characteristics inherent to an NGO model of development are lurking several challenges: too many actors, too many chiefs, and too much mission." An NGO has an advantage in that it can threaten to pull out of the delivery of humanitarian assistance at a place controlled by corrupt characters. But if there are too many actors involved in that part of the world, the unsavory characters would be replaced by another NGO. This makes the threat meaningless.[47]

In addition, international funding for development goes through various channels before it reaches the actual beneficiaries: "from the taxpayer to a bilateral aid agency, to an intergovernmental organization, to an international NGO, and finally to a local NGO before being finally spent on goods or services." How much of the allocated money for this endeavor ends up in the hands of the final beneficiaries is not exactly known. Furthermore, all NGOs have a mission statement that provides specific information about the service that is best for the beneficiaries. "Yet a less paternalistic — and a less expensive — mission could, in many cases, be a far more efficient modus operandi. One such alternative to the donor-knows-best approach is vouch-ers. A voucher given to beneficiaries ...could allow them to purchase goods and services." Such an approach would put the decision-making power in the hands of the intended beneficiaries.[48]

Another criticism of NGOs is that of the North-South bias. Some scholars note that when it comes to transnational cooperation among NGOs, and the distribution of power, influence, and resources, there is an obvious North-South bias. "Transnational NGOs are ... mostly a project of the north. Transnational civil society is less global but much more a projection of Western economic and political power.... There are at least three dimensions to the 'problem' of US-based NGOs: they are said to be unrepresentative; they drown out more 'legitimate' NGO voices and ... they are too closely tied to the US government in pressing their demands."[49] This is among the reasons why some NGOs are considered as an attempt by Westerners to impose their values upon non-Westerners.

Nadeem Malik and Ahsan Rana, in their examination of civil society in Pakistan, note that civil society grew up in the West with the rise of capitalism. More specifically, it grew up in secular, democratizing, pluralist states, most of which developed through social revolutions that came in waves in 1688, 1775–1820, 1848, 1871, and 1917–1923. In countries such as Pakistan, civil society concepts were exported by the West with the end of the Cold War and the "so-called triumph of the neoliberal economic paradigm. In a non-Western setting, civil society has gained currency through the discourse of projectization." What the authors' study has shown is what happens when concepts are introduced by the external development industry, "accompanied by the flow of resources from West to East in the form of projects."[50]

Malik and Rana suggest that these projects are not sustainable because donors change their priorities, and NGOs are compelled to end projects because funding is not available. The legitimacy of foreign-funded NGOs is questioned because they are not accountable to the people they serve, "but to their donors. The nature of the relationship between NGOs and communities is that of patronage rather than of equal partnership, and most beneficiaries in villages already have more immediate and unavoidable patrons.... It is complete reliance on foreign funding, and the discourse of the flow of resources from West to East which, at times, turns the discourse of civil society into an exclusive discourse of projectization."[51]

Afef Benessaieh makes associated arguments concerning the North-South bias as related to the existing global civil society. Benessaieh says that many scholars view the global civil society "as an open process and an extended imagined community, [and it] is not generally seen as constituting a monolithic grouping of like-minded social actors." However, many scholars often place too much emphasis on the diverse nature of global civil society and its shared progressive values. A lot of attention is given to members of the global civil society trying to promote human rights, environmental sustainability,

fair trade, etc., and much less attention is given to the extent INGOs and foreign donors "actually share the values they are said to promote or the ways in
which they negotiate their diversity of views. Few scholars in this field have
examined the extent to which the claimed globality of global civil society
includes the views and priorities of actors from the South."[52]

Benessaieh's work is based on a study of NGOs and other grassroots organizations in Chiapas, Mexico, between 2002 and 2004. The author chose
Chiapas for two main reasons. First, Chiapas gained much media attention
and support from many transnational actors during the Zapatista uprising in
1994. Second, Chiapas had a well-established NGO community that gained
strength in the 1980s, during a time of civil unrest in Central America, and it
grew even stronger in the 1990s because of the Zapatista uprising.[53]

LNGOs in Chiapas came to prioritize issues in the 1990s that were
important to INGOs because the relationship between LNGOs and INGOs
is full of "tension and power asymmetry.... Viewed from the South, global
civil society is a site of power relations in which strategic interest rather
than shared values or solidarity prevails. Local NGOs do not always adopt
donors' priorities as a result of like-mindedness; sometimes they do so in
order to secure funding that allows them to pursue other goals in tandem with
donor-supported projects."[54]

The access of SNGOs to global civil society is as direct as many individuals might expect. It is very much influenced by donors who not only set trends
but also behave as "door openers" for SNGOs. The influences on agenda setting are numerous as a result of the many players involved.

> However, Southern local NGOs are rarely in a position to identify for donors
> the salient themes of the day; more often they are required to translate these
> themes in ways that may allow recipient communities to match their needs with
> the priorities of donors.
>   Southern local NGOs actively participate in translating and labeling pri-
> orities between donors and recipient communities; they play a pivotal role in
> such transnational intermediation. If needed there is a transnationally resonant
> language into which they need to translate their concerns and priorities in order
> to be heard by and receive support from their donors, then global civil society
> is an asymmetrical field of play in which not all voices and ideas are heard on
> their own terms. As viewed by Southern local NGOs, global civil society is less
> a site of street theater accessible to all than a venue for a stage play for which
> they need to know the lines, mostly spoken in Northern tongues.[55]

What is missing here is many elements including the lack of consultation
between donors and beneficiaries, between Northern and Southern NGOs,
between NGOs and donors. In their study about housing in three communities in Port Vila, Vanuatu, Lisa Strychar and Jennifer Day found that even

though the "literature has spoken for years about putting people at the center of recovery, about inclusive design, and about consultation and participation … this is not yet the norm." The authors also concluded that despite the fact that NGOs and donors say that they desire community-based projects, and that "consultation and partnership lead to increased satisfaction and programmatic success," the all-inclusive approach is not followed.[56]

What then prevents NGOs and donors from consulting with recipients of aid, in this case housing? Strychar and Day cite time pressure after a disaster as one important reason. In such circumstances, NGOs operate in "an environment of trauma, grievance and emergency." The argument is that there is not enough time to implement "a locally contextual, participatory housing delivery scheme." Another reason mentioned by NGOs is the absence of donor support with funds and time. Finally, the authors note that the failure of consultation is the result "of complex and interrelated issues.… Our experience suggests that success is often measured by the number of people helped or houses built — a relevant measurement to be sure, but … agency mandate and measures are only a part of the story. Communities matter, too, and the cohesion impacts they suffer from non-participatory housing delivery models do not have to exist. Long-term satisfaction of recipients should be considered as a measure of success of housing programs."[57]

Karen Valentin and Lotte Meinert make a much more troublesome statement about the relationship between Northern and Southern NGOs, between donors and beneficiaries. They state that during colonial times part of the colonization mission was to "civilize the children of the savages," who in turn will civilize "the rest, that is the adult population and society at large.… In today's global South the idea of civilizing through children has continued with the development of mass schooling systems and various other child-focused development projects, many of which depend heavily upon financial support from foreign donors."[58]

Valentin and Meinert emphasize that the primary purpose of their article is to encourage debate about the role NGOs play "as civilizing institutions in the global South." To them, the "civilizing project is … not confined to today's children only, but reflects a historical process in which children have … become objects for adult and institutional intervention.… Such civilizing projects become even more visible in the context of development intervention targeting children of the global South, because they are linked to fundamental structural inequalities in the current global order. This implies a patronization not only of children and parents, but also of nations allegedly not able to take care of their own citizens. This leads to infantilized dependency …"[59]

Other scholars focus upon the power asymmetries between Northern and Southern NGOs. After examining partnerships between three Northern NGOs (Action Aid, Christian Aid, and ICCO) and their Southern counterparts in

Ghana, India, and Nicaragua, Willem Elbers and Lau Schulpen conclude that the Northern NGOs alone set the rules that govern the relationship, "based on their own norms, values, and beliefs; similarities and differences between the rules of the three agencies can, above all, be attributed to the corresponding and diverging nature of their norms, values, and beliefs; and informal rules allow more flexibility in their use. Whether this is beneficial for the Southern partners' room to maneuver depends on individual project officers, who are responsible for interpreting and applying the rules, and the partners' ability to conduct negotiations."[60]

In examining the role of NGOs in international climate change negotiations, Marika Gereke and Tanja Bruhl argue that even though NGOs play a greater role than before in the development of "international norms, in the implementation process as well as during monitoring and when a sanction is imposed," Northern and Southern NGOs "tend to pursue different perspectives which are unevenly represented" at these negotiations. The "NGO community consists of heterogenous actors who do not strive for universally admired principles, but rather promote particular interests."[61]

Because of the inequalities between "the Global North and the Global South, [Gereke and Rruhl assert that] Northern and Southern NGOs tend to have different perspectives on climate change which are very unevenly represented in international climate change negotiations. NGOs from the Global North up to now make up most NGOs taking part in international climate change negotiations, while the Global South is still underrepresented in these negotiations ..." Therefore, "the inclusion of NGOs does not necessarily enhance the legitimacy and democracy of international negotiations but, on the contrary, may contribute to an even more unjust system of global governance."[62]

A significant impediment NGOs are confronted with is their strong dependency on government financing, which then puts into question their connection to their constituents. NGOs can be understood as an extension of the state. Thus, NGOs in many cases try to conform to the expectations and demands of governments providing funding. Ultimately, the legitimacy of these NGOs is put at risk. Mulalic, who in her article on Muslim women's NGOs in Bosnia-Herzegovina is complementary of these NGOs, also notes that, being religious, "Muslim women's NGOs were not targeting Western donors. Besides, Western donors entirely neglected religious NGOs considering them as being exclusive and against [the] multiethnic state of Bosnia-Herzegovina. Therefore, Muslim [women's] NGOs were forced to seek support from Islamic donors. However, Islamic donors as Western ones have their own agendas in terms of allocating donated resources and, thus, the promotion of specific objectives through Muslim women's NGOs."[63] To combat the problem of dependency upon donors, Anna Qhanyan, in her article on the microfinance sector in Bosnia-Herzegovina after the 1995 Dayton Peace Accords, argues that "only under certain well-defined network conditions are NGOs able to defy donor policy preferences and pursue their own policy directions. Within such networks, donors witness an attenuation of their otherwise substantial financial and political power, and a consequent disconnect between their preferences and final policy outcomes as ultimately realized."[64]

As already discussed, LNGOs depend on the state as well as INGOs, other civil society groups, and philanthropic foundations. It is expected that at some point private aid will exceed funding from donor governments. This development raises questions not only of dependence but also about the impact and accountability of private development assistance. "These questions have been thrown into sharper relief by the recent emergence of 'philanthrocapitalism' — the use of business thinking by large new donors to transform philanthropy, coupled with the deployment of market mechanisms on a much larger scale to promote development and social change."[65]

Although "philanthrocapitalism" provides additional funding and ideas about development and a welcome challenge to more traditional ways of raising funds, "its potential impact and the depth of its innovation have been oversold in the current wave of publicity that surrounds the Clinton Global Initiative ... and others. Over time, and because the same lessons and constraints tend to operate on all development-assistance providers, 'philanthrocapitalism' will likely come to resemble other forms of private aid, integrating into the international system rather than replacing or displacing other actors, and that will be a cause for celebration."[66]

Such dependence upon the state affects the legitimacy of NGOs. When such dependence occurs, one could raise the following question: Whose interests do these NGOs represent? Do they represent the people whose voices are not being heard and who are in need of the NGO services? Or do they represent the interests of their donors? The legitimacy problem becomes more serious in states where the government is closely allied with certain NGOs. As in the case of Greece, the government often promotes NGO members to run for parliament. This problem is especially acute in nondemocratic states where governments establish their own NGOs or allow NGOs founded by individuals to operate under very strict guidelines (as in the case of China and other nondemocratic states). Of course, many of these NGOs, based on the definitions given previously, are not regarded by some as legitimate NGOs or they are "private organizations" or "hybrid" ones.

In some cases, because funding from the state and other sources is not available, NGOs become for-profit organizations to sustain themselves as Khieng and Dahles discuss in their article about NGOs in Cambodia. They argue that dependence on the state and other external sources of revenue leads to dependence, "goal displacement, reduced organizational autonomy, and top-down accountability. Funding from commercial activities is more predictable and potentially promotes bottom-up accountability and increases organizational autonomy but may conflict with the mission-drift of NGOs."[67]

In an associated work about Western-style NGOs in Kazakhstan and other Central Asian countries, Tamara G. Nezhina and Aigerim R. Ibrayeva, state that they "are weak and unsustainable." Many of these NGOs are dependent on foreign donors for financial resources and they do not develop local networks for support. Among the factors responsible for the ineffectiveness of NGOs in this region include the following: "[People] in Kazakhstan select government and family as major providers of social assistance when given a choice. NGOs in Kazakhstan are not effective in advocacy and service rendering because local culture is not conducive to smooth functioning of a new institution.... Western societal models do not fit Kazakhstan societal models and that 'one size does not fit all.' ... [Cultural] incompetence and arrogance may be a factor of institutional failure."[68]

Similar but more extensive comments about NGOs as well as grassroots organizations (GROs) are made by Michael Edwards and David Humle in their study on the impact of official aid on NGOs. The authors point out that since the end of the Cold War, bilateral and multilateral agencies have pursued a New Policy Agenda which put much emphasis on the role of NGOs and GROs in alleviating poverty, promoting social welfare, and developing civil society. In addition, the New Policy Agenda places much attention on good democratic governance as essential to a healthy economy.[69]

The primacy afforded to NGOs and GROs as the implementers of the New Policy Agenda has led to a dramatic increase in aid to and through them as well as NGOs becoming more dependent on foreign aid. Even though this is not a new phenomenon, it raises many questions about "NGO performance and accountability, NGO-state relations, and the ability of NGOs to act independently in pursuing their goals." Specifically, Edwards and Humle hypothesize that official funding:

Encourages NGOs to become providers of social and economic services on a much larger scale than hitherto, even though their long-term comparative advantage in this field is doubtful.

Compromises the performance of NGOs and GROs in other areas of development activity such as institutional development and advocacy.

Weakens the legitimacy of NGOs and GROs as independent actors in society.

Distorts the accountability of NGOs and GROs away from grassroots and internal constituencies, and overemphasizes short-term, quantitative outputs.

If these hypotheses, the authors note, are true, the ability of NGOs and GROs to be effective vehicles in delivering the New Policy Agenda could be in doubt.[70]

Edwards and Humle reach the following conclusions: The greater availability of funding has led to an explosion in the number of small and large NGOs. But the evidence does not necessarily support the position that NGOs provide services more cost-effectively than governments.

> Claims that NGOs reach 'the poorest of the poor' are often inaccurate, however, as had been demonstrated in the case of NGO credit schemes.... Even taken together, the largest NGOs in Bangladesh ... reach less than 20 percent of landless households in the country.[71]

Sustaining large-scale services by NGOs has also been questioned. Almost all NGOs involved in service delivery depend on subsidies from foreign donors, resources that are often denied to governments. "Were ministries of health and education allowed access to resources on this scale, it is argued, then over time they too would be able to provide services cost-effectively. Indeed, the widening gap between government and NGO resources makes state inefficiency a 'self-perpetuating reality.'" Many are concerned about the long-term impact on the quality of services for all. "Influential and well-funded NGOs may be able to concentrate resources in regions and sectors that might not be most important for national development, with a patchwork quilt of services of varying quality emerging against a background of weak central oversight."[72]

In examining the politics of international development aid in Sub-Saharan Africa (SSA) and more specifically Mozambique, Alex Arnall et al. note that scholars have paid much attention to the relationship between Western donors, national political elites, and the ruling Frelimo Party. "Relatively less consideration, however, has been directed towards the sharp rise in numbers of international and national NGOs across SSA since the commencement of IMF-induced economic reforms in the mid-1980s. In Mozambique, NGOs are primarily seen as service-deliverers, mainly to remote rural areas where state institutions have little reach. Many have also adopted an advocacy role, one that aims to reconfigure local power relationships to provide marginalized groups, such as women, with the opportunity to hold local leaders to account. However, concerns have been raised over the use of NGOs as 'legitimizing tools' in the New Policy Agenda being pursued by international financial institutions. These fears have led to claims that NGOs have fueled growing inequality in rural areas of Mozambique by channeling resources to local elites."[73]

Although there some success stories, numerous scholars lament the role of NGOs and GROs in the democratization process. Many NGOs are not likely to have an important impact in regard to political reform because governments are becoming more adept in containing the activities of NGOs through regulations and by trying to fragment the NGO movement, because NGOs themselves "have failed to develop effective strategies to promote democratization." Furthermore, the greater dependence on foreign funding has also put into question the legitimacy of NGOs. "[If] NGOs are becoming more responsive to external concerns, are substituting for government and are growing larger on this basis of foreign funding, what is happening to the links — to their values and mission, and to their relationships with the poor, supporters and others — through which they derive their right to intervene in development?"[74]

Based on the abovementioned arguments, how does the New Policy Agenda affect the accountability of NGOs and GROs? First, there is fear that foreign donor funding could "reorient accountability upward, away from grassroots, supporters and staff." Second, the large-scale donor funding "may result in problems of probity, especially where internal management and financial systems are originally based on informality and trust." Third, closer relations with donors could lead further away from self-regulation to greater regulation from the state. This, of course, does not mean that there are no problems with self-regulation, or that self-regulation would lead to greater accountability, "but the informal consultative processes and codes of ethics that characterize the voluntary sector in many countries have preserved a balance between flexibility, innovation and regulation. More formal procedures may reduce NGO capacities."[75]

In an article published in the *Guardian* on August 17, 2012, Mark Tran discusses the deepening faultline among NGOs over the future of development. Tran refers to a paper by Nicola Banks and David Hulme where the authors assert that NGOs have lost their way. Having begun as grassroots development bodies — heroic organizations with innovative agendas — NGOs have become "bureaucratic, depoliticized creatures that respond more to the dictates of donors than the people whose interests they claim to represent." In response to this paper, Duncan Green of Oxfam GB objected to the criticism by saying that it was based on "sweeping generalizations, argument by assertion, 'dodgy stats,' and the lack of case studies and interviews with NGOs themselves."[76]

A further difficulty confronting NGOs is their desire for survivability. This leads many of them to have multiple mandates, "which may diminish both their sense of mission and their capacity to provide effective services for their clients in the developing world." And by having many mandates, NGOs expand their roles — which in turn becomes problematic. There is danger "that some NGOs will become little more than contractors for government. The greater the level of financial dependence, the more fragile the degree of independence."[77]

Didem Danis and Dilara Nazli, in their work on the relationship between NGOs and the state in Turkey regarding Syrian refugees, use the term "sub-contractors" to describe that relationship (the kind of relationship that causes many to be highly critical of NGOs). Turkey has become an immigration country, unable to control the flow of refugees. "However, when it comes to controlling migrants' stay in Turkey, it seems that the Turkish state has not lost its grip." In fact, it developed new ways of controlling the lives of refugees inside Turkey. The party in power (AKP) promotes certain NGOs and other civil society groups, especially those supportive of the state, "to fulfil the requirements of the state's responsibilities. This new approach is a selective governance model where the state delegates some of its functions of refugee reception to NGOs that it considers to be ideologically and politically akin."[78]

This cooperation between the government and NGOs has led to the adoption of policies that emphasize social assistance but, at the same time, make it difficult to advocate for the human rights of refugees. In addition, the alliance has generated other actions, including "prevalence of informal practices (tolerated or deliberately overlooked by the state); lack of transparency; overlapping of state and civil society actors; monopolization and centralization of humanitarian assistance by certain NGOs favored by the leading political actors."[79]

Related to NGOs' desire for survival is what happened at the 2003 Convention for the Safeguarding of the Intangible Cultural Heritage (ICH). Even though NGO power was limited, NGO representatives not only tried to secure their position within the 2003 Convention, they also tried to entrench "an exclusionary canon of heritage expertise and reinstating the significance of geopolitical borders between the Global North and South." Maria Fernanda Escallon shows that NGOs utilized the convention to "consolidate global hierarchies of expertise.... Heritage has become an international language of political currency for pursuing recognition and financial investment.... NGO delegates use the language of expertise and the networks provided by ICH to create boundaries and protect their power among NGOs."[80]

Despite the dramatic growth in the number of NGOs, "the geographical imbalance and power differential between representatives are great. This situation highlights how ICH governance is paradoxically based on the creation and maintenance of borders, and a hierarchical interplay between members with unequal power." Furthermore, the 2003 Convention also shows that "the political debate around ICH is restructuring, moving further away from the protection of local communities' cultural rights, and closer to the entrenchment of hierarchical entitlements."[81]

In discussing the role of foreign donors in Cambodia, Khieng and Dahles note that the largest source of revenue is foundation grants. Such heavy dependence on foreign donors creates serious problems. Among them, the "fluctuation of donor money reduces the ability to sustain both activities and benefits to communities." There are examples of NGOs that modified their mission in their struggle for survival. "These NGOs are willing to engage in projects of any kind that could sustain their survival, even if the new engagement involves stepping out of their own expertise and mission."[82]

Masako Tanaka makes a comparable argument related to the desire for survivability and how it could be detrimental not only to NGOs but also to rights-based organizations (RBOs) while examining the changing roles of NGOs in Nepal. The author contends that NGOs in Nepal are at a crossroads. Some of them continue to receive funding on "behalf of RHOs for their own survival without trying to establish equitable relations with RHOs." Even though some of them employ people from excluded groups, there are few NGOs working with RHOs as partners and making attempts to build the capacity of RHOs. "NGOs either simply ignore them or avoid building the RHOs' capacities due to the fear of losing their own position and resources. … NGOs can fulfil their role as capacity developer and be accepted by RHOs if they are professional and committed to making them inclusive. NGOs have their own hidden agenda — to gain popularity in civil society, keep employment opportunities, and receive funding. Finding new roles may also fulfil their interests, but it is important for funding agencies to identify NGOs that can surely contribute to RHOs and inclusive aid."[83]

Johanna Simeant, in analyzing the internationalization/globalization of four French NGOs — Médecins du Monde, Médecins Sans Frontières, Action Contre la Faim, and Handicap International, concludes that even though "value diffusion" is a main reason for going global, the reasons for NGOs to go international are related to competition among them. The growing competition compels them "to adapt themselves in order to expand their ability to obtain human and financial resources, both public and private …"[84]

As stated previously, NGOs are special interest groups and as such many of them "suffer … from tunnel vision, judging every public act by how it affects their particular interest. Generally, they have limited capacity for large-scale endeavors, and as they grow, the need to sustain growing budgets can compromise the independence of mind that is their greatest asset. The fact that NGOs do not have to think about policy trade-offs, or the overall impact of their causes can even be harmful. A society in which the piling up of special interests replaces a single strong voice for the common good is unlikely to fare well."[85]

As interest groups, NGOs resemble political parties in that they depend on their members "for funding and answer to them for their policies." Since they depend on this grassroots funding for their survival, NGOs try to expand their base, which often leads to competition with other organizations. But NGOs differ from political parties as they are not accountable to the people. And even though they claim to speak on behalf of the public, "their main responsibility is always to themselves."[86]

The emphasis on maximizing membership leads to a "tendency to play to the gallery, and straightforward infighting." For organizations whose officers are not elected but have tremendous influence upon the lives of many people, trust is essential for their success. NGOs, especially aid ones, carry great responsibility because their work affects primarily the lives of the poorest among us. They tend to raise much money because they need it and because they are usually smaller and more flexible than government agencies. "However, some groups are themselves now as large as a small government agency — and as bureaucratic."[87]

NGOs are also expensive. According to a report written on behalf of UNICEF in 1995, health services set up by NGOs in Mozambique cost at least ten times more than those provided by the government. These NGOs were spending "more in two provinces than the entire national health budget — and that rather than use local doctors they were flying in foreign experts...." In another case, "aid agencies had concentrated too much on isolated projects instead of helping governments to provide essential services such as health and education. The success of aid agencies ... should be measured by how soon they leave a country, not by how long they stay." . . . "Yet however well intentioned, every NGO has to answer to the people who pay the bills. Accountability is central to the debate about NGOs' role in global decision-making. Critics claim that they are hardly a democratic substitute for governments.... After all, ..., democracies are often not very democratic."[88]

It is of import at this point to make a significant distinction between "practical accountability (for the use of inputs, the way activities are performed, and outputs) and strategic accountability for INGOs' performance in relation to their mission." Research has found that INGOs are inclined to use quality assurance programs to achieve practical accountability. However, "... this kind of accountability will not necessarily enable INGOs to achieve their mission to alleviate poverty and eliminate injustice." In addition, the heavy use of practical accountability has "led to a number of gaps in INGO accountability."[89]

For INGOs to achieve their mission, they must put much more emphasis on strategic forms of accountability. These forms will be geared toward dramatically changing "those social, economic, and political structures that promote poverty." One path that INGOs could follow to enhance "their strategic accountability is to establish a conceptual framework that enables them to integrate their mission and values into policies and practice."[90]

Democratic accountability is central to all kinds of NGOs including faith-based NGOs. Shawn Teresa Flanigan, in examining faith-based NGOs in Romania, focuses on "the freedom of expression rights of nonprofit organizations and the freedom of association rights of their clientele." The author notes that while the Romanian NGOs under consideration were able to maintain their freedom of expression rights when accepting public funding, their employees were involved "in overt evangelism of their clients." This, of course, infringed upon the clients' rights of association.[91]

As Western donors continue to praise the role of NGOs in international development, they become involved in development and democratization activities in countries that are suffering from ethnic and religious conflict. "While the ethnic and religious identities of NGOs may prove a benefit in reaching particular underserved communities, a history of contentious relationships between ethnic and religious groups may cause such development partnerships to demonstrate voluntary failure in ways previously unnoted. In the case of Romania … administrative discretion played a role in how NGO staff expressed their religious views toward clientele from a variety of faiths. While Romania has distinct ethnolinguistic and religious minority groups, conflict between these groups has been relatively peaceful in comparison to other countries in the Balkans. However, one can imagine that similar behavior by NGO staff in a country characterized by higher levels of discord could be much more problematic for development efforts."[92]

It was discussed previously that one of the primary reasons for the dramatic growth of NGOs during the past few decades is globalization and the neoliberal agenda. Neoliberals emphasize individual rights, the free market, and the necessity to limit the influence of the state as much as possible. Neoliberals are especially critical of what they consider control of the welfare state by NGOs. They believe that all individuals act in their own self-interest, and the only constraint on pursuing one's self-interest is the free market. As a result, neoliberals prefer private rather than public provision of goods. They are particularly critical of welfare spending and welfare lobbies. "They argue that the welfare state and its services operate in the interest of the well-paid bureaucrats and social workers who administer them rather than the interest of the disadvantaged consumers whom they are intended to serve. These producers of the welfare services (it is argued) have a vested interest in maintaining and expanding welfare services that has little to do with alleviating poverty and far more to do with enriching themselves."[93]

The prominence of the neoliberal agenda promoted by governments and various multinational organizations and institutions such as the IMF, the World Bank, and the WTO has led to a significant reduction in the welfare services offered by the state. This development has very much contributed to the increased role of NGOs in order to fill the gap in welfare services. NGOs have emerged as important "sources of resistance to the global free market agenda."[94]

But this, of course, is not the end of the story about NGOs as progressive organizations trying to promote more equal, participatory, and sustainable development. There are those who argue that NGOs have been "co-opted by neoliberalism, functioning in ways to maintain systemic inequality." The progressive element of NGOs has been compromised for many reasons. "NGOs may have initially grown within the cracks and fissures left by the unmet needs of a capitalist, patriarchal, and racist world system. However, the incredibly expansion of NGOs has primarily been a consequence of ... decades of a neo-liberal focus on privatization." Beginning with the Reagan/ Thatcher politics, bilateral as well as multilateral organizations put much emphasis on the rationale that "imperfect markets are better than imperfect states. As a compromise between funding social programs through governments and complete laissez-faire, NGOs became an important vehicle for development funds with consequences that seriously undermined their progressive potential."[95]

The critics of neoliberalism argue that through the adoption of market and business-based practices, donors often undermine the independence of NGOs. NGOs are seen by many as the spaces where social issues and needs are addressed through participatory practices. But the neoliberal practices leave little room for NGOs to maneuver. "It is commonly understood that as a result of increased donor control, much of [NGOs'] discretionary judgment is reduced, along with their ability to mobilize their local, contextualized knowledge for the public good."[96]

After examining a long-standing Canadian development NGO, CECI, Anne-Marie Duval and Yves Gendron note that NGOs could successfully respond to the "neoliberal hegemony" and "cultivate a counter-discourse promoting the creation of spaces for participation and deliberation ... The CECI case study suggests [NGOs] may attempt to shape ideas that circulate in the field by constructing a reputation of expertise in hybridizing donors' market imperatives to the social realities of the field. This expertise develops and plays out through tactics aiming to legitimize and make desirable some hybrid artifacts and, in so doing, promote certain underlying ideas — most notably how participatory imperatives can be taken into account when intervening in a given community."[97]

The neoliberal agenda and the emphasis on privatization have led to the reduction of government sponsored social services including health services. But as with most matters of contention, not everyone agrees with this assertion. In opposition to this argument, Amanda Murdie and Alexander Hicks assert that INGOs "create increased demand for governmental health services through three mechanisms: 1. Indirectly affecting the policy-making climate, 2. Aiding domestic NGO and health activists in their efforts, and 3. Directly pressuring governments for increased health spending themselves.

Given these mechanisms, health INGOs, although typically supplying health services of their own within the country, should augment pressure for public service provision by the state and, it follows, lead to increased state health spending."[98]

In many countries competition among NGOs for funding is immense. Often, those who succeed undertake a more compromising , "if not openly right-wing" position, and agree to promote the development agenda of the donors. The result of this is NGOs go from partners to contractors: "instead of forging partnerships with funders and communities, NGOs become contractors implementing the funder's agenda in the community.... Rather than contributing to sustainable poverty alleviation, NGOs, despite their best efforts, have, at a systemic level contributed to sustaining poverty. Maintaining poverty and inequality is an integral part of the new and old policy agenda of capitalism. The NGO phenomenon has supported this agenda most strongly by contributing to the delegitimation of the State."[99]

To the dismay of many, at times NGOs in numerous places, developed and developing, become corrupted. A clear and often in the news example is Nigeria. As Daniel Jordan Smith asserts, "[one] of the reigning jokes in contemporary Nigeria ... is that when students complete their education they have two options besides likely unemployment: founding a church or starting an NGO." The essence of this joke is a commentary about the difficulties related to poverty and the creativity of Nigerians trying to "seek advantage in circumstances of great constraint." It is obvious that only a small number of Nigerians can make a living by establishing a church or by finding an NGO. But the proliferation of NGOs and churches in Nigeria beginning in the 1990s has been dramatic, and it has led to significant "discourse about corruption in these domains."[100]

Elite control of the relationship between Nigeria and foreign donors is one of the major reasons for the corruption and the maintenance of inequality in the country. Wealthy donors, often Western ones, have embraced the neoliberal agenda with its emphasis on privatization and disdain for government offered social programs. The result has been more financial resources going to NGOs. The response from the Nigerian elites has been the creation of NGOs for the purpose of controlling these resources and funneling "a disproportionate share of development aid into their own pockets."[101]

Foreign donors "and their expatriate development agents in Nigeria" who "prefer to see themselves as watchdogs against corruption," often perpetuate inequalities. Stories about corruption in Nigeria are told by expatriates who reward themselves for "handsomely ... 'aiding' Nigeria. The reality is that while local elites are often stealing huge sums of money and expatriates are living lifestyles they could not afford even in their wealthy homelands, many ordinary Nigerians feel compelled to participate in what Westerners view as corruption [that] simply in order to survive. The stories about Nigerian corruption are so pervasive in expatriate discourse serve to mask the degree to which many development programs depend on collaboration between donors and local elites. The ideals promoted in development rhetoric are often belied by the realities of how development projects become vehicles for corruption and mechanisms for the reproduction of inequality."[102]

Glen W. Wright offers a critical assessment of NGOs as an instrument used to promote Western hegemony. Since the end of World War II, the author says, the number of NGOs has grown significantly under the New Policy Agenda, "with Western donor states emphasizing the role of NGOs in democratization and service provision. Donors have gained the power to set the development agenda and NGOs have slowly become Trojan horses for global neoliberalism."[103]

Wright argues that Western donors utilize NGOs to maintain their dominance through the following means: 1. By providing a significant percentage of the funding needed by NGOs and thus undermining their legitimacy; 2. By distorting accountability — instead of being accountable to their beneficiaries ("the people whose lives their activities affect"), NGOs become accountable to their foreign donors; 3. By the-*isation* of NGOs, which "refers to a number of processes, including bureaucratization, technicization, homogenization, and corporatization, which can turn NGOs into propagators of Western hegemony. This focus on technical management and bureaucracy has homogenized the approach to development, leaving no space for a heterogenous mix of ideas and approaches that arise from varied local contexts and that are necessary for social change. Instead, that context and diversity is eradicated by forcing in the Western perspective."; and 4. By using NGOs to provide services, Western donors displace governments of the developing world. "Thus, weakening state provision ... becomes self-perpetuating as Western donors both fail to provide the support needed to strengthen state provision, and further undermine it by providing superior private provision through NGOs. This again highlights the disjuncture between NGO and beneficiary, and the lack of accountability between the two."[104]

So, are NGOs progressive organizations or are they a neoliberal tool? They are both. "There are many reasons to believe that the NGO phenomenon is more business-as-usual: the agenda of NGOs is determined within the hegemonic world system, even progressive NGOs are co-opted, and even good strategies have a difficult time of success. Nonetheless, on the whole, NGOs still constitute one of the most widespread challenges to current development strategies, especially as they form linkages with other elements of civil society and foster the development of progressive social movements. The serious commitments many NGOs have to social justice and grassroots activism continue to make them an important force in the struggle for a fair and sustainable development."[105]

Many NGOs, like other organizations and institutions founded by human beings, play a positive role and contribute to the betterment of societies while others are characterized by corruption, mismanagement, etc. and have proven to be an impediment to progress.

NOTES

1. Beyer, 522.
2. Chapman and Fisher, 158.
3. Holmen and Jirsrom, 430.
4. Ibid., 441.
5. Ibid., 441–442.
6. Ibid., 442.
7. Grugel, 103.
8. Ibid., 103–104.
9. Joel Beinin, "Civil Society, NGOs, and Egypt's 2011 Popular Uprising," *The South Atlantic Quarterly* 113, no. 2 (Spring 2014): 397–398.
10. Euiyoung Kim, 878–880.
11. Ibid., 892.
12. Brian Grodsky, "Co-Optation or Empowerment? The Fate of Pro-Democracy NGOs after the Rose Revolution," *Europe-Asia Studies* 64, no. 9 (November 2012): 1684, 1702.
13. Ibid., 1702–1703.
14. Ibid., 1704–1705.
15. Orysia Lutsevych, "Black Sea Region: Missing Pieces of the Civil Society Puzzle," *German Marshall Fund of the United States* (2013): 1–3.
16. Ibid., 3–5.
17. Ibid., 7.
18. Pauline Jones Luong and Erika Weinthal, "The NGO Paradox: Democratic Goals and Non-Democratic Outcomes in Kazakhstan," *Europe-Asia Studies* 51, no. 7 (November 1999): 1275–1278.
19. Ibid., 1280–1281.
20. Ibid., 1281.
21. Fiona B. Adamson, "International Democracy Assistance in Uzbekistan and Kyrgyzstan: Building Civil Society from the Outside," in *The Power and Limits of NGOs: A Critical Look at Building Democracy in Eastern Europe and Eurasia*, ed. Sarah E. Mendelson and John K. Glenn (New York: Columbia University Press, 2002), 177–178, 199.
22. Ibid., 199–200.
23. Ibid., 200.

24. Wesley Longhofer et al., "NGOs, INGOs, and Environmental Policy Reform, 1970-2010," *Social Forces* 94, no. 4 (June 2016): 1743.

25. Ivan Franceschini, "Labor NGOs in China: A Real Force for Political Change?" *The China Quarterly* no. 218 (June 2014): 490.

26. Ibid., 490.

27. Phillips and Goodwin, 569–570.

28. Ibid., 570, 582.

29. Beyer, 528.

30. Thomas G. Weiss and Leon Gordenker, *NGOs, the UN, and Global Governance* (Boulder, Colorado: Lynne Rienner, 1996), 19.

31. Seamus Cleary, *The Role of NGOs under Authoritarian Political Systems* (London: MacMillan Press LTD., 1997), 3, 228–229.

32. Jae-Eun Noh, "The Role of NGOs in Building CSR Discourse around Human Rights in Developing Countries," *Cosmopolitan Civil Societies: An Interdisciplinary Journal* 9, no. 1 (2017): 13–14.

33. Ibid., 14.

34. Kristina Hahn and Anna Holzscheiter, "The Ambivalence of Advocacy: Representation and Contestation in Global NGO Advocacy for Child Workers and Sex Workers," *Global Society: Journal of Interdisciplinary International Relations* 27, no. 4 (October 2013): 497.

35. Francois Pierre-Louis, "The Haiti Earthquake of 2010: The Politics of a Natural Disaster," *Journal of Black Studies* 42, no. 2 (March 2011): 195–196.

36. Ibid., 186.

37. Ibid., 198–199.

38. Mark Schuller, *Killing with Kindness: Haiti, International Aid, and NGOs* (New Brunswick, New Jersey: Rutgers University Press, 2012), 173–174.

39. Ibid., 174.

40. Kevin Edmonds, "Beyond Good Intentions: The Structural Limitations of NGOs in Haiti," *Critical Sociology* 39, no. 3 (2013): 439.

41. Ibid., 450.

42. Chelsey L. Kivland, "Unmaking the State in 'Occupied' Haiti," *PoLAR: Political and Legal Anthropology Review* 35, no. 2 (November 2012): 248.

43. Philip Awekeya et al., "A Critical View on the Role of NGOs in Systemic Capacity Building: Insights from Projects for Promoting Access to Water and Self-Sufficiency in Food Production in Northern Ghana," *Journal of Organizational Transformation and Social Change* 14, no. 1 (2017): 1.

44. Ibid., 23.

45. Schuller, 175.

46. Ibid., 175–176.

47. Eric Werker and Faisal Z. Ahmed, "What Do non-governmental Organizations Do?" *The Journal of Economic Perspectives* 22, no. 2 (Spring 2008): 87–88.

48. Ibid., 88–89.

49. Beyer, 532.

50. Nadeem Malik and Ahsan Rana, "Civil Society in Pakistan: An Exclusive Discourse of Projectization," *Dialectical Anthropology* 44 (2020): 54.

51. Ibid., 54–55.

52. Afef Benessaieh, "Global Civil Society: Speaking in Northern Tongues?" *Latin American Perspectives* 38, no. 6 (November 2011): 69.

53. Ibid., 71.

54. Ibid., 83–84.

55. Ibid., 84.

56. Lisa Strychar and Jennifer Day, "Community Assessment of NGO Housing Delivery: Lessons from Port Vila, Vanuatu," *Development in Practice* 29, no. 4 (2019): 473–474.

57. Ibid., 474.

58. Karen Valentin and Lotte Meinert, "The Adult North and the Young South: Reflections on the Civilizing Mission of Children's Rights," *Anthropology Today* 25, no. 3 (June 2009): 23.

59. Ibid., 23.

60. Willem Elbers and Lau Schulpen, "Corridors of Power: The Institutional Design of the North-South NGO Partnerships," *Voluntas: International Journal of Voluntary and Nonprofit Organizations* 24 (2013): 48.

61. Marika Gereke and Tanja Bruhl, "Unpacking the Unequal Representation of Northern and Southern NGOs in International Climate Change Politics," *Third World Quarterly* 40, no. 5 (2019): 870.

62. Ibid., 871.

63. Mulalic, 442.

64. Anna Ohanyan, "Policy Wars for Peace: Network Model of NGO Behavior," *International Studies Review* 11, no. 3 (September 2009): 477.

65. Michael Edwards, "Why 'Philanthropicapitalism' Is Not the Answer: Private Initiatives and International Development," in *Doing Good or Doing Better: Development Policies in a Globalizing World*, ed. Monique Kremer, Peter van Lieshout, and Robert Went (Amsterdam: Amsterdam University Press, 2009), 237.

66. Ibid., 250.

67. Khieng and Dahles, 1412.

68. Tamara G. Nezhina and Aigerim R. Ibrayeva, "Explaining the Role of Culture and Traditions in Functioning of Civil Society Organizations in Kazakhstan," *ISTR* 24 (2013): 335, 356.

69. Michael Edwards and David Humle, "Too Close for Comfort? The Impact of Official Aid on non-governmental Organizations," *Current Issues in Comparative Education* 1, no. 1 (November 1998): 1.

70. Ibid., 3.

71. Ibid., 4.

72. Ibid., 4–5.

73. Alex Arnall et al., "NGOs, Elite Capture and Community-Driven Development: Perspectives in Rural Mozambique," *The Journal of Modern African Studies* 51, no. 2 (June 2013): 307.

74. Edwards and Hulme, 7–8.

75. Ibid., 11–12.

76. Mark Tran, "Is the Faultline among NGOs Over the Future of Development Deepening?," *Guardian*, August 17, 2012, https://www.globalpolicy.org/ngos/introduction/general-analysis-of-the-role-of-ngos/51841-is-the-faultline-among-ngos-Over-the-future-of-development .

77. Cited in Grugel, 102.

78. Didem Danis and Dilara Nazli, "A Faithfull Alliance between the Civil Society and the State: Actors and Mechanisms of Accommodating Syrian Refugees in Istanbul," *International Migration* 57, no. 2 (2019): 153.

79. Ibid., 153.

80. Maria Fernanda Escallon, "Negotiating Intangibles: The Power, Place, and Prestige of NGOs in Heritage Governance," *International Journal of Heritage Studies* 26, no. 8 (2020): 719, 732.

81. Ibid., 732–733.

82. Khieng and Dahles, 1424.

83. Masako Tanaka, "The Changing Roles of NGOs in Nepal: Promoting Emerging Rights-Holder Organizations for Inclusive Aid," *Voluntas: International Journal of Voluntary and Nonprofit Organizations* 22 (2011): 515.

84. Johanna Simeant, "What Is Going Global? The Internationalization of French NGOs 'Without Borders,'" *Review of International Political Economy* 12, no. 5 (December 2005): 851.

85. Michael Bond, "The Backlash against NGOs," in *The Globalization Reader*, eds. Frank J. Lechner and John Boli (Malden, MA: Blackwell Publishing, 2004), 279.

86. Ibid., 279.

87. Ibid., 279.

88. Ibid., 280.

89. Sue Cavill and M. Sohail, "Increasing Accountability: A Framework for International NGOs," *Development in Practice* 17, no. 2 (April 2007): 231.

90. Ibid., 231, 247.

91. Shawn Teresa Flanigan, "Paying for God's Work: A Rights-Based Examination of Faith-Based NGOs in Romania," *Voluntas: International Journal of Voluntary and Nonprofit Organizations* 18 (2007): 156, 173.

92. Ibid., 174.

93. Philip Mendes, "The NGO Wars: Why Neo-Liberals Are Trashing Non-Government and Advocacy Groups," *Social Alternatives* 24, no. 3 (2005): 40.

94. Ibid., 44.

95. Steven J. Klees, "NGOs: Progressive Force or Neo-Liberal Tool?," *Current Issues in Comparative Education* 1, no. 1 (2002): 49.

96. Anne-Marie Duval and Yves Gendron, "Creating Space for an Alternative Discourse in the Context of Neoliberal Hegemony: The Case of a Long-Standing NGO," *Administrative Theory and Praxis* 42 (2020): 62.

97. Ibid., 63, 81–82; Duval and Gendron show how CECI tries to expand its expertise "centered on a dynamic adaptation of the market and participatory (i.e., grassroots, solidarity-formed) discourses. By producing and disseminating what it hopes to be convincing hybrid artifacts (e.g., in the form of guidelines and articles) that exhibit this expertise, the NGO aims to establish the credibility needed for hybrid artifacts

(and the alternative participatory discourse that they carry) to be endorsed, solicited and eventually, adopted by donors," 62.

98. Amanda Murdie and Alexander Hicks, "Can International non-governmental Organizations Boost Government Services? The Case of Health," *International Organization* 67, no. 3 (Summer 2013): 541.

99. Klees, 50.

100. Daniel Jordan Smith, *A Culture of Corruption: Everyday Deception and Popular Discontent in Nigeria* (Princeton, New Jersey: Princeton University Press, 2007), 88.

101. Ibid., 110.

102. Ibid., 110–11.

103. Glen W. Wright, "NGOs and Western Hegemony: Causes for Concern and Ideas for Change," *Development in Practice* 22, no. 1 (February 2012): 123.

104. Ibid., 125–128.

105. Klees, 51–52.

Chapter 4

Non-governmental Organizations in the Global System

If NGOs operate across boundaries, as many do, and if NGOs are a force to be reckoned with, as many are, then it is imperative to survey their place in the global system. Once again, as with the functions performed by NGOs, NGOs have their supporters and detractors regarding their place in the global system.

It is contended that we live in a world of politics of astonishing size. In a world of so many large states, one might wonder why people are interested in investigating an even larger and more perplexing system, the system of global governance and the politics that influence it. Many scholars argue that for ethical and moral reasons human beings must pay attention to global governance. Different analysts try to explain the origins and nature of global governance and many give different answers to the moral questions raised.[1]

The most persuasive analysts emphasize the contemporary global governance avoids attacking state sovereignty, favors piece-meal responses to crises, and has emerged at a time when creative intellectual leadership was not matched by courageous political leadership. Consequently, for some time to come global governance and its politics will provide an insufficient answer to the moral questions that compel us to look at what world government there is. Global governance is likely to remain inefficient, incapable of shifting resources from the world's wealthy to the world's poor, pro-market, and relatively insensitive to the concerns of labor and the rural poor, despite the progressive role that it recently may have played in promoting liberal democracy and the empowering of women.[2]

This very pessimistic, or realistic to some, view of global governance is a compelling reason for insisting upon the examination of global governance and the roles performed not only by states but other organizations and institutions including NGOs.

While the label non-governmental organizations imply autonomy from government, "NGOs are often intimately connected with their home governments in relationships that are both ambivalent and dynamic, sometimes cooperative, sometimes contentious, sometimes both simultaneously.... [A] key factor affecting the orientation of NGOs and their ability to organize freely is sympathetic public space provided by governments. This space may be provided unwillingly and only when governments are prodded by INGOs or international development agencies. In the past decade, many governments in the third world have been forced by economic necessity and international agencies to cede recognition and autonomy to NGOs. Not surprisingly, governments, on their part, have often seen NGOs as undermining state hegemony and have attempted to bring them under control through government agencies set up to service them."[3]

Even though the relationship between governments and NGOs is heterogeneous and many times uneven, NGOs have played and continue to play an increasing role in the international system. As Steve Charnovitz shows, NGOs are not a twentieth century phenomenon. They have been with us for more than two hundred years. In his exploration of the history of NGO involvement in global governance, Charnovitz discusses the following periods of NGO involvement:

Period I — Emergence (1775–1918)
Organizing for Influence
Pre-League of Nations Involvement
Period II — Engagement (1919–1934)
Paris Peace Conference
League of Nations Activities
NGO Activity Outside the League
Period III — Disengagement (1935–1944)
League of Nations Activities
NGO Activity Outside the League
Period IV — Formalization (1945–1949)
Drafting the UN Charter
Implementing Article 71
NGOs in Other UN Organizations
NGO Activity Outside the United Nations
Period V — Underachievement (1950–1971)
Period VI — Intensification (1972–1991)
Period VII — Empowerment (1992–?)[4]

Charnovitz's main conclusion is that "[although] on the whole NGOs are more influential now than ever before, in some ways NGO penetration into international organization is no deeper that it was seventy years ago. The involvement of NGOs seems to rise when governments need them and to fall when governments and international bureaucracies gain self-confidence, suggesting a cyclical pattern."[5] This is to be expected because the states, overall, are still the most important actors in the international system, and as referenced earlier in this paper, NGOs operate under numerous constraints.

The multiplicity of NGOs and social movements at the international level invites continuing evaluation of the role they play in global politics. To the realists, the states continue to be the dominant actors and NGOs are nothing more than a sideshow of global politics. But according to the literature of transnational politics, NGOs are powerful enough to "represent a new sector of influence upon states — a 'global civil society' circumscribing states' relative autonomy." Ann Marie Clark et al. present a more nuanced view of global civil society for the evaluation of transnational actors.[6]

Clark et al. assert that NGOs are here to stay. They present important issues at UN conferences, and governments permit NGO participation at these conferences. In examining the role of NGOs at three global conferences (on the environment, human rights, and women), the authors note that even though the number of NGOs increased significantly, their achievement has been uneven. NGOs expanded interactions with each other, and new rules expanded their participation. But governments do not necessarily view such interactions as very significant. There is evidence "of a deepening society of global NGOs." While NGOs continue to disagree among themselves over many crucial issues, they do expand interactions and debates. These interactions have helped "to narrow the distance between them on substantive issues. But NGOs' interactions alone are not enough to establish the existence of a global society, and states only provisionally accept NGOs' contributions to UN conference processes. Governments are standing firm in their claims to ultimate sovereignty over issues that seem the most [to] affect their ability to control the distribution of power and resources, whether at home or abroad. Military defense and models of economic development are not negotiable. Moreover, certain countries see gender relations as yet another arena to block challenges to nation-state prerogatives."[7]

Chadwick F. Alger makes a similar claim by noting that despite the greater role NGOs play in the UN system, there are significant constraints. Among them are lack of knowledge about the complex and expanding universe of the UN system; the UN is asked to do much more than ever before; and there is lack of funding for strengthening relations with NGOs. Furthermore, James Paul, an active NGO representative, says that he feels uncomfortable "with the right to participate being 'extended through practice' and suggests the need for these practices to be codified. This too represents a challenge … Would efforts to codify practice into formal rules insure the longevity of practice? Or, might efforts to write formal rules incite responses that lead to restraints on evolving practice?"[8]

NGOS AND DEMOCRATIZATION

How a government responds to NGOs is often related to the intensity of NGO mobilizations. Responsiveness, however, does not mean acceptance of NGO positions.

> When NGOs seek to engage states, most states seem to respond by calculating their interests rather than by calculating a relationship with NGOs. On the other hand, states have an incentive to respond positively to NGO efforts to participate in intergovernmental forums: they can act as representatives of popular opinion or as informed observers of governance issues at the international level, as well as help governments in the implementation of international agreements. On the other hand, NGOs demand [government] resources and principled action that governments may not willingly provide or undertake. On issues that centrally address state sovereignty, more NGO visibility only means a more forceful negative response. In the final analysis, even new kinds of global conferences on new global issues with new global participants remain partially imprisoned by traditional roles and priorities of international politics. State sovereignty sets the limits of global civil society.[9]

The emphasis placed upon NGOs beginning with the late 1980s because of the focus on democratization and good governance enable NGOs to garner a degree of influence and greater access to resources. They are considered by many as essential to well-functioning civil society, and donors show their support for greater NGO economic and political roles. The assumption is that political democracy and economic development are mutually reinforcing. "The state, market, and civil society — which we will refer to as prince, merchant, and citizen — are related in a series of virtuous circles. A basic tenet of 'NGO love' is that NGOs promote and strengthen civil society, and thus subject the prince and merchant to greater public accountability." There is, however, an element of triumphalism in this discourse. Such statements about NGOs and civil society are difficult to digest in a world "characterized by instability, fragmentation, and deepening poverty."[10]

Even though NGO contributions to democratization are recognized by a myriad of people, "NGOs are often the providers of palliatives to competing factions in conflict. Rather than promoting accountability, NGOs are perhaps 'dancing the tune of the prince,' whether the prince is a government, an insurgency movement, or a local warlord." Generally, "ANGOs [the work cited is about NGOs in Afghanistan] have had to dance to the tunes both of the donor and of the prince. These roles need to be reversed in order to make a reality of the civil society rhetoric. A starting point might be to introduce mechanisms that empower organizations within civil society, whether these be NGOs or community groups, to help to set the agenda and so call the tune."[11]

The emphasis on decentralization and devolution since the 1980s has impacted the development discourse and practice. A fundamental characteristic of decentralization and devolution in developing countries has been the assumption that it will lead to greater democratization: "more power onto the local." The goal of democratization is to increase people's participation and thus raise the presence of groups that once were excluded from decision-making. "The concept of empowerment arose from such contexts. As the renewed democratic legislations have taken a proactive line on empowerment of civil society, NGOs have stepped up their socio-political position in the policy arena."[12]

Kaoko Takahashi addresses the issue of empowerment and empowerment policy while discussing the "formulation of a new housing approach named 'enablement.' Current housing development frameworks in the Philippines adhere to the line of enablement. The national government prepares enabling legislative/institutional settings toward the improvement of informal settlements with citizen empowerment, which are to bring forward participatory planning. Above all, great emphasis is put on the internalization of NGOs' contributions. NGOs are now prescribed as a catalyst to add further dynamism to the fostering of housing development for the poor."[13]

What has been observed, at least as the case of the Philippines indicates, is that an important attribute of community empowerment "lies in ensuring access to networks of NGOs. Optimistically it is hoped that NGO empowerment has diffusing effects leading to community empowerment." Yet the matter is more complicated. "Adverse effects like excessive dependency and distorted representation may arise, engendering structural disempowerment of the subjects to be empowered by NGOs. These counterproductive consequences have a considerable impact on the emergence of vertical relationships between NGOs and communities where an increase in accessibility to more resources would magnify the vulnerability of communities."[14]

NGOS AND PARTNERSHIPS WITH GOVERNMENTS

The World Bank, despite its problematic nature as a neoliberal institution, has played an important role in promoting the idea of partnerships between governments and NGOs. The development of such partnerships was first conceived in the 1980s for mostly practical reasons. NGOs were regarded as a source of expertise, skills, and resources for development. By the 1990s,

World Bank officials thought that NGO involvement as partners could lead to a more open and accountable way of governing in developing countries. Even though there were difficulties in the 1990s with pushing forward with these partnerships, significant changes have taken place over time, and more partnerships between governments and NGOs have come to fruition.[15]

Deborah A. Brautigam and Monique Segarra, after examining Guatemala, Ecuador, and Gambia, note that three possibilities could be listed for the change in attitude toward partnerships. The first is persistent pressure from the World Bank, using debt as leverage. But "reductions in debt over the period and (in Gambia) the growth of partnerships during a suspension of lending cast doubt on this as a complete explanation." The second is that crisis might lead a new leadership to new practices, and democratic transition might lead governments to allow a more vibrant civil society. The cases examined, however, do not bear this out. The third and most likely explanation for the change is strategic social learning.[16]

Strategic social learning by governments and NGOs "is likely to be affected by similar levels of professionalism and capacity among NGOs and their government counterparts; effective bridge builders, who essentially play the role of effective teachers; and the depth of horizontal conflicts and divisions between state and society.... [The] acceptance of these new relationships, even in relatively weak and aid-dependent states, is likely to be difficult. However, the trajectory of this institutionalization will be based only partly on the power of donors to impose their view, or states to resist. A more comprehensive explanation of the politics of partnership must incorporate the social learning that takes place over time, among the three partners, and the domestic politics that facilitate or impede this process."[17]

NGOs have played a role in nation-building efforts initiated by the international community and its members. The UN, its various agencies as well as members states have worked with NGOs to implement humanitarian assistance and development programs. By nation-building in this instance is meant maintaining peace and reconstruction. The expectation is for NGOs to help reintegrate civil war refugees, to stabilize the social situation by providing services, by setting up infrastructure and setting up schools, and by influencing the nature of the political system.[18]

Among the reasons why donors are looking toward NGOs for assistance in nation-building processes is the disarray of state structures in failed states or post-conflict countries. Another reason is the general trend at the end of the Cold War to grant development resources to NGOs rather than the governments of the target countries because of corruption or in order to promote human rights and pluralism. But the role of NGOs in nation-building is a contradictory one and could be problematic. "In times of war, it depends on the skill of the parties involved in the conflict as to how they make use of

NGOs for their strategies. NGOs rarely play an active role in this phase — if they want to adhere to the principle of neutrality. If NGOs actually do become actively and effectively involved in the nation-building process during a war, those with the greatest resources have to decide to support one of the parties in the conflict. It is precisely this, however, which is inconsistent with the principle of neutrality."[19]

During the reconstruction phase, there are again two sides to the role of NGOs. Regarding state institutions that are still unable to function effectively, NGOs are crucial for providing services. But at the same time, NGOs can be an "obstacle to the development of functional state structures because of the brain, loyalty and capacity drain." Furthermore, the role of NGOs in nation-building should not be overrated. "Other external factors and players perform more important roles, i.e., donors, UN, military aid, arms trading, and foreign interests also carry more weight."[20]

Dominik Zaum notes that NGOs have become an important factor of international intervention in civil wars and in post-conflict peacebuilding efforts because of their relationship with donor governments and international organizations. Being non-state actors, NGOs have been allowed access to places government agencies have not been allowed to go, and their expertise and skills have made them desirable partners for donors. But, as a result of this close relationship, the non-state character of NGOs has been questioned. "Similarly, their involvement in peacebuilding has undermined their claims that their work is non-political."[21]

Since the end of the Cold War, NGOs have increasingly become more involved in multilateral peacekeeping operations. Simultaneously, multilateral peacekeeping operations have moved into areas previously considered mostly of interest to NGOs. "The increasingly muddied waters of peacekeeping and peacebuilding in the 1990s" make it imperative to examine the changing relationship between NGOs and multilateral operations. "The activities of NGOs, particularly those involved in development, humanitarian relief and human rights, now cut across all phases of the peacekeeping process from advocates and advisers to governments and international organizations; to close contact in field operations; to unintentional but very real source of conflict in contested settings."[22]

The greater role NGOs play in peacekeeping activities is the result of many factors. Most important, it had coincided with the decision by states and multilateral organizations to withdraw from such activities and delegate these functions to NGOs. "This development has led to increased expectations about the capacity, efficiency, effectiveness and legitimacy of NGOs in addressing complex civil conflicts." And while the work performed by NGOs has not been that different from that of other actors, "the results threaten to undermine their long-term credibility in these and other areas." If the members of the international community continue to show little desire to engage in peacekeeping operations, NGOs will continue to be asked to fill in the gaps. "In this context, the challenges facing international NGOs today … are to recognize where things go wrong in order that they do no harm and to explore, develop, and implement programs that support local people who seek alternatives to conflict."[23]

As Francis Kofi Abiew and Tom Keating assert:

> NGOs may perhaps be better positioned to work hand in hand with local forces than other institutional actors are capable of doing. However, with the rise and subsequent decline of multilateral peacekeeping operations, it is imperative to recognize that donor governments, the UN, and even NGOs have perhaps reached their political limits in terms of their willingness and ability to invest in the people, resources and programs to address and resolve many of today's conflicts. Increasingly, the burden will have to shift to the local level and the development of indigenous initiatives and capacities in addressing the root causes of conflict and supporting conflict resolution processes. Ultimately, outside NGOs can play only a supporting role.[24]

Related to the provision of health care services by NGOs, Khan et al. make interesting comments and recommendations about the role of NGOs in the FATA (Federally Administered Area) of Pakistan, comments that are applicable to other regions also afflicted by violence and where governments have little or no control. Because of the government's inability to deliver health care services, the government now must share responsibilities with NGOs. It is imperative for NGOs to strive for support from many community actors before a project is launched. It is also important to work with grassroots organizations that have immediate contact "with communities in highly divided conflict-affected environments. Microlevel projects yield quick, tangible results and are very effective in building initial trust and working relationships, which can be leveraged for further long-term projects."[25]

NGOS AND THE STATE-CENTRIC NATURE OF THE GLOBAL SYSTEM

Dianne Otto, in her article about the role of NGOs in an emerging global civil society, notes that, regarding NGOs and ECOSOC, non-governmental actors have had a significant effect on global affairs. "International organizations and movements have been very influential in shaping the discourse within which international decision making and action occurs. Concern for the environment, for women's equality, and for disarmament would not have achieved international expression without the backdrop of social and political understandings promoted by NGOs. This civil activity has supported a 'quiet revolution' in the UN system."[26]

To many scholars there are advantages to the UN using NGO personnel . Some NGOs, especially large ones, have employees who are highly trained and experienced. Many NGO staff members have capacities and expertise that are as strong as those working for international organizations. "NGO personnel are available without the customary long recruitment process or without long-term contracts." Their numbers could be expanded or contracted depending on need. "Their assignment is not subject to the vagaries of geographical distribution that inhibit UN appointments.... This expertness and flexibility could thus be particularly advantageous when western parliaments insist upon restructuring and continual adaptations that are relevant to organizational shibboleths for many domestic audiences."[27] For NGOs to expand their role even more and to assist in building a global civil society, the UN must also undergo significant transformation. The UN must reorient itself and go from being state-centric to being more "inclusive of peoples as well as states."[28] Not an easy task if we consider the state-centric worldview of the past 350 years.

A worldview that is not only state-centric, but male dominated as well. Lotsmart Fonjong brings to our attention the success NGOs have had in increasing women's access to resources such as health, credit, etc. But NGOs have had limited success in "reversing discrimination against and subordination of women. In other words, their strategic gender needs have not yet been met.... This is because the provision of strategic gender needs touch on fundamental cultural and institutional changes that might be interpreted as foreign intervention on domestic issues from international NGOs.... Interventions by the state, local and other international agencies are therefore indispensable for long-term results.... Such interventions will complement the work already done by NGOs at the level of practical gender needs. This is because the government, and men, seem to have a vested interest in women's subordination."[29]

James A. Paul points out that NGOs are diverse and of no equal influence. "In addition to the great organizations dealing with human rights, environmental protection and humanitarian assistance, there are NGOs representing industry associations ... narrowly zealous religious organizations and advocates of obscure causes ... While some NGOs are fiercely independent, others are known as the creatures of governments, businesses or even criminal interests. ... With such diversity, generalizations about NGOs can be difficult." But the one generalization Paul makes is that even though states and international organizations at times find NGOs to be "a nuisance or even threatening to their interests," officials look toward NGOs for new ideas, information, as well as credibility.[30]

Paul Almeida, in his work on social movements, makes a similar argument as James A. Paul regarding generalizations about collective mobilization by NGOs in developing countries. Almeida asserts that variations in culture, population size, economic and technological development, available natural resources, system of government, and links to the international community affect the ability of excluded groups to mobilize and the "form mobilization takes when collective action materializes."[31]

After examining central challenges facing civil society groups in developing countries with an emphasis on state repression, globalization, and transnational movements, Almeida notes that one must be cautious about generalizing regarding mobilization processes. Instead, the emphasis should be on the processes that drive large-scale mobilization and the likelihood of establishing "ties across countries in the form of transnational movements. These processes included movements resisting non-democratic governments, acts of state repression, and eroding rights. The organizational basis of the resistance is found in civil society organizations and everyday institutions such as religious bodies and public schools. In the twenty-first century, the deepening of free market globalization continues to present new challenges and harms, which in turn initiate campaigns of resistance.... Climate change acts as a more recent ecological threat, bringing [developing nations] together in transnational movement campaigns."[32]

As already mentioned, the state-centric nature of the international system is one of the major constraints placed upon NGOs. Another is restrictions imposed by individual governments, democratic and especially nondemocratic ones. For example, the Law of the People's Republic of China on Administration of Activities of Overseas Non-Governmental Organizations in the Mainland of China (Overseas NGO Law) was adopted on April 28, 2016, and came into force on January 1, 2017. To the Chinese government, the new law was an attempt to "standardize and guide the activities of overseas non-governmental organizations." But the response to this law of foreign NGOs was concern and anxiety.[33] Multiple other examples of governments imposing restrictions upon NGOs have been discussed throughout this work.

Yongjiao Yang et al. argue that although some of the provisions related to the Overseas NGO Law have been abolished for some NGO categories, "maintaining close relationships with the government remains a key survival strategy for them. It is clear that the way forward for future relationships is for the government to shift its role from that of parent to that of a client or partner of NGOs through building value-based partnerships. Further, with the increasing significance of public donations as funding sources, it is clear that the generation of public trust will be indispensable for the sustainable development of NGOs."[34]

Furthermore, Yang et al. assert that establishing these kinds of relationships and developing public trust will be a difficult task. "The NGO sector is operating on shifting sands. China is in a transitional stage, experiencing probably the largest urbanization in human history. Mass migration brings together people with different value systems and different traditions. In particular, the rural/urban interface remains fluid and is still being negotiated. Compromises must be made, consensus has yet to be reached and a cohesive understanding of national values has yet to emerge. Both the government and NGOs are having to adapt themselves to this swiftly changing society and establishing value-based partnerships in these circumstances can be fraught with difficulties."[35]

A related example of the unsteady ground upon which Chinese NGOs stand is the tension between "official and unofficial outlets of worker voice." Officially, Chinese workers are represented by the All-China Federation of Trade Unions (ACFTU). Unofficially, workers, individually and collectively, are speaking out by using a variety of methods. This tension illuminates the dilemma confronting the Chinese leadership in its efforts to prevent "worker unrest from boiling over."[36]

Chinese leaders are concerned about the growth in the number of NGOs devoted to improving the lives of Chinese workers "as potential seedbeds of independent organized labor activism." But at the same time, labor NGOs try to deal with the needs of workers and, by extension, of the regime. The regime's suspicious posture toward labor NGOs reflects in part a broader skepticism toward civil society; yet the rise of workers' collective disputes, and the involvement of some labor NGOs in those disputes, also triggers the particular anxieties that surround independent labor activism." Chinese workers, and especially migrant workers, who are even more marginalized than the rest of the workers, have looked for and have formed organizations to represent their interests. Such labor organizations represent "a challenge to the ACFTU's official monopoly on collective worker representation and attract official scrutiny and skepticism. But they are also part of a growing civil society that gradually achieved a modicum of legitimacy ... and is now under pressure."[37]

Similar conclusions are reached by Ya-Wen Lei while examining the public sphere in China. The government of China, especially under the current leadership of Xi Jinping, has used the issues of social stability and national security to justify aggressive measures "to cope with the contentious public sphere." The government has used with greater efficacy regulations, laws, and technology to enhance censorship and surveillance to legalize its actions and to penalize unwanted behavior, "as well as the promotion of big data science and cloud computing for the purpose of control." The Chinese government has also attacked important actors who have contributed to the rise of public opinion incidents, actors such as "public opinion leaders, the disadvantaged, rights defense and public interest lawyers, journalists, and activists — and staged national media trials to counteract these actors' publicity strategies." The Communist Party has also attempted to exert greater control over the media, NGOs, and Internet companies. In addition, the Chinese leadership has attempted "to promote official discourse and ideology and to assert China's cyber-sovereignty."[38]

The outcome of these measures has led to mixed results and consequences. The Chinese government has made it much more difficult for social networks to be effective and has undermined their efforts to mobilize public opinion. But the activists have not been completely silenced, and the government continues to encounter resistance from many different quarters. "Friction within the party-state can still be exploited to enable the media to speak up and challenge censorship. In addition, a highly educated middle class has not been significantly influenced by the crackdown in terms of their capacity to unite themselves and make their voices heard." Unlike the middle class, the disadvantaged find it more difficult to mobilize public opinion without help from activists, NGOs, etc. "The contentious public sphere may continue to survive and thematize some problems, but it is unlikely to become a space for the middle class if the disadvantaged do not receive support. Given no other outlet of expression or redress, the disadvantaged in China could develop a more extreme and radical response to their grievances. And if discussion of societal problems significantly decreases, the contentious public sphere could develop into a venue dedicated primarily to the expression of nationalism."[39]

Jessica C. Teets describes the relationship between the state and civil society in China as consultative authoritarianism. She argues that the decision to decentralize public welfare and to promote the delivery of "goods supported the idea of local government-civil society collaboration. This idea was undermined by international examples of civil society opposing authoritarianism and the strength of the state-led development model after the 2008 economic crisis." Teets concludes by saying that she notices "growing convergence on a new model of state-society relationship that [she calls] 'consultative authoritarianism,' which encourages the simultaneous expansion of a fairly autonomous civil society and the development of more indirect tools of state control. This model challenges the conventional wisdom that an operationally autonomous civil society cannot exist inside authoritarian regimes and that the presence of civil society is an indicator of democratization." She also notes that consultative authoritarianism leads to more resilient authoritarianism and better governance.[40]

May Farid, while recognizing the difficulties facing NGOs operating under an authoritarian regime, argues that Chinese NGOs contribute to policy innovation and implementation. Farid distinguishes between government organized NGOs, NGOs that have close ties with private foundations and foreign NGOs, and grassroots Chinese NGOs. She notes that the first category of NGOs, because of their ties to government, is well positioned to "serve policy advisory functions" and the second, because of their financial power, is able to exert "influence on collaborating departments." The third category consists of indigenous groups operating in rural areas and small cities. These groups have no preexisting connections to the Chinese government, international organizations, or foreign governments. But even this group of NGOs has an impact on policy.[41]

How do small indigenous Chinese NGOs influence policy at the local level and beyond? "A context characterized by diminished bureaucratic capacity, policy discretion and experimentation provides them with opportunities to participate in the formulation and implementation of policy on issue areas in which they work. Particularly in areas where regulatory infrastructure and capacity is limited, NGOs can model innovations or act as agents of policies hitherto ignored by local officials. Officials, in turn, demonstrate 'benign neglect' and a heightened tolerance of such 'deviations' on the part of NGOs, not from a lack of administrative capacity, but this arrangement allows officials to avoid risks and appropriate successes."[42]

Despite the obstacles indicated above, despite Chinese civil society being in its infancy, and despite the uncertain implementation of some of the reforms related to NGOs, "it seems clear now that the legitimacy of grass-roots NGOs' work is already winning them broad societal support. Companies and individuals are donating money, volunteers are giving their time, and even government officials unable to offer formal approval are helping to make space for these groups to operate."[43] If the recent developments related to COVID-19 are an indication, the Chinese government's control over social media and the transmission of information is very tenuous. Furthermore, the government's initial response and the response of many organizations including NGOs has shown and "highlighted the latent power of Chinese civil society."[44] As mentioned above, similar positive as well as negative developments are occurring across the globe, in democratic and nondemocratic societies.

NGOS AND MULTINATIONAL CORPORATIONS

It could also be said that partnerships between NGOs and multinational corporations are fraught with difficulties and at the same time provide opportunities. To most people, corporations and NGOs have different missions, strategies, and cultures, and for some time, corporations and NGOs have had to learn more about each other. Both had to find out how the other functions and the constraints under which they operate. More important, especially since the 1990s, we have experienced the emergence of strategic alliances between businesses and NGOs. These alliances go beyond philanthropic practices; they include collaborative thinking to find solutions and to pool resources to achieve common goals.

Laurence Schwesinger Berlie in his work about business and NGO partnerships gives two important reasons for the greater number of such alliances. 1. "There is increasing importance of the concepts of sustainable development and corporate social responsibility; this has created essential common ground between NGOs and companies and has brought to light the need to establish partnerships in order to resolve complex economic, social and environmental issues." 2. "The professionalism and credibility of NGOs has increased; if NGOs were not powerful, the need to form partnerships with them would not be felt. Their influence on society and governments, their knowledge, their ability to manage problems in ways that are different yet complementary to that of companies and their ability to lead destructive campaigns against firms has led businesses to considering forming partnerships with NGOs."[45] It is to the advantage of businesses and NGOs to collaborate for each to achieve their goals and objectives. "Corporate management is increasingly aware of the need to position their firms to serve social preferences well beyond the basic market model. This awareness is reflected in the burgeoning CSR efforts. For their part, managers of NGOs see increased opportunities to leverage the extensive human and material resources of the business enterprise in order to achieve the social impact desired by the NGO."[46]

Despite the expanding number of such alliances, the phenomenon is still limited. "Both for businesses and NGOs, an alliance is fundamentally the result of a gamble about the future which makes them think that this engagement will be beneficial. Businesses which establish alliances do so because they think that sustainable development is an inevitable structural element of tomorrow's economic system. They therefore position themselves so that they can profit from a first-mover benefit, enabling them to be the leaders of tomorrow's markets."[47]

Berlie cites a few examples of alliances between companies and NGOs. Of course, there are many more.

BirdLife International — Rio Tinto

The goals of the partnership are:

To have an influence on Rio Tinto's practices of land stewardship.

To help the Rio Tinto Group achieve its commitments in terms of sustainable development.

To improve the capabilities and environmental awareness of Rio Tinto employees and other shareholders.

To educate local communities, since it is from them that Rio Tinto draws its human resources.

To embed the concept of sustainable development in the mindset of all Rio Tinto's stakeholders.

Lafarge — World Wide Fund for Nature Partnership

The primary goal of the partnership is:

To reduce Lafarge's carbon dioxide emission and protect biodiversity through the rehabilitation of quarries.

Agrupación Sierra Madre — CEMEX

The goals of the partnership are:

To develop the environmental culture, through publications.
To collaborate in the conservation of biodiversity.[48]

In a related article and after examining the case of Cambodia Trust, Eoghan Walsh and Helena Lenihan assert that NGOs will benefit by adapting business tools. Walsh and Lenihan note that NGOs already play an important role in the development field, and they enjoy more support from people than governments and international organizations. One way to improve their effectiveness and to strengthen accountability is by utilizing tools developed by for-profit businesses. Many NGOs are poorly run and managed. It will be to their benefit to "invest more resources in their organizations, set clear objectives, and become accountable to their beneficiaries."[49]

The authors highlight the experiences of Cambodia Trust after having utilized a business tool, the Quality Management System (QMS) and argue that the same tool could be applied in an NGO setting. "By improving its organizational management, the Trust has secured extra funding. This has strengthened the Trust on a number of other fronts: as a capacity-building exercise; by empowering national staff, in particular women; and by bridging the accountability gap — both downwards and upwards."[50]

However, and as it was mentioned earlier, firms do not always welcome this kind of collaboration or the extended influence of NGOs. In a study of the relationship between businesses and NGOs in the public arena in Spain, Carmen Valor and Amparo Merino observe that "[while] approach and cooperation are observed in [the] private arena, companies and NGOs have a conflicting relationship." Businesses have pressed for the withdrawal of advocacy NGOs from public forums "whose main purpose was policy-making in the CSR [Corporate Social Responsibility] field." The reason given is the "lack of foundational legitimacy of NGOs. Firms understand that these NGOs are not legitimized to be a counterbalancing force of corporations."[51]

By making such an argument, firms implicitly acknowledge another reason for withdrawal: "political NGOs are putting pressure on the government so that it enforces compulsory disclosure and verification of social and environmental performance. These are the means of achieving the main goal of political NGOs: a system change." By educating the public about these means, "a new model of businesses is brought up: companies must create value for all stakeholders." Thus, firms desire withdrawal of political NGOs "from the public arena out of fear of a change of paradigm."[52]

Withdrawal has been met with conflict on the part of NGOs.

"Advocacy NGOs have adopted a conflicting approach in the public arena. Bargaining is excluded from the battery of tactics at disposal since it is understood as a symptom of co-optation. Withdrawal from policymaking is the price to be paid for not removing the issue of verification from the agenda.
The withdrawal-conflict dynamics between businesses and advocacy NGOs in the public arena has had two main outcomes. At a macroeconomic level, it may help to maintain capitalism in tension; therefore reducing the potential negative externalities of the current economic paradigm. At a microeconomic level, it is shifting the locus of rulemaking. Regulation is not actually concocted in the public arena but within the company, with the assistance of NGOs. Nonetheless, in the private relationship between the agents, NGOs actively take part in self-regulatory corporate systems.[53]

Reflecting upon the relationship between corporations, more specifically those in the mining industry, and NGOs in the era of neoliberalism, Stuart Kirsch reaches interesting conclusions. He notes that "the politics of space enabled critics of the industry to exert pressure on mining companies everywhere they operate. The mining industry responded to its heightened exposure by establishing new forms of collaboration among companies that previously regarded each other as fierce competitors. These industry initiatives led NGOs to establish international networks that could share information, promote reforms in the investment policies of multilateral organizations and financial institutions, and set the agenda for a global campaign against the mining industry."[54]

Despite the limited resources and power, indigenous movements have raised the consciousness of people about the mining industry, which long avoided heavy public scrutiny. The industry can no longer assume that governments are the only negotiating partners and that indigenous groups have no capacity to challenge corporations. "The mining industry faces increasing pressure from NGOs mobilizing the discourses of environmentalism and indigenous rights.... [Political] movements and their NGO allies have been able to raise the status of these conflicts to the level of an existential threat to the mining industry, attract regular media coverage, demand attention at the highest levels of the state, and provoke debates at the World Bank and the United Nations. The mining industry has had to modify its policies and practices, although it has done so in ways that simultaneously push back against their critics."[55]

ARE NGOS TOO POWERFUL?

Are NGOs too powerful or just a side-show in a global system still dominated by states? There are scholars who say yes and there are others who say no. For example, Kenneth Anderson asserts that "[when] international NGOs assume power and authority to join with international organizations such as the United Nations on the grounds that they represent what the UN Charter calls the 'peoples of the world' and claim authority to act on their behalf, then indeed they have too much power — or, at least, they claim power on the basis of a false premise."[56]

Anderson notes what other scholars have also noted, that since the end of the Cold War the number of INGOs, especially those focusing on human rights, the environment, and women's rights, increased substantially and began to claim that the time had come for them to take their rightful place in globalization — for them to go global. That meant expanding their membership, activities, and organizational structures as well as seeing the UN "as a fruitful — indeed, a *rightful* — place to lobby, advocate, and organize." Such a stance implied that INGOs did not merely claim to advise, advocate, or lobby on the basis of their expertise, but also to "[sit] at the table of global governance on the basis of *speaking for* the 'peoples of the world.' Representation, in a word: international NGOs, rather than governments, would represent people."[57]

But who elects them to represent the world's peoples? How many members do they have? Anderson answers these questions by saying that NGOs wield too much power "when they inflate themselves into global civil society, representing supposedly vast populations with which, in fact, they have no real contact at all." NGOs' claims "to representativeness and intermediation are thus gravely suspect, and to the extent that international NGOs rely upon such claims … they exercise, or seek to exercise, too much power. Or, more precisely, they seek to exercise power from a source to which they are not legitimately entitled." It is incumbent upon states and organizations such as the UN to tell INGOs "no" when "they overreach from claims of expertise to claims …of representation of the peoples of the world. NGOs do not represent the people; they represent themselves, and their power ought to be tied strictly to that condition."[58]

Marlies Glasius disagrees with Anderson and says that NGOs are not too powerful. He says that INGOs have greatly contributed to strengthening certain characteristics of democratic governance — especially as related to transparency, equality, and deliberation.

> They should not be seen as offering a form of representation of the global *demos*, however, or at least not representation in its traditional form. Their activism could be conceptualized as a form of participation, but in practice this participation is so limited and so uneven that international NGOs cannot entirely be considered an adequate "functional equivalent" or"'alternative mechanism" to parliamentary democracy, operating at the global level. NGOs do contribute to making international decision-making processes more democratic than they might otherwise be, but a democratic deficit remains. Another contribution made by NGOs, however, has received much less attention that the democratizing aspect: that of moral values.[59]

Glasius concludes by noting that:

> The existence of a democratic deficit at the global level, and the fact that NGOs cannot entirely fill it, should not be denied. But the number of victims created by states violating human rights over the past century is staggering. Some of these governments were flawed democracies, too. This is why it is worth giving up some national democratic supremacy in exchange for international law — first, to frame norms on human rights, disarmament, and the environment; and second, to actually enforce them. And NGOs should be there to help make these laws and get them enforced; to strengthen transparency, equality, and deliberation in international decision-making processes; and to help inch states from narrow interests toward global common interests.[60]

On the positive side, Michael Edwards says, NGOs have helped to accomplish the following, although with often limited success:

They "[changed] the terms of the debate on globalization, leading to the emergence of a new orthodoxy about the need to manage the downside of this process, level the playing field, and expend 'policy space' for developing countries."

They "[kept] the spotlight on the need for reforms in international institutions and global governance on issues such as unfair terms of trade and investment, global warming, Africa, and the kind of warped humanitarian intervention represented by the war in Iraq."

On the negative side, NGOs have not had sufficient success in the following areas:

They have not been very innovative in finding ways to effect greater changes regarding the structures that perpetuate poverty and abuses of human rights.

They have not been able to transform power relations in the significant areas of class, gender, and race. They have not confronted the challenge of internal change in any important way. They have not established strong links with social movements to be able to effect sustained change. And they have not "gotten to grips with the rise of religion as one of the most powerful forces for change in the world today. ..."

Equally important, development NGOs have not innovated in any significant sense in the form and nature of their organizational relationships. For example, little concrete attention is paid to downward accountability or the importance of generating diverse, local sources of funds for so-called 'partners' in the south ... They have internalized functions that should have been distributed across other organizations ... franchising global brands instead of supporting authentic expressions of indigenous civil society, and crowding out southern participations in knowledge creation and advocacy in order to increase their own voice and profile, as if the only people with anything useful to say about world development were Oxfam and a handful of others."[61]

Some other negative consequences that might result from the growing number of NGOs and the increase in numbers include the following: "A society where the piling up of special interests replaces a single strong voice for the poor is unlikely to fare well." Single-issue voters become polarized, which often freezes public debate. Civil society becomes more fragmented, "producing a weakened sense of common identity" and less willingness to invest in public goods. More and more groups promote narrow interests threatening democratic government. There are about two hundred states. Add to that number hundreds of influential non-state actors — multinational corporations, NGOs, ethnic and religious groups, etc., and the result could be too many voices and the inability of any one of them to advance their own interests.[62]

> Severely weakened states will encourage conflict, as they have in Africa, Central America, and elsewhere. Moreover, it may be that only the nation-state can meet crucial social needs that markets do not value. More international decision-making will also exacerbate the so-called democratic deficit, as decisions that elected representatives once made shift to unelected international bodies ... It also arises when legislatures are forced to make a single take-it-or-leave-it judgment on huge international agreements, like the several-thousand-page Uruguay Round trade accord. With citizens already feeling that their national governments do not hear individual voices, the trend could well provoke deeper and more dangerous alienation, which in turn could trigger new ethnic and even religious separatism. The end result could be a proliferation of states too weak for either individual economic success or effective international cooperation.[63]

Ole Jacob Sending and Iver B. Neumann take a somewhat different position in relation to those who say that NGOs are too powerful and those who say the opposite. Sending and Neumann note that according to the literature on global governance the state has lost power to non-state actors. But the authors argue that rather than focusing on the power of states and non-state actors, the emphasis must be "on the sociopolitical functions and processes of governance in their own right and seek to identify their rationality as practices of political rule." According to this point of view, "the role of nonstate actors in shaping and carrying out global governance-functions is not an instance of transfer of power from the state to nonstate actors but rather an expression of a changing logic or rationality of government ... by which civil society is redefined from a passive object of government to be acted upon into an entity that is both an object *and* a subject of government." After studying two cases, the international campaign to ban landmines and international population policy, the authors conclude by saying that "the self-association and political will-formation characteristic of civil society and nonstate actors do not stand in opposition to the political power of the state, but is a most central feature of how power, understood as government, operates in late modern society."[64]

WHAT SHOULD BE THE PLACE OF NGOS IN THE GLOBAL SYSTEM AND HOW TO ENHANCE THEIR PERFORMANCE?

Despite the many shortcomings and criticisms of NGOs, NGOs could and often do play a significant role in the international system. As referenced at the beginning of this work, NGOs. especially since the end of the Cold War. have performed a leading role in numerous areas including providing relief during calamities, contributing to social and economic development, raising education standards, monitoring various transnational actors, lessening the divide between North and South, enhancing transparency, providing expertise and information, and contributing to the enhancement of civil society. It is difficult to deny the positive role performed by NGOs such as Doctors without Borders, Oxfam, the International Red Cross, the various organizations interested in banning and removing landmines, etc. Imagine conditions for refugees and other displaced people in Turkey, the Middle East, Greece, Italy, and elsewhere in Europe, Africa, Asia, and the Americas. How much more difficult would their lives be without NGOs? There was and still is great need for different kinds of grassroots organizations including NGOs.

NGOs ought to be part of the global governance process, the opposition to this argument notwithstanding, because of the positive role they could play. As already mentioned, NGOs provide information and they could help in improving efficiency of global governance and promote greater legitimacy. "They can take over the role of bringing scientific and practical expert knowledge into the discourse and thus also into the social deliberation process and finally into the political decision-making process. This would happen even if only the results of social deliberation contributed to the agenda-setting of international negotiations."[65]

Enhancing the participatory rights of NGOs in international governance could lead to political change within international organizations. "In the best case, this political change will be accompanied by a process of learning. This intra-organizational learning process should lead to the willingness on the part of the international organizations to enable more integration of NGOs.... The forms of soft power that are informally performed by NGOs within the framework of global governance would then be increasingly institutionalized. This could contribute to strengthening the legitimacy of global governance. The output legitimacy and also the participation of civil society could be enhanced."[66]

As discussed previously, the states are often resistant to expanding the participatory role of NGOs in global governance. Traditionally, the states have been the sole legitimate players in global relations. The states themselves were the ones that negotiated agreements, accepted binding international arrangements, and tried to enforce international obligations. But the world has been dramatically transformed for numerous reasons including globalization. "[The] traditional concept of international law as the 'law of nations' no longer reflects the realities of international society." Today's global society includes many other actors beyond the states who desire greater voice in international organizations and processes.[67]

In today's world, there is need for an updated system of global governance where states continue to provide leadership and assume responsibility that has transboundary implications. But in this system of governance the states are not the only providers of security. Other players are involved in governance processes and they help manage and resolve future challenges. In the case of Southeast Asia, for example, and despite bilateral tensions and territorial disputes, "we see a pattern of security governance where state and non-state actors work together to address a host of non-traditional security (NTS) threats. There are numerous regional frameworks focused on such threats, including regional agreements to regulate transboundary air pollution, institutionalize disease surveillance and reporting to prevent the spread of pandemics, speed up operations in disaster relief and emergency response, promote peaceful use of nuclear energy, and manage the movements of people through strengthening norms and practices on preventing trafficking in persons."[68]

The shock of Brexit and Donald Trump's victory show that a significant number of voters view internationalism and globalization as sources of economic inequality a and threat to their future. They view globalization and global governance as elite projects that led to few benefits and much pain. It will be difficult to convince the Brexit supporters as well as the supporters of Trump, the National Front in France, and others elsewhere that international cooperation is a good thing. But despite these developments, those who hold different opinions must come together and make stronger arguments in support of global governance. "Such an international coalition could bring together warring MNCs and NGOs in the face of a future international disorder based on nationalism and unilateralism, dominated by unconstrained great powers. Forging such a coalition, already visible in climate change, will be a long-term enterprise.... [There] are bases for optimism. The global order rests on multiple supports, even in the face of a skeptical or disruptive US government. And one of those supports is growing: nearly all public opinion surveys suggest that citizens of the future — the young — lean in favor of global openness and collaboration."[69]

Non-state actors, including NGOs, play a significant role in multiple governance processes taking place at different levels. "With their expert knowledge and linkages with governments, epistemic communities have made important contributions in helping shape the agenda of regional cooperation on a number of issues." Civil society organizations and NGOs have also been important in pushing governments to observe norms and promote best practices. Furthermore, limited knowledge of local circumstances, lack of understanding of people's needs, and poor cultural sensitivity results "in a mismatch between the assistance and support provided and a community's needs, leading to ineffective governance.... Civil society groups are familiar with local context and maintain good access to people at the local level are in a better position to access local risks and gaps in capacity.... Working closely with local communities, civil society groups [that] and NGOs come in and provide the critical intervention areas that are either missed or overlooked by government and intergovernmental mechanisms."[70]

NGOs and other civil society actors not only promote best practices and pressure governments to observe norms, they are also able to help establish norms. It is generally accepted that "norms are limited when contradicted by power, but they are not extinguished. Norms based on principles of right and wrong suffer disadvantage when power is primary." If a country's security is very much dependent upon competition, norms about respecting others and being willing to accommodate others "are prevented from emerging."[71] But this is not always the case. NGOs can play a role in the norm generation process.

The generation of norms is a slow process. But such process does not mean that the creation of norms is a "fait accompli as long as the principled actor remains steadfast." And it does not mean that "norms automatically triumph given the right formula.... The process is a process of repeated trial and frequent error." NGOs and governments are often at opposite ends. "[It] is fair to assume that states generally want to minimize or place stringent conditions on multilateral accountability for human rights, while NGOs disregard state protests of sovereignty in favor of an emphasis on conformity with demands based on moral principles. Conceived in the terms of the potential influence of civil society on governance, NGOs may be successful in engendering norms if they are able to use their knowledge and influence to propagate their own interpretations of governmental decisions within the public sphere, thus catalyzing broader support and pressure for change. The degree to which NGOs are linked to principle rather than political interests enhances the legitimacy and moral force of their arguments."[72]

Among those multinational organizations that ought to expand the role of NGOs is the WTO. NGOs not only ought participate in the policymaking side of the WTO, they ought to also participate in the dispute settlement side as well for the following reasons: First, "the relatively closed nature of the WTO dispute resolution process undermines public confidence in the fairness and authoritativeness of WTO decisions." Participation of NGOs affected by the decisions will provide greater credibility to the process. Second, "allowing NGOs to make submissions to the panels would also be constructive. In cases where the scope of a case goes beyond the boundaries of trade law ... non-governmental organizations might be especially illuminating thereby leading to better informed...panel decisions."[73]

Hannah Murphy maintains that even though NGOs are excluded from the formal decision-making process at the WTO, they are important players within the "global public policy networks." After examining two NGO campaigns directed at the WTO (campaigns related to intellectual property and multilateral investment rules), Murphy concludes that the campaigns played a significant role in "broadening the trade agenda by publicizing neglected trade-related issues, building coalitions and boosting the negotiating sources of developing member countries."[74]

These campaigns demonstrate that NGOs should be regarded as "highly strategic, entrepreneurial actors, not just norm-disseminators, in attempting to impact international policy deliberators. NGOs work to link their campaign issues to objectives of states, contribute to the brokerage and maintenance of coalitions of developing member states, and lend their knowledge and financial resources to support developing members inside the WTO arena. ... NGOs also play roles in the governance of international trade through monitoring, publicizing and analyzing developments in trade negotiations, as well as participating in broader global public policy networks, in which they interact with international organizations to highlight and discuss the impacts of WTO rules and air alternative perspectives on trade policy matters."[75]

Those who oppose direct NGO access to the WTO propose the idea that NGOs "filter comments through their sovereign governments." But there are problems with this argument. "Firstly, international NGOs do not fit the traditional citizen-government model. Secondly, NGOs from countries who are not members of the WTO are not represented ... Thirdly, a government may not want to present a point urged by one of 'its' NGOs." In order to improve conditions, the WTO must establish formal procedures to avoid incoherence and government briefs to the panels should become public, not including, of course, documents designated as confidential.[76]

Not only the WTO ought to expand the role of NGOs, the IMF and the World Bank ought to do the same as well. Both are being accused of being secretive, unaccountable, and ineffective. Their critics demand that they become more transparent, more accountable, and more participatory. To their credit, these organizations have begun to recognize non-state actors, including NGOs. They now make more information and analysis available to NGOs than ever before. Both now "consult with lobbying organizations in Washington DC and grassroots organizations in member countries.... These contacts are taking place at regional, country and local levels."[77]

It is important to point out that "NGOs have not taken place as major 'stakeholders' in the institutions: they have not acquired control, nor a formal participatory role in decision-making. However, where Northern NGOs have allied with or used political leverage in major shareholding countries they have exercised considerable informal power and influence. Indeed, in such cases the position of some NGOs starts looking much stronger than that of many smaller developing countries — whose formal right to participate in decision-making is diluted" by their many domestic problems as well as problems related to representation in these international institutions.[78] It is not an easy task to democratize international institutions that are structured in a nondemocratic manner.

Similar comments could be made about the EU, at least in relation to security and defense matters. It is true that the EU has for a time recognized the role of non-state actors as important contributors in dealing with social problems. The EU relies on the expertise and resources of non-state actors including NGOs in crisis management. "The cooperation between the EU and NGOs has been traditionally rooted in the field of development. In 2006, the *European Consensus on Development* included civil society organizations as fully-fledged stakeholders in all stages of the development process. This evolution has been confirmed in the post-Lisbon phase [the Treaty of Lisbon came into effect on December 1, 2009]: the *Agenda for Change*, the new framework for EU development and cooperation proposed by the European Commission in October 2011, acknowledges the need to strengthen the links between the EU and civil society organizations, social partners and local authorities through dialogue and the use of best practices. It also advocates the EU's support for the emergence of an organized local civil society able to act as a watchdog and partner in dialogue with national governments."[79]

But when issues about security and defense arise, cooperation between the EU and NGOs "has been less regular or structured. Again, the European Commission has been very active in reaching out to civil society actors in the sectors of conflict prevention and peacebuilding. However, despite the EU's recognition of the value of the potential contribution of NGOs, cooperation in early warning and situation assessment, particularly concerning the strategic and operational planning of CSDP [the Common Security and Defense Policy] missions, is still suboptimal. The difficulty of identifying relevant expertise in the civil society realm is accompanied by an enduring lack of trust on the part of national diplomatic and EU officers in the non-governmental sector, by a scarce availability of resources and by a limited knowledge of EU crisis management processes and needs by NGOs."[80]

Andre Broome, in considering the circumstances under which NGOs can potentially act as an important source of change in the international economic regime, argues that NGOs must keep in mind three lessons: First, their arguments must be evidence-based as it was the case in the early 1990s against the claims of the World Bank and the IMF "that a debt crisis in a large group of low-income countries did not exist." Second, NGOs must take advantage of specific circumstances that might enable NGOs to exert influence on public decision-making processes. "The impact of the NGO debt campaign during the 1990s and early 2000s was partly enabled by a window of opportunity for changing the international sovereign debt regime by a leadership change at the World Bank, as well as changes in government in the United Kingdom and the United States where … political leaders made greater debt relief for heavily indebted poor countries a foreign policy priority.… In addition, the damage done to the IMF's reputation during the Asian financial crisis may have made it more difficult for the IMF to resist the expansion of debt relief beyond the terms agreed for the 1996 HIPC Initiative [heavily indebted poor countries]." And third, even though the role of NGOs has expanded, "their impact on formal policy change is likely to continue to depend on the extent to which they are able to influence the political agendas of major states. This is hardly surprising, as international organizations such as the IMF and the World Bank remain at heart state-driven agencies, … [Because for] the most part their [NGOs] influence is channeled through states, this does suggest the recent claims that NGOs are at the vanguard of an emergent global civil society that can help to generate transnational democracy without accessing formal decision-making structures should be treated with skepticism."[81]

The current information revolution provides NGOs with an important tool to influence public values and norms on a global scale, and thus presents a challenge to the "traditional state-centric, realist paradigm in international relations." The proliferation of NGOs and other members of the global civil society "present a different set of priorities than those traditionally associated with the state system, and it is in this respect that it represents a phenomenon worthy of broad theoretical analysis. In the short term, social movements and NGOs are motivated by their interest in revising particular policies of states and international organizations.… Thus, global civil society represents not a mutually exclusive paradigm from state-centric realism. Rather it points to a particular relationship between the global citizenry and the state, whereby the former is seen not as the passive object of the latter's machinations but rather as an active participant in shaping not only immediate policies but also the long-term parameters of legitimacy of the state." This, of course, does not mean that civil society alone can resolve the many problems of interest to its members, though in some instances devolution and local autonomy could be more preferable to interference from removed state-based bureaucracies such as the IMF and the World Bank.[82]

Furthermore, and despite these developments, the global civil society is no more than "marginally significant in the grand arena of power politics — [it commands] no armies and few corporate sponsors. Nevertheless, global civil society does represent an emerging phenomenon that is notable not for its raw power but for its distinctiveness from the assumed characteristics of the traditional state system."[83]

NGOs, as referenced previously, are confronted with many problems and challenges. Among them are their structure and identity, commercialization, governance and management, and the roles they perform. Some other related problems are "loss of independence and values, and possibly loss of civic vision and energy, replaced by the emergence of more organically-based social movements and other civil society groups. Indeed ... many NGOs fail to align and be clear about their operational and organizational strategies. This shortcoming works against ensuring that who they are will enable them to effectively deliver what they want to do! The resulting gap between words and deeds is a sort of debilitating schizophrenia that invites public mistrust."[84] While examining the role of NGOs one must always keep in mind what has been evidenced throughout this work, that NGOs operate differently depending on the nature of a country's governmental system, the nature of its economic system, its state of development, and its historical legacy. "[One] needs to [for example] think about the role of NGOs in global politics in the transitional economies in a more nuanced way. In as much as NGOs rely on public trust as their source of legitimization as political actors, and public trust in NGOs cumulates over time, scholars need to think of NGO strength as a stock variable, not merely as a flow variable. ... This ... will provide a theoretically persuasive way of thinking of the effectiveness of NGOs as political actors."[85]

Albert Arhin, in his examination of the role of NGOs in advancing the UN's 2015 Sustainable Development Goals (SDGs) as specifically related to Ghana, makes a number of important observations about the environment in which NGOs operate. He notes that the aim of the SDGs is to "end hunger and poverty, protect the planet, and promote prosperity by 2030." Arhin also notes that NGOs play an important role in service delivery, advocacy, and facilitation to advance the SDGs. Yet the author's study shows that the changing development landscape in Ghana presents NGOs with three challenges. First, "although the changing development landscape in Ghana presents opportunities, it is also generally causing uncertainty in the mobilization of financial resources that NGOs need to perform their diverse goals." Second, "the changing development landscape may affect the institutional capacity of several NGOs to deliver programs that would advance the SDGs. Respondents highlighted the difficulty in maintaining office and operational costs, the high turnover of competent staff, closure of programs, and difficulty in investing in the capacity of staff to meet the changing technological developments ..." Third, the changing development landscape may affect the identity of NGOs. The importance and legitimacy of NGOs very much depends on their closeness to grassroots populations and the expectation that they are not-for-profit and nonpartisan. But "the need to generate resources to survive can place commercial interests above voluntarism and altruistic motivations that have driven NGOs.... [The] necessity to charge user fees for services provided by NGOs can potentially shift attention away from advocacy functions to predominantly service provision and facilitation."[86]

NGOs are known for questioning the performance of governments and businesses. But NGOs themselves are being questioned for their effectiveness, accountability, and even their legitimacy. "Their accountability and transparency have been increasingly questioned, and their practices and activities are not always in the service of a 'good society' ..." As a consequence, many in the international community look at NGOs with skepticism and public opinion is not as favorable as in the past. "Rather than a 'choice and voice' for the people, NGOs are now often regarded as primarily supportive of themselves and their agenda, along with that of their donors ... In the end, they seem to be no more than groups of individuals organized for multiple reasons that include human aspirations and self-interests that prevail over the search for the common good. While they remain key players in the development arena globally, they have lost the favorable view once held uncritically by the international community."[87]

For NGOs to better survive, they must adjust and transform themselves. Because of the economic, social, political, and technological changes caused by globalization, NGOs have derived many benefits. But globalization has also presented NGOs with many challenges. Many factors in a globalizing world make change difficult.

Adapting to Speed and Contagion

Innovations in communication technology make it possible for information to cross the globe instantly. This results in limited time available to organizations to respond to the changing circumstances. "Thus, globalization's compression of time and space has made organizational change even more difficult. The financial crisis of 2008 illustrates the time limits facing organizations. By the time Lehman Brothers collapsed on September 14, 2008, the 'contagion' had spread across Europe and Asia resulting in the economy of one country after another falling into recession."

Pressures to Harmonize and Centralize

During the past few decades, NGOs have been confronted with growing pressure from internal as well as external sources for greater centralization and conformity, which in turn have limited their capacity to change and adapt. The benefits of globalization set aside, internationalization has affected global strategies, and has led to increased bureaucratization, which often stifles innovation and slows decision-making.

Culture as Constraint to Transformation

"Large INGOs have developed an organizational culture that is not support-ive of change and adaptation.... As new employees begin to learn the char-acteristics of an organization's culture, their strategies and choices become constrained, at first strategically and then, over time, habitually by those characteristics."

Learning Disabilities and Feedback Shortcomings

"Failure to become learning organizations has further reduced large INGOs' ability to change, since learning is a key attribute that allows organizations to adapt to an uncertain future. INGOs' failure to invest in information technol-ogy also means that they have not developed the processes and systems that may help to offset the drag of an increasingly bureaucratic culture. Making the situation worse, INGOs have generally lacked a sufficiently compelling motivation to overcome the internal barriers to change. While for-profit organizations have the discipline of markets (disputed by many) and demo-cratic governments the ballot box, the largest INGOs do not face any similar accountability mechanism.... The result is that despite widespread under-standing about many of the problems facing INGOs, they continue to recur."[88]

A frequently cited example of NGOs becoming learning organizations willing to adapt is microfinance institutions in Bangladesh. Bangladesh has one of the largest and among the most successful microfinance sectors in the world. One of the reasons for the success is the homegrown delivery modes that have emerged from "experimentation by providers within the country.... NGOs and the Grameen Bank have proven effective at delivering microfi-nance services through a well-established infrastructure that reaches down to sub-village level and allows them to have face-to-face weekly meetings with their members. Part of the success MFIs [Monetary Financial Institutions] have had with outreach is also associated with innovations that were intro-duced after problems were identified with the early microfinance models." Many MFIs replaced early rigid approaches that were considered necessary for fiscal discipline and to secure capital for lending with more flexible prod-ucts and greater variety of services, which in turn proved more attractive to rural families.[89]

Yet another example of an MFI willing to learn, to adapt, and to show flexibility is the most prominent of all, the Bangladesh Rural Advancement Committee (BRAC) . As indicated above, MFIs (including BRAC) have been successful in their efforts to help people, especially in rural areas, through microfinancing. It was not until 1992 when BRAC, recognizing the immense problem of urban poverty, started providing services to the urban poor.

"However, after two decades of successful urban service delivery, BRAC realized that service delivery alone will not transform the lives of the urban poor. Consequently, BRAC has started focusing on learning from its successful rural experience and developing a comprehensive and holistic approach to go beyond the symptoms and address the root cause of urban poverty."[90]

To realize its vision, BRAC decided to focus on a number of strategies. First, in order to effectively deal with the problems facing the urban poor, BRAC has to collect precise data on many topics, including . . . "the dynamics of new migrants and dynamics of urban poverty over time, number of street dwellers ... and so on." By doing so, BRAC can use the information "to design existing programs and customize new ones accordingly to the findings." Second, "a combined development policy/program that incorporates both community and facility-oriented services for vulnerable slum dwellers needs to be developed to address the multiple dimensions of urban poverty." Third, as with many developing countries local authorities in Bangladesh do not have the capacity to deal with urban poverty. "In order to ensure the rights of the urban poor to the services that they are entitled to, BRAC needs to work extensively to strengthen local governments' ability to implement programs and policies aimed at poverty reduction. And fourth, "a strong legal and justice system is essential to reduce the vulnerabilities of various groups, with the aim of freeing slum residents from being exploited by slum lords and other influential leaders, promote safe working environment and proper wage rates for low-paid workers, and reduce incidences of violence and discrimination against domestic workers and protect street dwellers from crime, sexual and drug abuse."[91]

It has been observed that over the past few years there has been an expansion of humanitarian aid with more and more actors involved offering their services. This development has made humanitarian action even more complicated than previously. Many organizations and institutions created for other purposes are today involved in work related to humanitarian action. This trend continues to grow for numerous reasons. "The reasons vary for this 'humanitarian tendency' and sudden conversion to humanitarianism of many bodies and institutions. The motives behind these humanitarian efforts, however, are not always altruistic. For example, many acts of humanitarianism are driven by the search (amongst others) for public legitimacy, pure image, simple opportunism, [and] diversification of securing supplies of resources. Whatever the case, what is certain is that humanitarian acts, regardless of their motives, have a quasi-domino effect, in that they seem to motivate the involvement of other actors whether it be to participate directly in humanitarian actions or at least [to] take cognizance of the changes taking place in the field of humanitarianism."[92]

The significant increase in the number of actors involved has not necessarily led to improved efficiency. In fact, in some cases it has contributed to confusion, less enthusiasm, and wasting of resources. One of the major problems is the lack of cooperation and coordination among the various bodies involved in humanitarian activities. While coordination is always important in a catastrophe, it is even more important in complex emergencies where "a mixture of political factors, conflicts and extreme vulnerabilities is at play."[93]

Lack of coordination is, of course, problematic under any circumstances. Ivica Petrikova demonstrates the case in her work on the effectiveness of three NGOs working with child laborers in El Salvador. Each NGO chose to approach child labor in a different way. One views it as an inevitable consequence of poverty and "cannot be addressed separately from other developmental problems." Another considers it "a violation of children's human rights in need of imminent eradication." And the third "falls somewhere in between, promoting child-labor bans in theory but not fully enforcing them in practice." These NGOs did not communicate with each other and did not coordinate their activities with each other. "As a result, the overall effect of their work is hindered by small-scale projects, high transaction costs, potential duplication, and contradicting strategies to addressing child labor." The situation could be improved by mutual coordination. But even if this were to take place, greater coordination alone would not necessarily lead to greater efficiency in addressing the problems associated with child labor, "as it appears that the NGOs devise their strategies and projects on the basis of their donors' preferences rather than on the basis of their beneficiaries' needs."[94]

The following ought to take place to improve coordination:

Leadership: The need for one agency to exert leadership to carry out tasks of coordination in complex emergencies.

Defining the common principles and the tasks where each complements the others: Reaching agreements and consensus on the context and the framework of the crisis and on the priorities of aid in terms of vulnerability; and taking advantage of the growing specialization among agencies.

Establishing the practical mechanisms of coordination at all levels: . . .

Devoting resources . . .

Incorporation of all humanitarian actors . . .

Setting up mechanisms of information with other actors . . .[95]

Coordination aside, NGOs must remain true to their mission. This means, for example, in the case of rights-based approaches, "holding duty-bearers accountable for fulfilling direct obligations to themselves, and those they are responsible for, under standards of due diligence. While in the classic understanding of human rights, the state is considered to be the primary duty-bearer, governments are increasingly handing over their function of delivering health services to non-state actors, including NGOs. The state must retain ultimate responsibility for respecting, protecting, and fulfilling human rights. NGOs, however, especially those claiming to be rights-based in their operations, should also be seen as duty-bearers, upholding rights through their services and activities — even if this requires challenging state policies and their implementation."[96]

NGOs must also improve accountability for the sector to reestablish public confidence in it. One way to do so is through the introduction of "collective self-regulation." Mick Moore and Sheelagh Stewart argue that "collective self-regulation could make a significant contribution to solving four generic problems faced by development NGOs in poor countries, NGOs that depend to a significant extent on foreign funding. Those are labelled the 'account-ability', 'structural growth', 'evaluation', and 'economics of scale' problems, respectively."[97]

NGOs, like various professional associations, should, Moore and Stewart note, introduce "self-policing standards." By these standards they mean the introduction of norms rather than rules, and norms that are not too rigid to allow for flexibility and adaptability. The norms or codes of practice should

> "embody ... a range of statutes, with corresponding obligations, determined by the size of the organization, its age, or other factors that appeared relevant. ...
> The typical list is likely to include several of the following issues:
> Timelines of issuing of annual reports.
> Issues to be included in the annual report such as degree of disclosures of assets and liabilities, of salaries and all other benefits paid to staff, directors, board members, and consultants.
> Employment, recruitment, and staff development policies and practices.
> Sources of finance.
> Arrangements for internal or external scrutiny of financial transactions, employ-ment practices, organizational policies, etc.
> Arrangements for the evaluations of organizational performances.[98]

It is of interest to mention that some of these actions are being taken, espe-cially by humanitarian NGOs as well as other kinds of NGOs. An example is the case of the Humanitarian Accountability Partnership-International (HAP-I), which is a "voluntary, self-regulatory collective accountability initiative, to investigate the processes through which NGOs define collec-tive rules, standards, and practices for accountability." Maryam Zarnegar Deloffre, in her study on global accountability, finds "that transnational coor-dination of NGO accountability practices results from social learning that generates a global accountability community (GAC) constituted by mutual engagement, joint enterprise, and a shared repertoire of practices.... GACs both regulate the behavior of members and constitute their social identities, interests, and practices."⁹⁹

Some other examples of self-regulatory initiatives of NGOs include Accountable Now, the Sphere Standards, and the Red Cross Code of Conduct, and most importantly the INGO Accountability Charter. The charter was signed in June 2006 as a response to pressure from the media, businesses, and governments for greater transparency and accountability. Some of the founding members include Amnesty International, Oxfam International, Greenpeace International, and World Vision. These founding members recognized the need "for a global, cross-sectoral code which reflected the values and priorities of the NGO sector. The Charter text codifies practices for INGOs in the areas of respect for universal principles; responsible advocacy; effective programs; non-discrimination; transparency; good governance; ethical fundraising; and professional management."¹⁰⁰ All "these initiatives provide voluntary standards for NGOs to regulate their own behavior, but they have been criticized because they rarely include any compliance and enforcement mechanisms, and this leads to patchy and inconsistent implementation. Over the past 25 years, the increasing influence acquired by NGOs in global governance has not been accompanied by a parallel process of regulation, in contrast to other non-state actors …"¹⁰¹ It would be a mistake not to mention the *WANGOs Code of Ethics and Conduct for NGOs* as yet another effort to promote accountability.

All these efforts to improve accountability demonstrate that in the opinion of numerous individuals NGOs are facing a crisis of trustworthiness. The so-called accountability agenda has gained traction as a way of solving this crisis. Vincent Charles Keating and Erla Thrandardottir are encouraging people to be cautious because most proponents of the accountability agenda promote the rational model of trust, which is based on "transparency and external oversight." According to this model, NGO trust is a function of the amount of information the donors have about the NGO and "the ability to structure their interests through the threat of external penalties. In other words, the increased availability of information about an NGO increases the likelihood of donors correctly identifying trustworthy NGOs to support or to work with."¹⁰²

Scholars, Keating and Thrandardottir say, do not take into consideration the "social characteristics of trust [social trust] between donors and NGOs. … [Trust] is not simply a mechanism through which we place a bet on the behavior of others when we believe the expected values are positive. In addition to the rational and observational component, trust is a social phenomenon that is affected by social conditions and relations." The rationalist model does not take into consideration these perceptions, which could lead to long-term negative consequences for NGOs. "[It] is not only incorrect in its understanding of why many donors trust NGOs but tragically might do the opposite of what it intends to do among individual donors. Instead of creating greater donor trust in NGOs, it might create and sustain greater distrust by promoting a gulf of unfamiliarity that will make these costly practices permanent." The authors, of course, do not argue for the abandonment of the rational model. Instead, they note that the potential effects of both the rational and social trust models must be examined.[103]

Related to the need for greater coordination and accountability among NGOs as well as productive innovations is the work of Sarah Sunn Bush and Jennifer Hadden about the stagnation in the founding of new INGOs. As has been discussed earlier in this work, it is common for scholars to comment about the explosion in the number of NGOs. But Bush and Hadden are raising doubts about the present-day validity of this commentary. They argue that based on an analysis of a new dataset on American INGOs from 1992 to 2012 there has been stagnation in their growth because of the "now dense environment" in which they operate.[104] There are, in the authors' opinion, too many INGOs.

The stagnation in one population can give an opportunity to another population to emerge.

> Given the recent stagnation of INGOs foundings, along with the bureaucratization [of NGOs in general], it is reasonable to wonder if we may see new organizational forms emerging to challenge the dominance of INGOs as the main nonstate service providers and advocates in world politics. For example, the growth in internet-enabled campaign groups like Cherge.org, MoveOn, or Avaaz may mark the emergence of a new organizational model in which activists move easily across the virtual and physical, national and international, and sectoral boundaries that often demarcated the identities of traditional INGOs. Direct-giving campaigns — often internet-enabled through platforms such as Give Directly, Go Fund Me, or Kiva — are also gaining popularity as an alternative to organization-led programming. Whereas an entrepreneur in an earlier time period may have turned to creating an INGO to pursue social change, the density and competitiveness of the INGO population may make new forms more appealing. These new entrants may enhance innovation within global governance, but also bring with them the potential for substantial disruption as the modes of service delivery and advocacy evolve in new directions. Government agencies may also be able to spur new forms of nonstate action in the same way they have done in the past.[105]

The greater population density and competition among INGOs could lead to greater efficiency and improved performance. But the increased density makes coordination and cooperation among INGOs more difficult, which could result in duplications as well as conflicts. Hence, INGO founders must put much emphasis on "developing policies and performance metrics" to enhance coordination "and productive innovations within highly dense and mature INGO populations."[106] And because NGOs must interact with a plethora of actors and populations, they must take even more seriously their role as intermediaries between beneficiaries, governments, and international relief/development organizations. One example of success in that role was how NGOs acted after the 2001 earthquake in Gujarat, India. Bipasha Baruah found that NGOs "can play important roles in facilitating the design and construction of high-quality, culturally appropriate housing; revitalizing and diversifying livelihoods; and reducing physical and social vulnerability to future disasters." Of course, NGO performance was not without any problems. To avoid some of the problems Baruah recommends NGOs have "clearly defined roles, responsibilities, and accountability measures in post-disaster reconstruction projects, [and] they also need a certain amount of autonomy to protect their organizational philosophies and flexibility to make day-to-day decisions."[107]

To overcome these limitations and to improve their effectiveness, NGOs not only must be cognizant of what was mentioned above, they must take some additional steps. They must increase their links with governmental power without becoming victims such links, they must be inclined to develop solidarity with other NGOs — they must learn to trust other NGOs and they must develop their ability to clearly set their agendas placed before people and before the many appropriate organizations and institutions. Most important, NGOs must remain true to their mission and they must be closely guided by the WANGOs *Code of Ethics and Conduct for NGOs*. NGOs must be responsible, public-service-minded, concerned with people everywhere and not just those within the nation of their origin, and they must put much emphasis on human rights and the dignity of every human being. They must be transparent and truthful, they must not be for-profit, they must be independent of government as much as possible, and they must do all necessary to gain the public trust.

As James McGann and Mary Johnstone say, "[as] 'the conscience of the world' they must be beyond reproach so that they remain the keepers of the public trust."[108]

NOTES

1. Craig N. Murphy, "Global Governance: Poorly Done and Poorly Understood," *International Affairs* 76, no. 4 (October 2000): 789.

2. Ibid., 789.

3. William F. Fisher, "DOING GOOD? The Politics and Antipolitics of NGO Practices," *Annual Review of Anthropology* 26 (1997): 451.

4. Steve Charnovitz, "Two Centuries of Participation: NGOs and International Governance," *Michigan Journal of International Law* 18, no. 2 (1997): 183–184.

5. Ibid., 190.

6. Ann Marie Clark et al., "The Sovereign Limits of Global Civil Society: A Comparison of NGO Participation in UN World Conferences on the Environment, Human Rights, and Women," *World Politics* 51, no. 1 (October 1998): 1.

7. Ibid., 33–34.

8. Alger, 422–423.

9. Ibid., 34–35.

10. Jonathan Goodhand and Peter Chamberlain, "Dancing with the Prince: NGOs survival strategies in the Afghan conflict," in *Development, NGOs and Civil Society*, ed. Jonathan Goodhand and Peter Chamberlain (London: Oxfam GB, 2000), 91.

11. Ibid., 91, 106.

12. Kaoko Takahashi, "Assessing NGO Empowerment in Housing Development Frameworks: Discourse and Practice in the Philippines," *International Journal of Japanese Sociology* no. 18 (2009): 123.

13. Ibid., 123.

14. Ibid., 123.

15. Deborah A. Brautigam and Monique Segarra, "Difficult Partnerships: The World Bank, States, and NGOs," *Latin American Politics and Society* 49, no. 4 (Winter 2007): 149, 173.

16. Ibid., 173–174.

17. Ibid., 174.

18. Jeanette Schade, "Between Projectitis and the Formation of Countervailing Power NGOs in Nation-Building Processes," in *Nation-Building*, ed. Jochen Hippler (London: Pluto Press, 2005), 125.

19. Ibid., 125–126, 133.

20. Ibid., 134.

21. Zaum, 34.

22. Francis Kofi Abiew and Tom Keating, "NGOs and UN Peacekeeping Operations: Strange Bedfellows," *International Peacekeeping* 6, no. 2 (Summer 1999): 89.

23. Ibid., 107.

24. Ibid., 107.

25. Khan et al., 227.

26. Otto, 127.

27. Leon Gordenker and Thomas G. Weiss, "Devolving Responsibilities: A Framework for Analyzing NGOs and Services," *Third World Quarterly* 18, no. 3 (1997): 448.

28. Otto, 128.

29. Lotsmart Fonjong, "Fostering Women's Participation in Development through Non-Governmental Efforts in Cameroon," *The Geographical Journal* 167, no. 3 (September 2001): 233–234.

30. James A. Paul, "NGOs and Global Policy-Making," *Global Policy Forum* (June 2000): 2,

https://www.globalpolicy.org/empire/31611-ngos-and-global-policy-making.html? tmpl=component&print=1&page .

31. Paul Almeida, *Social Movements: The Structure of Collective Mobilization* (Oakland, CA: University of California Press, 2019), 147.

32. Ibid., 171.

33. Chongyi Feng, "The NGO Law in China and Its Impact on Overseas Funded NGOs," *Cosmopolitan Civil Societies: An Interdisciplinary Journal* 9, no. 3 (2017): 95.

34. Yongjiao Yang et al., "Beyond the Abolition of Dual Administration: The Challenges to NGO Governance in 21st Century China," *ISTR* 27 (2016): 2307.

35. Yongjiao Yang et al., 2307.

36. Cynthia Estlund, *A New Deal for China's Workers?* (Cambridge, MA: Harvard University Press, 2017), 44.

37. Ibid., 45, 63.

38. Ya-Wen Lei, *The Contentious Public Sphere: Law, Media, and Authoritarian Rule in China* (Princeton, New Jersey: Princeton University Press, 2018), 201–202.

39. Ibid., 202.

40. Jessica C. Teets, "Let Many Civil Societies Bloom: The Rise of Consultative Authoritarianism in China," *The China Quarterly* no. 213 (March 2013): 19, 36.

41. May Farid, "Advocacy in Action: China's Grassroots NGOs as Catalysts for Policy Innovation," *Studies in Comparative International Development* 54 (2019): 529.

42. Ibid., 545.

43. Spires, Tao, and Chan, 89.

44. Minxin Pei, "China's Coming Upheaval: Competition, the Coronavirus, and the Weakness of Xi Jinping," *Foreign Affairs* (May–June 2020): 95.

45. Laurence Schwesinger, *Alliances for Sustainable Development: Business and NGO Partnerships* (New York: Palgrave/Macmillan, 2010), xi, 21.

46. Lee Tavis, "Multinational Enterprises: Interacting with Non-governmental Organizations," in *Peace through Commerce: Responsible Corporate Citizenship and the Ideals of the United Nations Global Compact*, ed. Oliver F. Williams (South Bend, Indiana: University of Notre Dame Press, 2008), 413.

47. Schwesinger, 22.

48. Ibid., 162–173.

49. Eoghan Walsh and Helena Lenihan, "Accountability and Effectiveness of NGOs: Adapting Business Tools Successfully," *Development in Practice* 16, no. 5 (August 2006): 422.

50. Ibid., 423.

51. Carmen Valor and Amparo Merino, "The Relationship between NGOs and Businesses in the Public Arena: An Empirical Analysis for Spain," *Journal of Public Affairs* 9 (2009): 31.

52. Ibid., 31.

53. Ibid., 31–32.

54. Stuart Kirsch, *Mining Capitalism: The Relationship between Corporations and Their Critics* (Oakland, CA: University of California Press, 2014), 225.

55. Ibid., 232–233.

56. Kenneth Anderson, "Do NGOs Wield Too Much Power? Yes," in *Controversies in Globalization: Contending Approaches to International Relations*, ed. Peter M. Haas et al. (Washington, DC: CQ Press, 2010), 364.

57. Ibid., 365–366.

58. Ibid., 368–369, 370.

59. Marlies Glasius, "Do NGOs Wield Too Much Power? No," in *Controversies in Globalization: Contending Approaches to International Relations*, ed. Peter M. Haas et al. (Washington, DC: CQ Press, 2010), 380.

60. Ibid., 382.

61. Michael Edwards, "Have NGOs 'Made a Difference'? From Manchester to Birmingham with an Elephant in the Room," in *NGO Management: The Earthscan Companion*, ed. Alan Fowler and Chiku Malunga (London and Washington, DC: Earthscan Publishing, 2010), 20–21.

62. Mathews, 274.

63. Ibid., 275.

64. Ole Jacob Sending and Iver B. Neumann, "Governance to Governmentality: Analyzing NGOs, States, and Power," *International Studies Quarterly* 50, no. 3 (September 2006): 651.

65. Beyer, 534.

66. Ibid., 535.

67. Zhengling, 485.

68. Melly Caballero-Anthony, *Negotiating Governance on Non-Traditional Security in Southeast Asia and Beyond* (New York: Columbia University Press, 2018), 218–219.

69. Miles Kahler, "Global Governance: Three Futures," *International Studies Review* 20, issue 2 (June 2018): 245.

70. Caballero-Anthony, 230–233.

71. Ann Marie Clark, *Diplomacy of Conscience: Amnesty International and Changing Human Rights Norms* (Princeton, New Jersey: Princeton University Press, 2001), 21–22.

72. Ibid., 36.

73. Zhengling, 495.

74. Hannah Murphy, "Rethinking the Roles of Non-Governmental Organizations at the World Trade Organization," *Australian Journal of International Affairs* 66, no. 4 (August 2012): 468.

75. Ibid., 480.

76. Zhengling, 496–497.

77. Ngaire Woods, "Making the IMF and the World Bank More Accountable," *International Affairs* 77, no. 1 (January 2001): 83, 95.

78. Ibid., 96.

79. Nicoletta Pirozzi, "The European Union's Crisis Management after Lisbon: Addressing New Security Challenges in the 21st Century," *Instituto Affari Internationali* (IAI) (2013): 11.

80. Ibid., 12.

81. Andre Broome, "When Do NGOs Matter? Activist Organizations as a Source of Change in the International Debt Regime," *Global Society: Journal of Interdisciplinary International Relations* 23, no. 1 (January 2009): 76–78.

82. Scott Turner, "Global Civil Society, Anarchy and Governance: Assessing an Emerging Paradigm," *Journal of Peace Research* 35, no. 1 (January 1998): 39–40.

83. Ibid., 40.

84. Brian Pratt, "Strategic Issues Facing NGOs into the Foreseeable Future," in *NGO Management: The Earthscan Companion*, ed. Alan Fowler and Chiku Malunga (London and Washington, DC: Earthscan Publishing, 2010), 165–166.

85. Nives Dolsak, "Climate Change Policies in the Transitional Economies of Europe and Eurasia: The Role of NGOs," *Voluntas: International Journal of Voluntary and Nonprofit Organizations* 24 (2013): 397–398.

86. Albert Arhin, "Advancing Post-2015 Sustainable Development Goals in a Changing Development Landscape: Challenges of NGOs in Ghana," *Development in Practice* 26, no. 5 (2016): 555, 565–566.

87. Cecilia Tortajada, "Non-governmental Organizations and Influence on Global Politics," *Asia and the Pacific Policy Studies* 3, issue 2 (May 2016): 266, 272.

88. Paul Ronalds, "The Change Challenge: Achieving Transformational Organizational Change in International NGOs," in *NGO Management: The Earthscan Companion*, ed. Alan Fowler and Chiku Malunga (London and Washington DC: Earthscan Publishing, 2010), 204–206.

89. Henry Scheyvens, "The Role of Microfinance and Microfinance Institutions in Climate Change Adaptation: Learning from Experiences in Bangladesh," *Institute for Global Environmental Strategies* (April 1, 2015): 26–27, http://www.jstor.com/stable/resrep00725.10 .

90. Mushtaque Raza Chowdhury, et al., "Developing Urban Space: The Changing Role of NGOs in Bangladesh," *Development in Practice* 27, no. 2 (2017): 261.

91. Ibid., 269.

92. Francisco Rey, "The Complex Nature of Actors in Humanitarian Action and the Challenge of Coordination," in *Reflections on Humanitarian Action: Principles, Ethics and Contradictions*, ed. The Humanitarian Studies Unit (London: Pluto Press, 2001), 99.

93. Ibid., 100.

94. Ivica Petrikova, "NGO Effectiveness: Evidence from the Field of Child Labor in El Salvador," *Forum for Development Studies* 42, no. 2 (2015): 225.

95. Rey, 115–116.

96. Susannah Mayhew et al., "Balancing Protection and Pragmatism: A Framework for NGO Accountability in Rights-Based Approaches," *Health and Human Rights* 9, no. 2 (2006): 181.

97. Mick Moore and Sheelagh Stewart, *Development NGOs and Civil Society* (London: Oxfam GB, 2000), 80–81.

98. Ibid., 86.

99. Maryam Zarnegar Deloffre, "Global Accountability Communities: NGO Self-Regulation in the Humanitarian Sector," *Review of International Studies* 42, part 4 (2016): 724.

100. INGO Accountability Charter, https://ingoaccountabilitycharter.org/about-the-charter (accessed August 5, 2020; Angela M. Crack offers useful insights on the effectiveness of the charter in her article titled: "The Regulation of International NGOs: Assessing the Effectiveness of the INGO Accountability Charter," *Voluntas: International Journal of Voluntary and Nonprofit Organizations* 29, issue 2 (April 2018): 419–429.

101. Domenico Carolei, "What Happens When NGOs Are Accused of Violating Human Rights?," *openDemocracy: free thinking for the world* (April 16, 2019), https://www.opendemocracy.net/en/transformation/what-happens-when-ngos-are-accused-violating-human-rights/.

102. Vincent Charles Keating and Erla Thrandardottir, "NGOs, Trust, and the Accountability Agenda," *The British Journal of Politics and International Relations* 19, issue 1 (2016): 134, 138.

103. Ibid., 140, 146.

104. Sarah Sunn Bush and Jennifer Hadden, "Density and Decline in the Founding of International NGOs in the United States," *International Studies Quarterly* 63 (2019): 1133.

105. Ibid., 1145.

106. Ibid., 1145.

107. Bipasha Baruah, "NGOs as Intermediaries in Post-Disaster Rural Reconstruction: Findings for Research in India," *Development in Practice* 25, no. 7 (2015): 951.

108. James McGann and Mary Johnstone. "The Power Shift and the NGO Credibility Crisis," Brown Journal of World Affairs 11, issue 2 (Winter/Spring 2005): 169.

BIBLIOGRAPHY

Abeles, Marc. "Rethinking NGOs: The Economy of Survival and Global Governance." *Indiana Journal of Global Legal Studies* 15, issue 1 (January 1, 2008): 241–258.

Abderlrahman, Maha. "The Transnational and the Local: Egyptian Activists and Transnational Protest Movements." *British Journal of Middle Eastern Studies* 38, no. 3 (December 2011): 407–424.

Abiew, Francis Kofi and Tom Keating. "NGOs and UN Peacekeeping Operations: Strange Bedfellows." *International Peacekeeping* 6, no. 2 (Summer 1999): 89–111.

Adamson, Fiona B. "International Democracy Assistance in Uzbekistan and Kyrgyzstan: Building Civil Society from the Outside." In *The Power and Limits of NGOs: A Critical Look at Building Democracy in Eastern Europe and Eurasia*, edited by Sarah E. Mendelson and John K, Glenn, 177-206. New York: Columbia University Press, 2002.

Agbenyiga, DeBrenna LaFa and Lihua Huang. "Impact of the Organizational Networks on the Roles of NGOs in Eldercare: Perspectives from HelpAge Ghana Day Cantres." *Aging International* 37 (2012): 338–355.

Ahmed, Shamina and David M. Potter. *NGOs in International Politics*. Boulder, Colorado: Kumarian Press, 2013.

Alger, Chadwick F. "Evolving Roles of NGOs in Member State Decision-Making in the UN System." *Journal of Human Rights* 2, no. 3 (September 2003): 407–424.

Almeida, Paul. *Social Movements: The Structure of Collective Mobilization*. Oakland, CA: University of California Press, 2019.

Anderson, Kenneth. "Do NGOs Wield Too Much Power, Yes." In *Controversies in Globalization: Contending Approaches to International Relations*, edited by Peter M. Haas, John A. Hird, and Beth McBratney, 364–370. Washington, DC: CQ Press, 2010.

Arhin, Albert. "Advancing Post-2015 Sustainable Development Goals in a Changing Development Landscape: Challenges of NGOs in Ghana." *Development in Practice* 26, no. 5 (2016): 555–568.

Arnall, Alex, David S. G. Thomas, Chasca Twyman, and Diana Liverman. "NGOs, Elite Capture and Community-Driven Development: Perspectives in Rural Mozambique." *The Journal of Modern African Studies* 51, no. 2 (June 2013): 305–330.

Aspinall, Edward and Marcus Mietzner. "Indonesia: Economic Crisis, Foreign Pressure, and Regime Change." In *Transitions to Democracy: A Comparative Perspective*, edited by Kathryn Stoner and Michael McFaul, 144–167.

Ateljevic, Jovo. "Building Institutional, Economic and Social Capacities through Discourse: The Role of NGOs in the Context of Bosnia-Herzegovina and Serbia." *Journal of Southern Europe and the Balkans* 10, no. 3 (December 2008): 347–362.

Awekeya, Philip, Kansoe ReCas, and Roland Brady. "A Critical View on the Role of NGOs in Systemic Capacity Building: Insights from Projects for Promoting Access to Water and Self-Sufficiency in Food Production in Northern Ghana." *Journal of Organizational Transformation and Social Change* 14, no. 1 (2017): 78–97.

Baruah, Bipasha. "NGOs as Intermediaries in Post-Disaster Rural Reconstruction: Findings for Research in India." *Development in Practice* 25, no. 7 (2015): 951–965.

Bayat, Asef. "Activism and Social Development in the Middle East." *International Journal of Middle East Studies* 34, no. 1 (February 2002): 1–28.

Baydas, Lana. "Civic Space in India between the National Security Hammer and the Counterterrorism Anvil." *Center for Strategic and International Studies* (CSIS) (2018): 61–72.

Beinin, Joel. "Civil Society, NGOs, and Egypt's 2011 Popular Uprising." *The South Atlantic Quarterly* 113, no. 2 (Spring 2014): 396–406.

Bello, Walden. "The Rise of the Relief-And-Reconstruction Complex." *Journal of International Affairs* 59, no. 2 (Spring/Summer 2006): 281–296.

Benessaieh, Afef. "Global Civil Society: Speaking in Northern Tongues?" *Latin American Perspectives* 38, no. 6 (November 2011): 69–90.

Berlie, Laurence Schwesinger. *Alliances for Sustainable Development: Business and NGO Partnerships*. New York: Palgrave/Macmillan, 2010.

Bernath, Julie and Ratana Ly. "Forward to the Working Paper Series on Cambodia." *Swisspeace* (2019): 7–12.

Beyer, Cornelia. "Non-Governmental Organizations as Motors of Change." *Government and Opposition* 42, no. 4 (2007): 513–535.

Beznosova, Olga and Lisa McIntosh Sundstrom. "Western Aid and the State-Society Balance in Novgorod and Khabarovsk." *Problems of Post-Communism* 56, no. 6 (2009): 21–35.

Bibi, Ghanem, Julie Peteet, and Joe Stork. "The NGO Phenomenon in the Arab World." *Middle East Report*, no. 193 (March-April 1995): 26–27.

Blue, Sarah A. "Including Women in Development: Guatemalan Refugees and Local NGOs." *Latin American Perspectives* 32, no. 5 (September 2005): 101–117.

Bond, Michael. "The Backlash against NGOs." In *The Globalization Reader*, edited by Frank J. Lechner and John Boli, 277–283. Malden, MA: Blackwell Publishing, 2004.

Borgh, Chris van der and Carolijn Terwindt. "Shrinking Operational Space of NGOs — a Framework of Analysis." *Development in Practice* 22, no. 8 (November 2012): 1065–1081.

Boulding, Carew E. "NGOs and Political Participation in Weak Democracies: Evidence on Protest and Voter Turnout from Bolivia." *The Journal of Politics* 72, no. 2 (April 2010): 456–468.

Boulding, Carew E. and Jami Nelson-Nunez. "Civil Society and Support for the Political System." *Latin American Research Review* 49, no. 1 (2014): 128–154.

Boussaguet, Laurie and Charlotte Halpern. "NGOs, Civil Society and Policy Analysis: From Mutual Disinterest to Reciprocal Investment." In *Policy Analysis in France*, edited by Charlotte Halpern, Patrick Hassenteufel, and Philippe Zittoun, 243–260. Bristol, UK: Bristol University Press, Policy Press, 2018.

Bradley, Matthew Todd. "Chinese-Built Dams, Africa, and Economic Growth: Is There a Role for African NGOs?" *Journal of the Indiana Academy of the Social Sciences* 14, issue 1 (2010): 88–96.

Brautigam, Deborah A. and Monique Segarra. "Difficult Partnerships: The World Bank, States, and NGOs." *Latin American Politics and Society* 49, no. 4 (Winter 2007): 149–181.

Broome, Andre. "When Do NGOs Matter? Activist Organizations as a Source of Change in the International Debt Regime." *Global Society: Journal of Interdisciplinary International Relations* 23, no. 1 (January 2009): 59–78.

Bukenya, Badru. "From Social Accountability to a New Social Contract? The Role of NGOs in Protecting and Empowering PLHIV in Uganda." *The Journal of Development Studies* 52, no. 8 (2016): 1162–1176.

Burroughs, John and Jacqueline Cabasso. "Confronting the Nuclear-Armed States in International Negotiating Forums: Lessons for NGOs." *International Negotiation* 4 (1999): 457–480.

Bush, Sarah Sunn and Jennifer Hadden. "Density and Decline in the Founding of International NGOs in the United States." *International Studies Quarterly* 63 (2019): 1133–1146.

Caballero-Anthony, Melly. *Negotiating Governance on Non-Traditional Security in Southeast Asia and Beyond*. New York: Columbia University Press, 2018.

Campbell, Susanna, Matthew DoGiuseppe, and Amanda Murdie. "International Development NGOs and Bureaucratic Capacity: Facilitator or Destroyer?" *Political Research Quarterly* 72, no. 1 (2019): 3–18.

Carapico, Sheila. "NGOs, INGOs, GO-NGOs and DO-NGOs: Making Sense of Non-Governmental Organizations." *Middle East Report*, no. 214 (Spring 2000): 12–15.

Carolei, Domenico. "What Happens When NGOs Are Accused of Violating Human Rights?." *openDemocracy: free thinking for the world* (April 16, 2019), https://www.opendemocracy.net/en/transformation/what-happens-when-ngos-are-accused-violating-human-rights/. .

Carothers, Thomas. "The Closing Space Challenge: How are Funders Responding?" *Carnegie Endowment for International Peace* (2015): 1–37.

Castells, Manuel. "Global Governance and Global Politics." *Political Science and Politics* XXXVIII, no. 1 (2004): 9–16.

Cavill, Sue and M. Sohail. "Increasing Strategic Accountability: A Framework for International NGOs." *Development in Practice* 17, no. 2 (April 2007): 231–248.

Chapman, Jennifer and Thomas Fisher. "The Effectiveness of NGO Campaigning: Lessons from Practice." *Development in Practice* 10, no. 2 (May 2000): 151–165.

Charnovitz, Steve. "Two Centuries of Participation: NGOs and International Governance." *Michigan Journal of International Law* 18, no. 2 (1997): 182–286.

Chowdhury, Mushtaque Raza, Ferdous Jahan, and Rehnuma Rahman. "Developing Urban Space: The Changing Role of NGOs in Bangladesh." *Development in Practice* 27, no. 2 (2017): 260–271.

Clark, Ann Marie, Elizabeth J. Friedman, and Kathryn Hochstetler. "The Sovereign Limits of Global Civil Society: A Comparison of NGO Participation in UN World Conferences on the Environment, Human Rights, and Women." *World Politics* 51, no. 1 (October 1998): 1–35.

Clark, Ann Marie. *Diplomacy of Conscience: Amnesty International and Changing Human Rights Norms.* Princeton, New Jersey: Princeton University Press, 2001.

Cleary, Seamus. *The Role of NGOs under Authoritarian Political Systems.* London: MacMillan Press LTD., 1997.

Code of Ethics & Conduct for NGOs, 1–42, www.WANGO.org .

Cosgrove, Serena. "Levels of Empowerment: Marketers and Microenterprise-Lending NGOs in Apopa and Nejapa, El Salvador." *Latin American Perspectives* 29, no. 5 (September 2002): 48–65.

Crack, Angela M. "The Regulation of International NGOs: Assessing the Effectiveness of the INGO Accountability Charter." *Voluntas: International Journal of Voluntary and Nonprofit Organizations* 29, issue 2 (April 2018): 419–429.

Crotty, Jo. "Making a Difference? NGOs and Civil Society Development in Russia." *Europe-Asia Studies* 61, no. 1 (January 2009) 85–108.

Cummings, Sarah, Richard Heeks, and Marleen Huysman. "Knowledge and Learning in Online Networks in Development: A Social-Capital Perspective." *Development in Practice* 16, no. 6 (November 2006): 570–586.

Danis, Didem and Dilara Nazli. "A Faithful Alliance between the Civil Society and the State: Actors and Mechanisms of Accommodating Syrian Refugees in Istanbul." *International Migration* 57, no. 2 (2019): 143–157.

Danopoulos, Constantine P., Nila Kapor-Stanulovic, and Konstantinos S. Skandalis. "Children and Armed Conflict: The Yugoslav Experience." *Journal of Balkan and Near Eastern Studies* 14, no. 1 (March 2012): 151–163.

Dany, Charlotte. "Exploring the Political Agency of Humanitarian NGOs: Médecins Sans Frontières." *Global Society: Journal of Interdisciplinary International Relations* 33, no. 2 (2019): 184–200.

Deloffre, Maryam Zarnegar. "Global Accountability Communities: NGO Self-Regulation in the Humanitarian Sector." *Review of International Studies* 42, part 4 (2016): 724–747.

Deng, Guosheng. "The Influence of Elite Philanthropy on NGO Development in China." *Asian Studies Review* 39, no. 4 (2015): 554–570.

Diamond, L. "Toward Democratic Consolidation." In *The Global Resurgence of Democracy*, edited by L. Diamond and M. Plattner, 227–240. Baltimore: The Johns Hopkins University Press, 1996.

Diamond, Larry. *Developing Democracy: Toward Consolidation*. Baltimore: The Johns Hopkins University Press, 1999.

Dolsak, Nives. "Climate Change Policies in the Transitional Economies of Europe and Eurasia: The Role of NGOs." *Voluntas: International Journal of Voluntary and Nonprofit Organizations* 24 (2013): 382–402.

Douglas, Melonee, Rachel Levitan, and Lucy W. Kiama. "Expanding the Role of NGOs in Resettlement." *Forced Migration Review*, issue 54 (February 2017): 34–37.

DuBois, Thomas David. "Before the NGO: Chinese Charities in Historical Perspective." *Asian Studies Review* 39, no. 4 (2015): 541–563.

Duval, Anne-Marie and Yves Gendron. "Creating Space for an Alternative Discourse in the Context of Neoliberal Hegemony: The Case of a Long-Standing NGO." *Administrative Theory and Praxis* 42 (2020): 62–89.

Edmonds, Kevin. "Beyond Good Intentions: The Structural Limitations of NGOs in Haiti." *Critical Sociology* 39, no. 3 (2013): 439–452.

Edwards, Michael and David Humle. "Too Close for Comfort? The Impact of Official Aid on Nongovernmental Organizations." *Current Issues in Comparative Education* 1, no. 1 (November 1998): 1–21.

Edwards, Michael. "Why 'Philanthrocapitalism' Is Not the Answer: Private Initiatives and International Development." In *Doing Good or Doing Better: Development Policies in a Globalizing World*, edited by Monique Kremer, Peter van Lieshout, and Robert Went, 237–254. Amsterdam: Amsterdam University Press, 2009.

Edwards, Michael. "Have NGOs 'Made a Difference'? From Manchester to Birmingham with an Elephant in the Room." In *NGO Management: The Earthscan Companion*, edited by Alan Fowler and Chiku Malunga, 13–25. London and Washington, DC: Earthscan Publishing, 2010.

Elbers, Willem and Lau Schulpen. "Corridors of Power: The Institutional Design of North-South NGO Partnerships." *Voluntas: International Journal of Voluntary and Nonprofit Organizations* 24 (2013): 48–67.

El-Gawhary, Krista Masonis. "Egyptian Advocacy NGOs: Catalysts for Social and Political Change?" *Middle East Report*, no. 214 (Spring 2000): 38–41, http://www.jstor.org/stable/1520194 .

Escallon, Maria Fernanda. "Negotiating Intangibles: The Power, Place, and Prestige of NGOs in Heritage Governance." *International Journal of Heritage Studies* 26, no. 8 (2020): 719–136.

Estlund, Cynthia. *A New Deal for China's Workers?* Cambridge, MA: Harvard University Press, 2017.

Fagan, Adam and Indraneel Sircar. "Compliance without Governance: The Role of NGOs in Environmental Impact Assessment Processes in Bosnia-Herzegovina." *Environmental Politics* 19, no. 4 (July 2010): 599–616.

Farid, May. "Advocacy in Action: China's Grassroots NGOs as Catalysts for Policy Innovation." *Studies in Comparative International Development* 54 (2019): 528–549.

Feng, Chongyi. "The NGO Law in China and its Impact on Overseas Funded NGOs." *Cosmopolitan Civil Societies: An Interdisciplinary Journal* 9, no. 3 (2017): 95–105.

Fisher, William F. "DOING GOOD? The Politics and Antipolitics of NGO Practices." *Annual Review of Anthropology* 26 (1997): 439–464.

Flanigan, Shawn Teresa. "Paying for God's Work: A Rights-Based Examination of Faith-Based NGOs in Romania." *Voluntas: International Journal of Voluntary and Nonprofit Organizations* 18 (2007): 156–175.

Flowers, Petrice R. "Failure to Protect Refugees? Domestic Institutions, International Organizations, and Civil Society in Japan." *Journal of Japanese Studies* 34, no. 2 (Summer 2008): 333–361.

Fonjong, Lotsmart. "Fostering Women's Participation in Development through Non-Governmental Efforts in Cameroon." *The Geographical Journal* 167, no. 3 (September 2001): 223–234.

Forkuor, David and Seth Agyemang. "Fighting Urban Poverty in Ghana: The Role of Non-Governmental Organizations." *Urban Forum* 29 (2018): 127–145.

Franceschini, Ivan. "Labor NGOs in China: A Real Force for Political Change?" *The China Quarterly* no. 218 (June 2014): 474–492.

Frangonikopoulos, Christos A. "Politics, the Media and NGOs: The Greek Experience." *Perspectives on European Politics and Society* 15, no. 4 (2014): 606–619.

Frangonikopoulos, Christos A. and Stamatis Poulakidakos. "Revisiting the Public Profile and Communication of Greek NGOs in Time of Crisis." *International Journal of Media and Cultural Politics* 11, no. 1 (2015): 119–127.

Frey, Monique and Gerhard Meili. "Social Inclusion and Cultural Identity of Roma Communities in South-Eastern Europe." *Swisspeace* (2011): 50–56.

"Funding Opportunities for NGOs." *European Union*, 1-2, https://ec.europa.eu/info/funding-tenders/how-eu-funding-works/who-eligible-funding/funding-opportunities-ngos_en .

"Funds, Programs, Specialized Agencies and Others." *United Nations*, 1–4, https://www.un.org/en/sections/about-un/funds-programmes-specialized-agencies-and-others/ .

Gereke, Marika and Tanja Bruhl. "Unpacking the Unequal Representation of Northern and Southern NGOs in International Climate Change Politics." *Third World Quarterly* 40, no. 5 (2019): 870–889.

Glasius, Marlies. "Do NGOs Wield Too Much Power? No." In *Controversies in Globalization: Contending Approaches to International Relations,* edited by Peter M. Haas, John A. Hird, and Beth McBratney, 371–382. Washington, DC: CQ Press, 2010.

Goodhand, Jonathan and Peter Chamberlain. "Dancing with the Prince: NGOs' Survival Strategies in the Afghan Conflict." In *Development, NGOs and Civil Society*, edited by Jonathan Goodhand and Peter Chamberlain, 91–108. London: Oxfam GB, 2000.

Gordenker, Leon and Thomas G. Weiss. "Devolving Responsibilities: A Framework for Analyzing NGOs and Services." *Third World Quarterly* 18, no. 3 (1997): 443–455.

Grodsky, Brian. "Co-Optation or Empowerment? The Fate of Pro-Democracy NGOs after the Rose Revolution." *Europe-Asia Studies* 64, no. 9 (November 2012): 1684–1708.

Grugel, Jean. "Romancing Civil Society: European NGOs in Latin America." *Journal of Interamerican Studies and World Affairs* 42, no. 2 (Summer 2000): 87–107.

Guerra, Junia Fatima do Carmo and Walter Mswaka. "Knowledge and Power of Civil Society: An Empirical Study of Brazilian Professionals Working in NGOs." *Cosmopolitan Civil Societies Journal* 8, no. 1 (2016): 64–85.

Hahn, Kristina and Anna Holzscheiter. "The Ambivalence of Advocacy: Representation and Contestation in Global NGO Advocacy for Child Workers and Sex Workers." *Global Society: Journal of Interdisciplinary International Relations* 27, no. 4 (October 2013): 497–520.

Hasmath, Reza, Timothy Hildebrandt, and Jennifer Y. J. Hsu. "Conceptualizing Government-Organized Non-Governmental Organizations." *Journal of Civil Society* 15, no. 3 (2019): 267–284.

He, Baogang and Hannah Murphy. "Global Social Justice at the WTO? The Role of NGOs in Constructing Global Social Contracts." *International Affairs* 83, no. 4 (2007): 707–727.

Heinrich, Volkhart Finn. "The Role of NGOs in Strengthening the Foundations of South African Democracy." *Voluntas: International Journal of Voluntary and Nonprofit Organizations* 12, no. 1 (2001): 1–15.

Heurlin, Christopher. "Governing Civil Society: The Political Logic of NGO-State Relations under Dictatorship." *Voluntas: International Journal of Voluntary and Nonprofit Organizations* 21, issue 2 (June 2010): 220–239.

Holmen, Hans and Magnus Jirstrom. "Look Who's Talking! Second Thoughts about NGOs as Representing Civil Society." *Journal of Asian and African Studies* 44, no. 4 (2009): 429–448.

Holtom, Paul and Mark Bromley. "Non-Governmental Monitoring of International Arms Transfers." *Stockholm International Peace Research Institute* (2011): 26–32.

"How Does the U.S. Spend Its Foreign Aid?" *Council on Foreign Relations*, 1–10, https://www.cfr.org/backgrounder/how-does-us-spend-its-foreign-aid .

Howell, Jude, Armine Ishkanian, Ebenezer Obadre, Hakan Seckinelgin, and Marlies Glasius. "The Backlash against Civil Society in the Wake of the Long War on Terror." *Development in Practice* 18, no. 1 (February 2008): 82–93.

Hsu, Jennifer Y. J. and Reza Hasmath. "The Local Corporatist State and NGO relations in China." *Journal of Contemporary China* 23, no. 87 (2014): 516–534.

INGO Accountability Charter, https://ingoaccountabilitycharter.org/about-the-charter .

International Committee of the Red Cross, *Britannica Online Encyclopedia*, 1, https://www.britannica.com/print/article/290788 .

Islam, Ekhtekharul. "Governmental Organizations and Non-Governmental Organizations Involvement in Managing Drinking Water: Disaster Affected Coastal Rural Area of Bangladesh." *The Global Studies Journal* 6 (2014): 45–54.

Kahler, Miles. "Global Governance: Three Futures." *International Studies Review* 20, issue 2 (June 2018): 239–246.

Kaldor, Mary. *Global Civil Society: An Answer to War.* Malden, MA: Polity Press, 2003.

Kanji, Nazneen, Carla Braga, and Winnie Mitullah. "Promoting Land Rights in Africa: How Do NGOs Make a Difference." *International Institute for Environment and Development* (2002): 31–34.

Keating, Vincent Charles and Erla Thrandardottir. "NGOs, Trust, and the Accountability Agenda." *The British Journal of Politics and International Relations* 19, issue 1 (2016): 134–151.

Kegley, Charles W. and Gregory A. Raymond. *Exorcising the Ghost of Westphalia: Building World Order in the New Millennium.* Upper Saddle River, New Jersey: Prentice Hall, 2002.

Khan, Muhammad Ammad, Jian Xiaoying, and Nazish Kanwal. "Armed Conflict in the Federally Administered Tribal Areas of Pakistan and the Role of NGOs in Restoring Health Services." *Social Work in Public Health* 31, no. 4 (2016): 215–230.

Khieng, Sothy and Heidi Dahles. "Resource Dependence and Effects of Funding Diversification Strategies among NGOs in Cambodia." *Voluntas: International Journal of Voluntary and Nonprofit Organizations* 26 (2015): 1412–1437.

Kim, Euiyoung. "The Limits of NGO-Government Relations in South Korea." *Asian Survey* 49, no. 5 (September/October 2009): 873–894.

Kim, Jungin. "A Study of the Roles of NGOs for North Korean Refugees' Human Rights." *Journal of Immigrant & Refugee Studies* 8 (2010): 76–90.

Kim, Sunhyuk. "NGOs and Social Protection in East Asia: Korea, Thailand and Indonesia." *Asian Journal of Political Science* 23, no. (2015): 23–43.

Kirsch, Stuart. *Mining Capitalism: The Relationship between Corporations and Their Critics.* Oakland, CA: University of California Press, 2014.

Kivland, Chelsey L. "Unmaking the State in 'Occupied' Haiti." *PoLAR: Political and Legal Anthropology Review* 35, no. 2 (November 2012): 248–270.

Klees, Steven L. "NGOs: Progressive Force or Neo-Liberal Tool?." *Current Issues in Comparative Education* 1, no. 1 (2002): 49–54.

Kluczewska, Karolina. "Questioning local ownership: Insights from Donor-Funded NGOs in Tajikistan." *Journal of Civil Society* 15, no. 4 (2019): 353–372.

Lambrou, Yianna. "The Changing Role of NGOs in Rural Chile after Democracy." *Bulletin of Latin American Research* 16, no. 1 (1997): 107–116.

Lazzarini, Mia. "The Top 10 Influential NGOs," 1–10, https://www.peoplebrowsr.com/blog/the-top-10-influential-ngos .

Lei, Ya-Wen. *The Contentious Public Sphere: Law, Media, and Authoritarian Rule in China.* Princeton, New Jersey: Princeton University Press, 2018.

Leipold, Gerd. "Campaigning: A Fashion or the Best Way to Change the Global Agenda?." In *Development and Advocacy*, edited by Oxfam GB, 74–83. London: Oxfam GB, 2002.

Lester, Eve. "A Place at the Table: The Role of NGOs in Refugee Protection: International Advocacy and Policy-Making." *Refugee Survey Quarterly* 24, no. 2 (2005): 125–142.

Lewis, David and Nazneen Kanji. *Non-Governmental Organizations and Development.* New York: Routledge, 2009.

Longhofer, Wesley, Evan Schofer, Natasha Miric, and David John Frank. "NGOs, INGOs, and Environmental Policy Reform, 1970–2010." *Social Forces* 94, no. 4 (June 2016): 1743–1768.

Luong, Pauline Jones and Erika Weinthal. "The NGO Paradox: Democratic Goals and Non-Democratic Outcomes in Kazakhstan." *Europe-Asia Studies* 51, no. 7 (November 1999): 1267–1284.

Lutsevych, Orysia. "Black Sea Region: Missing Pieces of the Civil Society Puzzle." *German Marshall Fund of the United States* (2013): 1–8.

Makita, Rie. "New NGO-Elite Relations in Business Development for the Poor in Rural Bangladesh." *Voluntas: International Journal of Voluntary and Nonprofit Organizations* 20, no. 1 (March 2009): 50–70.

Malik, Nadeem and Ahsan Rana. "Civil Society in Pakistan: An Exclusive Discourse of Projectization." *Dialectical Anthropology* 44 (2020): 41–56.

Martens, Kerstin. "Mission Impossible? Defining Nongovernmental Organizations." *Voluntas: International Journal of Voluntary and Nonprofit Organizations* 13, no. 3 (September 2002): 271–285.

Mathews, Jessica T. "Power Shift." In *The Globalization Reader*, edited by Frank J. Lechner and John Boli, 270–276. Malden, MA: Blackwell, Publishing, 2004.

Mayhew, Susannah, Megan Douthwaite, and Michael Hammer. "Balancing Protection and Pragmatism: A Framework for NGO Accountability in Rights-Based Approaches." *Health and Human Rights* 9, no. 2 (2006): 180–206.

McGann, James and Mary Johnstone. "The Power Shift and the NGO Credibility Crisis." *Brown Journal of World Affairs* 11, issue 2 (Winter/Spring 2005): 159–172.

McGrew, Anthony. "Globalization and Global Politics." In *The Globalization of World Politics: An Introduction to International Relations*, edited by John Baylis, Steve Smith, and Patricia Owens, 14–33, 4th ed. Boulder, Colorado: Lynne Rienner Publishers, Inc., 2008.

Mendes, Philip. "The NGO Wars: Why Neo-Liberals Are Trashing Non-Government and Advocacy Groups." *Social Alternatives* 24, no. 3 (2005): 40–45.

"Most US Foreign Aid Flows through US Organizations." *PolitiFact Global News Service*, 1–8, https://www.politifact.com/global-news/statements/2017/mar/08/raj-shah/yes-most-us-foreign-aid-flows-through-us-organizat/ .

Mulalic, Muhidin. "Fostering of Civil Society by Muslim Women's NGOs in Bosnia and Herzegovina." *Journal of Muslim Minority Affairs* 34, no. 4 (2014): 438–448.

Murdie, Amanda and Alexander Hicks. "Can International Nongovernmental Organizations Boost Government Services? The Case of Health." *International Organization* 67, no. 3 (Summer 2013): 541–573.

Murphy, Craig N. "Global Governance: Poorly Done and Poorly Understood." *International Affairs* 76, no. 4 (October 2000): 789–803.

Murphy, Hannah. "Rethinking the Roles of Non-Governmental Organizations at the World Trade Organization." *Australian Journal of International Affairs* 66, no. 4 (August 2012): 468–485.

Natsios, Andrew S. "NGOs and the UN System in Complex Humanitarian Emergencies: Conflict or Cooperation?" In *The Politics of Global Governance: International Organizations in an Interdependent World*, edited by Paul F. Diehl, 381–397. Boulder, Colorado: Lynne Rienner Publishers, Inc., 2005.

Nezhina, Tamara G. and Aigerim R. Ibrayeva. "Explaining the Role of Culture and Traditions in Functioning of Civil Society Organizations in Kazakhstan." *ISTR* 24 (2013): 335–358.

"NGO Monitor: Making NGOs Accountable," 1–9, https://www.ngo-monitor.org/funder/united_states/ .

Nichols, Briana, Karla Umana, Tamara Britton, Lisette Farias, Ryan Lavalley, and Rachel Hall-Clifford. "Transnational Information Politics and the 'Child Migration Crisis': Guatemalan NGOs Respond to Youth Migration." *Voluntas: International Journal of Voluntary and Nonprofit Organizations* 28 (2027): 1962–1987.

Noh, Jae-Eun. "The Role of NGOs in Building CSR Discourse around Human Rights in Developing Countries." *Cosmopolitan Civil Societies: An Interdisciplinary Journal* 9, no. 1 (2017): 1–19.

Nyamugasira, Warren. *Development and Social Action*. London: Oxfam GB, 1999.

Ocantos, Ezequiel Gonzales. "Persuade Them or Oust Them: Crafting Judicial Change and Transitional Justice in Argentina." *Comparative Politics* 46, no. 4 (July 2014): 479–498.

Ogunseye, Balaji. "NGOs and Which 'Civil Society'?" *International Institute for Environment and Development* (1997): 10–13.

Ohanyan, Anna. "Policy Wars for Peace: Network Model of NGO Behavior." *International Studies Review* 11, no. 3 (September 2009): 475–501.

Oleinikova, Olga. "Foreign Funded NGOs in Russia, Belarus and Ukraine: Recent Restrictions and Implications." *Cosmopolitan Societies: An Interdisciplinary Journal* 9, no. 3 (2017): 85–94.

Olson, David J. and Andrew Piller. "Ethiopia: An Emerging Family Planning Success Story." *Studies in Family Planning* 44, no. 4 (December 2013): 445–459.

Otto, Dianne. "Non-Governmental Organizations in the United Nations System: The Emerging Role of International Civil Society." *Human Rights Quarterly* 18 (1996): 107–141.

Panday, Pranab Kumar and Shelley Feldman. "Mainstreaming Gender in Politics in Bangladesh: Role of NGOs." *Asian Journal of Political Science* 23, no. 3 (2015): 301–320.

Paul, Bimal Kanti. "Relief Assistance to 1998 Flood Victims: A Comparison of the Performance of the Government and NGOs." *The Geographical Journal* 169, no. 1 (March 2003): 75–89.

Paul, James A. "NGOs and Global Policy-Making." *Global Policy Forum* (June 2000): 1–3, https://www.globalpolicy.org/empire/31611-ngos-and-global-policy-making.html?tmpl=component&print=1&page= .

Pei, Minxin. "China's Coming Upheaval: Competition, the Coronavirus, and the Weakness of Xi Jinping." *Foreign Affairs* (May/June 2020): 82–95.

Petrikova, Ivica. "NGO Effectiveness: Evidence from the Field of Child Labor in El Salvador." *Forum for Development Studies* 42, no. 2 (2015): 225–244.

Petrova, Tsveta. "Citizens' Participation in Local Governance in Eastern Europe: Rediscovering a Strength of Civil Society in Post-Socialist World?" *Europe-Asia Studies* 63, no. 5 (July 2011): 757–787.

Phillips, Ruth and Susan Goodwin. "Third Sector Social Policy Research in Australia: New Actors, New Policies." *Voluntas: International Journal of Voluntary and Nonprofit Organizations* 25 (2014): 565–584.

Pierre-Louis, Francois. "The Haiti Earthquake of 2010: The Politics of a Natural Disaster." *Journal of Black Studies* 42, no. 2 (March 2011): 186–202.

Pilny, Andrew and Michlle Shumate. "Hyperlinks as Extensions of Offline Instrumental Collective Action." *Information, Communication & Society* 15, no. 2 (March 2012): 260–286.

Pirozzi, Nicoletta. "The European Union's Crisis Management After Lisbon: Addressing New Security Challenges in the 21st Century." *Instituto Affari Internationali* (IAI) (2013): 1–19.

Pitner, Julia. "Critiquing NGOs: Assessing the Last Decade." *Middle East Report* (Spring 2000): 34–37.

Pratt, Brian. "Strategic Issues Facing NGOs into the Foreseeable Future." In *NGO Management: The Earthscan Companion*, edited by Alan Fowler and Chiku Malunga, 165–174. London and Washington DC, 2010.

Rey, Francisco. "The Complex Nature of Actors in Humanitarian Action and the Challenge of Coordination." In *Reflections on Humanitarian Action: Principles, Ethics and Contradictions*, edited by the Humanitarian Studies Unit, 99–119. London: Pluto Press, 2001.

Richter, Thomas. "Reduced Scope for Action Worldwide for Civil Society." *German Institute of Global and Area Studies* (GIGA) (December 1, 2018): 1–12, https://www.jstor.org/stable/resrep21176 .

Riemann, Kim D. "A View from the Top: International Politics, Norms and Worldwide Growth of NGOs." *International Studies Quarterly* 50, no. 1 (2006): 45–67.

Ronalds, Paul. "The Change Challenge: Achieving Transformational Organizational Change in International NGOs." In *NGO Management: The Earthscan Companion*, edited by Alan Fowler and Chiku Malunga, 202–214. London and Washington DC: Earthscan Publishing, 2010.

Ross, Elizabeth. "The Role of Small NGOs: Building Quality International Education." *Harvard International Review* (Summer 2013): 40–44.

Sabbarwal, Smriti. "Indigenous Peoples' Concerns for Environment: Examining the Role of Non-Governmental Organizations." *Fourth World Journal* (Winter 2017): 27–39.

Schade, Jeanette. "Between Projectitis and the Formation of Countervailing Power — NGOs in Nation-Building Processes." In *Nation-Building*, edited by Jochen Hippler, 125–136. London: Pluto Press, 2005.

Scheyvens, Henry. "The Role of Microfinance and Microfinance Institutions in Climate Change Adaptation: Learning from Experiences in Bangladesh." *Institute for Global Environmental Strategies* (April 1, 2015): 19–28, http://www.jstor.com/stable/resrep00725.10 .

Schnellbach, Christoph. "The Role of NGOs in Promoting Minority Rights in the Enlarged European Union." *Perspectives on European Politics and Society* 13, no. 4 (December 2012): 497–512.

Schuller, Mark. *Killing with Kindness: Haiti, International Aid, and NGOs*. New Brunswick, New Jersey: Rutgers University Press, 2012.

Sending, Ole Jacob and Iver B. Neumann. "Governance to Governmentality: Analyzing NGOs, States, and Power." *International Studies Quarterly* 50, no. 3 (September 2006): 651–672.

Shieh, Shawn and Guosheng Deng. "An Emerging Civil Society: The Impact of the 2008 Sichuan Earthquake on Grassroots Associations in China." *The China Journal* no. 65 (January 2011): 181–194.

Shipper, Apichai W. "Foreigners and Civil Society in Japan." *Pacific Affairs* 79, no. 2 (Summer 2006): 269–289.

Short, Nicola. "The Role of NGOs in the Ottawa Process to Ban Landmines." *International Negotiation* 4 (1999): 481–500.

Sick, Timothy D. "South Africa: Enabling Liberation." In *Transitions to Democracy: A Comparative Perspective*, edited by Kathryn Stoner and Michael McFaul, 168–191. Baltimore, MD: The Johns Hopkins University Press, 2013.

Simeant, Johanna. "What Is Going Global? The Internationalization of French NGOs 'without Borders.'" *Review of International Political Economy* 12, no. 5 (December 2005): 851–883.

Smith, Daniel Jordan. *A Culture of Corruption: Everyday Deception and Popular Discontent in Nigeria*. Princeton, New Jersey: Princeton University Press, 2007.

Sotiropoulos, Dimitri A. "Civil Society in Greece in the Wake of the Economic Crisis." *ELIAMEP* (December 2017): 1–12.

Spires, Anthony J. Lin Tao, and Kin-man Chan. "Societal Support for China's Grass-Roots NGOs: Evidence from Yunnan, Guangdong and Beijing." *The China Journal* no. 71 (January 2014): 65–90.

Steger, Manfred B. and Ravi K. Roy. *Neoliberalism: A Very Short Introduction*. New York: Oxford University Press, 2010.

Steinberg, Gerald M. "International NGOs, the Arab Upheaval, and Human Rights: Examining NGO Resource Allocation." *Northwestern Journal of International Human Rights* 11, no. 1 (2013): 124–149.

Strychar, Lisa and Jennifer Day." Community Assessment of NGO Housing Delivery: Lessons from Port Vila, Vanuatu." *Development in Practice* 29, no. 4 (2019): 464–476.

Suleiman, Lina. "The NGOs and the Grand Illusions of Development and Democracy." *ISTR* 24 (2013): 241–261.

Takahashi, Kaoko. "Assessing NGO Empowerment in Housing Development Frameworks: Discourse and Practice in the Philippines." *International Journal of Japanese Sociology* no. 18 (2009): 112–127.

Tan, See Seng. "NGOs in Conflict Management in Southeast Asia." *International Peacekeeping* 12, no. 1 (Spring 2005): 49–66.

Tanaka, Masako. "The Changing Roles of NGOs in Nepal: Promoting Emerging Rights-Holder Organizations for Inclusive Aid." *Voluntas: International Journal of Voluntary and Nonprofit Organizations* 22 (2011): 494–517.

Tavis, Lee. "Multinational Enterprises: Interacting with Nongovernmental Organizations." In *Peace through Commerce: Responsible Corporate Citizenship and the Ideals of the United Nations Global Compact*, edited by Oliver F. Williams, 413–430. South Bend: Indiana: Notre Dame University Press, 2008.

Teets, Jessica C. "Let Many Civil Societies Bloom: The Rise of Consultative Authoritarianism in China." *The China Quarterly* no. 213 (March 2013): 19–38.

The World's Top Ten Charitable Foundations, 1–6, https://www.fundsforngos.org/ foundation-funds-for-ngos/worlds-top-ten-wealthiest-charitable-foundations .

Thomson, Elaine. "The Role of NGOs in Challenging the Conservative Agenda: Some Empirical Studies." *Social Alternatives* 23, issue 1 (First Quarter 2004): 43–49.

Tortajada, Cecilia. "Nongovernmental Organizations and Influence on Global Politics." *Asia and the Pacific Policy Studies* 3, issue 2 (May 2016): 266–274.

Tran, Mark. "Is the Faultline among NGOs Over the Future of Development Deepening?." *Guardian*, August 17, 2012, https://www.globalpolicy.org/ngos/ introduction/general-analysis-of-the-role-of-ngos/51841-is-the-faultline-among-ngos-over-the-future-of-development .

Tuijl, Peter Van. "Entering the Global Dealing Room: Reflections on a Rights-Based Framework for NGOs in International Development." *Third World Quarterly* 21, no. 4 (2000): 617–626.

Turner, Scott. "Global Civil Society, Anarchy and Governance: Assessing an Emerging Paradigm." *Journal of Peace Research* 35, no. 1 (January 1998): 25–42.

Turnock, David. "The Role of NGOs in Environmental Education in South-Eastern Europe." *International Research in Geographical and Environmental Education* 13, no. 1 (2004): 103–109.

Tzifakis, Nikolaos, Sotiris Petropoulos, and Asteris Huliaras. "The Impact of Economic Crises on NGOs: The Case of Greece." *Voluntas: International Journal of Voluntary and Nonprofit Organizations* 28, issue 5 (October 2017): 2176–2199.

Ui, S., L. Heng, H. Yatsuya, L. Kawaguichi, H. Akashi, and A. Aoyana. "Strengthening Community Participation at Health Centers in Rural Cambodia: Role of Local Non-Governmental Organizations (NGOs)." *Critical Public Health* 20, no. 1 (March 2010): 97–115.

Un, Kheang. "State, Society and Democratic Consolidation: The Case of Cambodia." *Pacific Affairs* 79, no. 2 (Summer 2006): 225–245.

Valentin, Karen and Lotte Meinert. "The Adult North and the Young South: Reflections on the Civilizing Mission of Children's Rights." *Anthropology Today* 25, no. 3 (June 2009): 23–28.

Valor, Carmen and Amparo Merino. "The Relationship between NGOs and Businesses in the Public Arena: An Empirical Analysis for Spain." *Journal of Public Affairs* 9 (2009): 20–34.

Walsh, Eoghan and Helena Lenihan. "Accountability and Effectiveness of NGOs: Adapting Business Tools Successfully." *Development in Practice* 16, no. 5 (August 2006): 412–424.

Warkentin, Craig. *Reshaping World Politics: NGOs, the Internet, and Global Civil Society*. New York: Rowman & Littlefield Publishers, Inc., 2001.

Watkins, Susan Cotts, Ann Swidler, and Thomas Hannan. "Outsourcing Social Transformation: Development NGOs as Organizations." *Annual Review of Sociology* 38 (2012): 285–315.

Watson, Alison MS. "Saving More Than the Children: The Role of Child-Focused NGOs in the Creation of Southern Security Norms." *Third World Quarterly* 27, no. 2 (2006): 227–237.

Weiss, Thomas G. and Leon Gordenker. *NGOs, the UN, and Global Governance*. Boulder, Colorado: Lynne Rienner, 1996.

Werker, Eric and Faisal Z. Ahmed. "What Do Nongovernmental Organizations Do?" *The Journal of Economic Perspectives* 22, no. 2 (Spring 2008): 73–92.

Willetts, Peter. "Transnational Actors and International Organizations in Global Politics." In *The Globalization of World Politics: An Introduction to International Relations*, edited by John Baylis, Steve Smith, and Patricia Owens, 330–347, 4th ed. Boulder, Colorado: Lynne Rienner Publishers, Inc., 2008.

Willetts, Peter. "The Role of NGOs in Global Governance." *World Politics Review* (September 27, 2011): 1–7, https://www.worldpoliticsreview.com/articles/10147/the-role-ngos-in-global-governance .

Winckler, Hugo, Francois Godement, and Agatha Kratz. "China: Waging 'Lawfare' on NGOs." *European Council on Foreign Relations* (2015): 1–8.

Wipfli, Heather L., Kayo Fujimoto, and Thomas W. Valentine. "Global Tobacco Control Diffusion: The Case of the Framework Convention on Tobacco Control." *American Journal of Public Health* 100, no. 7 (July 2010): 1260–1266.

Wolff, Jonas and Annika Elena Poppe. *Civil Society, NGOs and Foreign Funding: An Overview*. Frankfurt: Peace Research Institute Frankfurt, 2015.

Woods, Ngaire. "Making the IMF and the World Bank More Accountable." *International Affairs* 77, no. 1 (January 2001): 83–100.

Wright, Glen W. "NGOs and Western Hegemony: Causes for Concern and Ideas for Change." *Development in Practice* 22, no. 1 (February 2012): 123–134.

Yang, Yongjiao, Mick Wilkinson, and Xiongxiong Zhang. "Beyond the Abolition of Dual Administration: The Challenges to NGO Governance in 21st Century China." *ISTR* 27 (2016): 2292–2310.

Yi, Kang. "Sichuan, Year Zero?" In *Dog Days: Made in China Yearbook 2018*, edited by Ivan Franceschini, Nicholas Loubere, Kevin Lin, Elisa Nesossi, Andrea E. Pia, and Christian Sorace, 196–199. Canberra, Australia: ANU Press, 2019.

Zaum, Dominik. "International Non-Governmental Organizations and Civil Wars." *Civil Wars* 11, no. 1 (March 2009): 22–38.

Zhengling, Lin. "An Analysis of the Role of NGOs in the WTO." *Chinese Journal of International Law* 3, issue 2 (2004): 485–497.

Index

About the Author

George Kaloudis is professor emeritus of political science and history at Rivier University in Nashua, New Hampshire. He taught a variety of courses including courses on global politics, international law, modern Greece, democratization, globalization, and nongovernmental organizations. Professor Kaloudis has published multiple book reviews, essays, journal articles, and books on numerous topics related to the courses he taught over thirty-five years of a teaching career.

www.ingramcontent.com/pod-product-compliance
Lightning Source LLC
Chambersburg PA
CBHW022310280326
41932CB00010B/1045